RELIGION AND THE SECONDARY SCHOOL

COLIN ALVES

Religion and the Secondary School

A report undertaken on behalf of the
Education Department of the
British Council of Churches

SCM PRESS LTD

LONDON

SBN 334 01388 7

First published 1968
by SCM Press Ltd
56 Bloomsbury Street London WC1
© SCM Press Ltd 1968

Printed in Great Britain by
Billing & Sons Limited
Guildford and London

CONTENTS

LIST OF DIAGRAMS

FOREWORD

THIS IS not an official Report of the British Council of Churches, but the Council is glad to have been able, through its Education Department, to initiate the research project it describes. It was carried out, with the help of a generous grant from the Gulbenkian Foundation, by Mr Colin Alves, who is himself author of the Report. His conclusions should be assessed on their own merits and not necessarily as representing the views of the British Council of Churches. In the same way the Directing Committee, which has supervised the project under the Chairmanship of Mr D. G. O. Ayerst, C.B.E., is responsible for the Introduction and the inferences which it has drawn from the Report. As General Secretary of the British Council of Churches, I commend the Report and the findings to the careful consideration and study of all concerned with the important subject with which they deal.

October 1967   KENNETH SANSBURY
                                                     Bishop

Report of the Special Committee
appointed by the Education Department of the
British Council of Churches
to consider the state and needs of religious education
in county secondary schools[1]

1. In 1964 the British Council of Churches appointed a special
committee to carry out an enquiry into the state and needs of
religious education with particular reference to county schools.
Throughout our work we have been conscious that religious experience cannot be measured by any enquiry, however sympathetic,
nor assured by any administrative action, however well designed.
Yet this is what matters most. We have inevitably had to concern
ourselves mainly with the conditions within which teachers have to
work, and with those results which are capable of being assessed on
an objective basis. These means to an end, however, are of great
importance. On these matters we have come to the following
conclusions based on the evidence collected by our investigating
officer and on our own thinking about the issues involved. We
commend them to those who have power to act. We find enough
encouraging features to justify a New Deal; enough discouragement
to show how urgent is the need for it. In what follows we have
confined ourselves, as we had to confine our enquiry, to the situation
in county secondary schools. We regard it as of great importance
that this enquiry should be followed by a similar investigation of the
position in county primary schools. It is not safe to assume that what
applies in the one will hold true in the other.

[1] 'A county school is one which is built, maintained and staffed by the local
education authority. Its full cost falls on public funds.'

2. We have found it necessary to attempt an expansion of the phrase 'the spiritual (and) moral development of the community' to which the 1944 Education Act says local education authorities 'should contribute'. What kind of contribution ought they to make? If their duty were to teach the young the Christian religion in such a way that when they grew up they would become informed members of a Christian denomination, we should have to say that they have failed. But preparation for church membership is the duty of the churches, not the schools.

3. This is very far from saying that there is nothing that schools can or ought to do about the spiritual development of the community. The first job of the county school today in this respect is in our view to open the eyes of pupils to values which would otherwise lie outside their field of vision. These values come to us as part of a living tradition according to which we believe God is active in human experience. Schools have a duty to make their pupils aware of this inheritance, and to enable them to feel the strength and the challenge which it offers. Their pupils need help also in forming discriminating intellectual and moral judgments in ethical and religious matters. They will not all, of course, form the same judgments; nor will they all put them into practice, though we hope and believe that as a result of what they learn at school many more will live their lives responsibly than would otherwise do so. Clearly the duty of schools thus defined includes, but is not limited to, religious education in the particular sense.

4. At some time during their years at a secondary school boys and girls normally take up positions which will play an important part in determining their adult patterns of belief and behaviour. This can happen either consciously and responsibly, or simply by thoughtless conformity to what they see around them. Schools have a double duty – to set higher standards in their own living than prevail in the world of mass communications, and to bring boys and girls to a deliberate choice of standards. We think they are more successful in the former than in the latter task. It is true that for some pupils the choice may well have to depend more on imitation of an admired and trusted person than on intellectual discrimination; but the choice can still be a valid personal decision. Indeed the element of imitation is an important element in most decisions about behaviour.

But schools should not rest content with setting an example. They should try to secure that decisions are made in as much of the light of reason as possible. The answers given by sixth formers to our questionnaires suggest that this is the area in which religious education is least successful. Other subjects, too, call for the formulation of responsible judgments. We suspect that the same difficulty is encountered by those who teach them.

5. We recognize that these aims inevitably give rise to situations in which pupils will seek personal advice either at school or elsewhere. When it is sought in school, teachers must be prepared to meet the need. This is neither to advocate professional counselling, nor to rule it out; but there is an obligation on all teachers who are asked for help to give it. Where on our criteria we have found a school with good religious education, we have usually found this being done. Christians in particular, whether in school or outside it, have a duty to give help without religious strings. There is a Christian duty to behave simply as a good human being.

6. Religious education in the particular sense in county secondary schools is to be interpreted as Christian. It cannot effectively be anything else in our country. Certainly pupils have a right to be put in a position where they can make up their own minds about the faith for which so much is claimed and in which so many find satisfaction and inspiration.

7. But this does not mean that God is absent from other religious experience or that those who are not aware of a personal God have no spiritual experience. We can, and should, learn from men of other faiths, theistic and non-theistic and they from us. This has always been true in its own right. The county secondary school ought to find room for it in its programme of religious education. The presence among our fellow citizens of an increasing number of followers of other faiths makes this provision urgent. In addition to the Jews there are now other communities in Britain practising non-Christian religions. The sample of schools on which our work was based did not include any schools in which this problem directly arose. We are, however, aware of both the distinct and the common religious needs of Christians and others in schools which both attend. Thought should be given to the best way of meeting them.

8. The success that we feel entitled to claim for schools which take their religious education seriously and tackle it with professional competence is limited. Some of the limiting factors are outside the control of the schools and the authorities which maintain them. Among these intractable factors perhaps the most important is the environment. It is important to recognize the relative failure of religious education in the south-east contrasted with the relative success of the South-east in most of the things that men value highly in our society, including efficient education.[2] The South-east is the quintessence of twentieth-century urbanism; this is increasingly the setting in which all schools have to work.

9. The first of the limiting factors clearly within the power of the educational system to remove concerns the supply, training and deployment of teachers for religious education in secondary schools.

(*a*) There are too few teachers as a result of the failure of the central and local authorities to take seriously their responsibility for seeing that there is a sufficient supply of men and women suitably trained. They have deceived themselves into believing that any teacher who is willing is able to do the job. This may once have made sense. It is now quite out-of-date.

(*b*) The qualifications available are often in our judgment unsuitable. We need teachers as highly qualified as their colleagues, but the type of higher education available has until recently almost everywhere been insufficiently aligned to the major issues of the day. We welcome these new degree courses in theological departments and faculties in which theological and social studies can be followed side by side. We hope that those concerned with planning B.Ed. courses will realize the special contribution they can make by laying stress on the understanding of the development of the human personality without which success is impossible in religious education.

(*c*) Higher theological education without professional training for teaching is shown by our survey to be an insufficient preparation, but in recent years this has been the background of a number of specialist teachers. A man trained only as a minister of religion is

[2] The Newsom Report (*Half Our Future*) drew attention to the longer school life and higher average standards in reading comprehension found in the South-east (pp. 187, 196, 200).

so far from being a ready-made effective teacher that his experience of preaching may at first prove a hindrance in acquiring the teacher's art of listening.

(*d*) Our evidence shows the value of academically respectable qualifications obtained by practising teachers as a result of further study. The distinct success of teachers who have qualified themselves in this way is in our opinion a reflection of two factors – the knowledge they have acquired, and the purposefulness they have brought to it. We do not believe that the second factor would be weakened if the former were recognized on a wider basis than at present by salary increments. Not all part-time qualifications would be suitable, but those awarded by a university ought to be. We think, however, that the content of these courses probably needs the same kind of re-consideration that is being given to degree courses in theology.

(*e*) It is essential that religious education should receive its full share of attention under the greatly increased provision for in-service training now being envisaged. The education service must not rely on the churches to do its work for it. They have not the special skills required on the professional side, though clearly they will have much expert knowledge to contribute in the field of content. Some Institutes of Education have done a good deal in recent years for in-service training of teachers of religion; but there is need for much more provision of this kind, in which the Department of Education and Science, the Institutes, the colleges of education and the local education authorities can all take part. We are glad to note that four local education authorities have appointed advisers in religious education. More should.

(*f*) We suspect that there are proportionately fewer outstanding and good teachers in religious education than in other subjects. We think that there would be more if the scales of professional advancement were not as markedly loaded against religious education specialists as our survey shows. The failure of so many heads and governing bodies to award special responsibility and head of department posts to religious education specialists has a most discouraging effect. With the coming of big secondary schools we consider that there should be a regular establishment of posts for religious education carrying emoluments above the basic

Burnham scale and providing a reasonable career prospect. This might be linked with a nation-wide provision of advisory posts instead of the present four.

(*g*) We are concerned with the way in which too many schools deploy their specialists. To spread them thinly over the whole school so that one teacher may be expected to teach as many as 800 pupils once a week is to provide working conditions which virtually ensure failure. We doubt if any teacher can do the difficult job now demanded of him for more than 200 pupils a week or, to put it another way, to pupils whom he sees only once a week.

(*h*) The churches ought to take far more active steps to make known to their members the need for teachers who are Christians. This need is not confined to teachers of religious knowledge; it extends to teachers of all subjects since the pupil is more important than the subject matter. We feel that the churches have done far more nationally to provide for the training of teachers than they have done locally to bring the claim of teaching as a vocation before their younger members.

10.   We are aware that a good many teachers and older pupils regard religious education with some suspicion and contempt as a kind of admittedly ineffective brain-washing. Our desire is to make it at once more effective and less suspect. This involves first of all an 'open' approach in the class-room such as pupils expect in other subjects. By this we mean that pupils should not feel inhibited from expressing any opinions they may honestly hold or asking any questions which seem to them important. We mean, too, that teachers must be seen to address themselves scrupulously to the whole of the evidence, following where the argument leads. Success also involves such an integration with the teaching of other subjects as to make cross-reference easy and effective. To achieve this some modification of the system of an isolated, all-purpose religious instruction period is desirable at the top of the school. We think that this can be achieved in various ways. One is by providing in the later years of the secondary course a variety of options within the broad field of religion, philosophy and ethics. This would enable pupils to exercise a fair degree of choice in their own education and provide a reasonable way of protecting tender consciences, whether

parental or adolescent. This pre-supposes a fairly large school; but these are in most places now becoming the rule. A second alternative route is by making religious education part of an integrated course instead of letting it stand on its own. This would remove the special status with its tacit assumption of being beyond criticism which we believe lies behind at least many of the humanist objections to religious education. Christians ought to welcome the opportunity for the study of their faith to take its place on level terms with other disciplines.

11. Too much of the work we have seen seems more closely aligned to the older conception of religious education than to the new. This is partly because of the nature of a good many of the Agreed Syllabuses. An Agreed Syllabus is necessary to fulfil the present law; and has a useful part to play subject to certain reservations. These are as follows:

(*a*) Too many of the syllabuses are set in a traditional mould mainly designed to introduce the pupil to as much of the Bible as possible. Unfortunately the great majority of syllabuses do not sufficiently encourage schools to start with questions arising for the pupils both in their daily life and in the world at large. This involves great flexibility, and an Agreed Syllabus should provide freely for it. While each Agreed Syllabus should be kept constantly under review, it can only be revised at considerable intervals of time. It ought not, therefore, to attempt to set out too detailed or binding a plan of work.

(*b*) A clearer recognition ought to be given to the fact that many secondary schools have efficient, professional religious education departments and that all should have them. These ought to be capable of drawing up their own schemes of work, sometimes in co-operation with other school departments. This ought to be recognized in the Agreed Syllabus.

(*c*) There are almost certainly too many different syllabuses. It is true that a good many authorities have not made their own, but adopted another authority's, but this has happened in an eclectic way up and down the country without producing any clear geographical groupings. Agreement on a common syllabus over a fairly wide area would simplify the task of in-service training.

In future more attention needs to be paid to strictly educational considerations of this kind.

(*d*) Agreed Syllabuses, which were not invented by the 1944 Act, date from a time when school life was much shorter than it is now. It is soon to become a year longer for all. In these circumstances we think it important that an Agreed Syllabus should take cognisance in a constructive way of the G.C.E. and C.S.E. examinations which many pupils will be taking in this field; and that these examinations should themselves be carefully related to the whole plan of religious education. We have not thought it our duty to suggest how this should be done, but we draw attention to the use that could be made of the professional experience which members of the subject panels of the various examining boards possess.

12.   A quite different, but perhaps even more necessary, change concerns the morning assembly. We recognize that there has recently been strong criticism of it. We believe, however, that it can have great value of a spiritual kind beyond any justification it may deserve as an expression of corporate life. As many as possible should be encouraged to take part as fully as possible in it. This means in our judgment that, while the assembly will usually be Christian, at other times it will be a sincere expression of spiritual values which are not avowedly Christian, though the Christians among the staff and pupils will give them more profound significance in the light of their religious understanding. We think it reasonable to assume that the great majority of teachers and pupils would be prepared to take part in daily assemblies which had this latitude of expression.

13.   We are convinced that the conscience clauses protecting both teachers and parents must be retained. We think that they will need to be invoked even less frequently than at present if religious education and worship are developed in the ways we have indicated. These developments will, we think, provide, among other things, some safeguard for adolescent consciences which have at present no official recognition. We do not think that anything we suggest is inconsistent with the present law. And we consider that the law provides positively for something for which there is a real demand. We draw attention to the wishes of the overwhelming majority of all

parents for Christian education as shown by two opinion polls, to the similar demand by the parents of grammar school sixth formers discovered by Mr. Edwin Cox, and to the views of the pupils themselves which our investigation has made clear.

14. We are impressed with the valuable work done in schools by such voluntary agencies as the Christian Education Movement, and by the outward-going practical work of a social nature which nearly all schools undertake. We hope that this may be regarded as a Christian obligation. We notice with pleasure how often this work is in fact largely undertaken under the leadership of the head of the religious education department. It is important, however, that this should not be regarded as in any sense a prerogative or preserve of the RE Department.

15. We wish to draw particular attention to the descriptions of enterprising work in which Mr Alves' account of his investigation abounds. We do not think we are being partial when we say that the initiative and insight this work displays would grace any subject.

16. We owe a very great debt of gratitude to the trustees of the Calouste Gulbenkian Foundation for the grant which made possible this exploration of the best of religious education in county secondary schools. The Arthur Yapp trust has also given us generous financial help. King Alfred's College, Winchester, not only released Mr Colin Alves for two years to undertake the investigation, but made it possible for him to take up the appointment by paying the difference between his salary and what we could afford. The local education authorities and the schools which have taken part in the enquiry have made the task of the visitors pleasant and, we hope they will agree, profitable. Dr Curnow of the University of Reading Department of Applied Statistics and Professor J. Wrigley of the University of Southampton have ungrudgingly given statistical advice which we hope has kept the enquiry on sound lines. In the launching of the enquiry and throughout three-quarters of its progress we have been able to rely not only on the advice but also on a good measure of the time of the Rev. J. A. Wainwright, secretary of the Education Department of the British Council of Churches until May 1966. He has helped us greatly. On Mrs Margaret Stroh there has fallen an avalanche of clerical work which she has never allowed to submerge

her. Many volunteers have worked hard at scoring the answers to our test questions. To all these we are grateful; but our greatest personal debt is to Mr Colin Alves whose imperturbability, industry and insight have carried a heavy load a long way in a short time. In expressing our thanks to him, we commend with confidence his work to those who have responsibility under the Education Act for contributing towards the spiritual and moral development of the community.

D. G. O. AYERST (*Chairman*)	J. E. T. HOUGH
R. L. ARUNDALE	H. BRAMWELL HOWARD
JOHN BEDFORD	D. S. HUBERY
KATHLEEN BLISS	O. JESSIE LACE
E. L. CLARKE	J. P. LEE-WOOLF
F. A. COCKIN	A. G. MACWILLIAM
A. T. DALE	H. F. MATHEWS
J. C. DANCY	W. R. NIBLETT
R. E. DAVIES	G. R. OSBORN
F. W. DILLISTONE	T. R. NEWELL PRICE
R. J. GOLDMAN	J. B. RAPP
JOYCE HARDING	E. C. D. STANFORD
A. S. HERBERT	A. WHIGHAM-PRICE
G. B. HEWITT	F. I. VENABLES
F. H. HILLIARD	J. A. WAINWRIGHT (*Secretary*)

July, 1967

AUTHOR'S ACKNOWLEDGMENTS

THE WHOLE committee is very grateful to the Chief Education Officers of the following Education Authorities for permission to use some of their schools in one or more stages of the survey. (The Authorities are listed here under the regional divisions used for analysis.)

South-west:	Cornwall, Devonshire, Plymouth, Somerset, Bath, Dorset, Wiltshire, Gloucestershire.
South-east:	Bournemouth, Isle of Wight, Hampshire, Southampton, Portsmouth, East Sussex, West Sussex, Eastbourne, Surrey, Croydon, Kent, Canterbury, Berkshire, Reading, Hillingdon, Hounslow, Richmond-upon-Thames, Merton, Bromley, Bexley, Inner London, Ealing, Harrow-on-the-Hill, Brent, Barnet, Haringey, Enfield, Newham, Barking, Havering, Oxfordshire, Oxford, Buckinghamshire, Luton, Essex, Southend-on-Sea, Bedfordshire, Cambridgeshire, West Suffolk, East Suffolk, Ipswich, Northamptonshire, Northampton.
Midlands:	Herefordshire, Worcestershire, Worcester, Warwickshire, Birmingham, Solihull, Coventry, Leicestershire, Leicester, Peterborough, Huntingdonshire, Isle of Ely, Norfolk, Norwich, Great Yarmouth, Shropshire, Staffordshire, Smethwick, West Bromwich, Stoke-on-Trent, Derbyshire, Derby, Nottinghamshire, Nottingham, Lindsey, Kesteven, Holland.
Wales:	Glamorganshire, Cardiff, Swansea, Merthyr Tydfil, Monmouthshire, Newport, Pembrokeshire, Cardiganshire, Radnorshire, Anglesey, Caernarvonshire, Denbighshire.
North:	Cheshire, Birkenhead, Stockport, Wallasey, West Riding of Yorkshire, Barnsley, Bradford, Dewsbury, Doncaster, Huddersfield, Leeds, Rotherham, Sheffield, East Riding, Kingston upon Hull, York, North Riding, Middlesbrough, Lancashire, Blackburn, Blackpool, Bootle,

Liverpool, Manchester, Oldham, Preston, Rochdale, St. Helens, Salford, Southport, Westmorland, Cumberland, Durham, Gateshead, Sunderland, West Hartlepool, Northumberland, Tynemouth.

We are also very grateful to the headmasters, headmistresses, staff and pupils of all the schools involved, particularly those who received the full load of four questionnaires and a couple of days' visiting.

We would also like to thank all those who gave of their time either to carry out these visits to the schools or to assess the sixth-form essay-questions (or, in some noble cases, to do both).

Thanks are also due to the Master of Marlborough College for his hospitality to the members of the sub-committee on a great number of occasions, and also to Bishop Cockin on whose shoulders fell the task of the drafting and redrafting of all the sub-committee's reports.

Finally a word of thanks to those who gave me direct, personal assistance in the preparation of this report, particularly to my wife (my long-suffering wife, one must say), to Mrs Alice Kember and to Mrs Hilda van de Lagemaat, as well as to all the others (too many to name) who gave of their advice, counsel and time, without which the report would never have been completed.

PART I

I

The Purpose and Planning
of the Survey

We have now had about ten years' experience of the operation of the provisions made in the Education Act for religious worship and teaching, and
it is but common sense to take stock and compare notes. In the past,
religious education suffered grievously from an excess of views and opinions
based on inadequate knowledge of actual practice within the schools . . .
For intelligent and constructive stock-taking, we need above all else
knowledge of what has been happening during the last ten years, based on
actual experience.

So WROTE Professor W. O. Lester Smith, the Chairman of the
Research Committee which in 1954 produced the report called
Religious Education in Schools (London: SPCK, 1954) on behalf of
the Institute of Christian Education. In those days any form of
research into Religious Education (hereafter referred to as RE) was
a comparatively rare thing, at least in this country, and it is noteworthy that the 1954 Report contained no bibliography whatsoever.
During the past ten years, however, interest and activity in this area
of research have come to appear by contrast almost overwhelming
in its profusion, as the bibliography on pp. 220–2 will reveal.

And yet, among all this research there has been comparatively
little concerned with the particular area covered by the 1954 Report.
'Actual practice within the schools' has been largely ignored, and
attention has been concentrated on the stages and processes of
individual religious development. While this has had a dramatic
impact on the whole pattern of thought and planning in the field of
religious education, certain questions have been left unanswered,
particularly those concerned with the community setting within
which religious development takes place. In short, the balance of

recent research into religious education has been in the area of psychology rather than sociology. A great deal of investigation has been done to assess children's reactions; far less has been done to assess the influence of the teachers concerned and of school society in general.

Therefore, when the Education Department of the British Council of Churches set up a special committee to do some 'intelligent and constructive stock-taking' after *twenty* years' experience of the 1944 Act, it was obvious that some survey would have to be made of current practice in the schools, as well as some assessment of the results of this practice. Only with such knowledge firmly behind them could the committee make a considered judgment on the present situation and produce recommendations as to the most profitable direction the subject should (or could) take during the next decade. My appointment as Survey Officer to the committee was the result of this need for factual information.

Two similar surveys were in fact already in process, one being conducted by Dr R. B. Dierenfield (Associate Professor of Education at Macalester College, Saint Paul, Minnesota), the other by Harold Loukes (as a follow up to his book *Teenage Religion* [London, SCM Press, 1961]). It was decided to work on from these surveys, particularly the latter, and I am very grateful to these two researchers for the use they allowed me to make of their material, as well as for the stimulation and guidance their thought and comment provided.

The immediate purpose of the British Council of Churches' survey was to find 'growing points' in the current situation, to discover some of the places where RE was meeting with success, and then to attempt to identify the factors underlying such success.

At this point the committee was faced with a fundamental problem. By what criteria can one judge success in this field? On what grounds can one say 'In this school RE is doing what is required of it'? Was it, in practical terms, to be my task as Survey Officer to travel from school to school until I found one where certain procedures were being carried out which had been previously defined by the British Council of Churches committee as being 'good' procedures, and then describe what I had found? The basic weakness of this method of investigation was the circular nature of the argument involved – 'We think on *a priori* grounds that the *x* approach is good; we have discovered *x* operating in *y* school; therefore *y* school has a good approach to RE, namely, x.' Something a little more objective than this obviously had to be found.

Eventually it was decided that I should work from 'end results'. The weakness here is, of course, that any educational process does not really exhibit its 'end results' until the end of life itself, but I had to content myself with the immediate 'end results' of the actual time spent in school. Having discovered the schools with the best 'end results' I would then visit these schools, or obtain the further information required by some other means, so that I could describe the methods by which they achieved their results. One could then at least say, 'X methods appear to be associated with y results; if you want y results, we recommend x methods to you; if you want to use x methods, you will probably achieve y results; if you want to use z methods, you may possibly not achieve y results.' This much, at any rate, would have a certain measure of objective factual ground on which to stand.

But how does one measure the 'end results'? And how was one to find the schools which were likely to produce good results? Time was not unlimited, and it would have been foolish to spend it on a long process of sifting good results from bad if I could find some means of ensuring that a large proportion of the schools I approached were likely to produce good results. Such a means was in fact available. As a first step towards his recent survey Harold Loukes had circularized all the Local Education Authorities, University Departments and Colleges of Education, Diocesan Education Committees, and others, asking for lists of secondary schools worthy of recommendation for the work they were doing in RE. From the replies he received he had been able to compile a list of about 300 schools, and he generously offered to make this list available to us.

At this point in our planning, however, it was realized that it would not be enough simply to find and describe 'successful' schools, even if their success was vouched for both by recommendation and also by the results of whatever objective instrument we eventually produced. What was also needed was a contrasting group of schools, ones which had not been recommended, or ones where objective results were poor, so that we could isolate the features of the successful schools which were not to be found in the unsuccessful schools. Without the possibility of making such comparisons and contrasts one might have taken as being 'characteristic of a successful school' features which were in fact common to *all* schools.

To provide a source of material for the required contrast-group a second list of schools was drawn up on a strict basis of random selection (see p. 46). When the joint list was finally compiled it contained schools from 155 different Local Education Authorities. Each Local Education Authority was approached for permission to use their schools, and it was most encouraging at this stage of the planning to receive full support and co-operation from 144 of the Chief Education Officers involved. There was in fact only one direct refusal made, on the very understandable grounds that the schools in this particular area had recently been inundated with far more than their fair share of questionnaires, etc., and that it would be wrong to inflict yet another on them at this moment.

The next step was to approach the schools, and again the response was most encouraging. Altogether 637 schools were invited to take part, and 539 (i.e. approximately 85%) accepted the invitation; nineteen headmasters/headmistresses wrote to apologize for not being able to take part, explaining the reasons for their decision; twelve simply refused the invitation, and the other sixty-seven did not reply. When one realizes that many surveys do not get more than a 40–50% response, the support received from the Heads can be seen as striking evidence of the importance they attach to this subject, and possibly also of their awareness of the problems surrounding its teaching under present circumstances.

Then came the separating of these schools into 'successful' and 'less successful'. groups. This was done by means of a questionnaire (hereafter referred to as 'Survey 65', as it was sent out in the Spring term of 1965). The details of this questionnaire are set out on pp. 36–45 but it would be appropriate at this point to consider the principles round which it had been built up.

Fields Affected by RE

One of my first tasks as Survey Officer had been to assess the general consensus of opinion within the committee as to what were the aims of RE, particularly in the county school situation. This was a question to which we were continually having to return, but our first foray into the realm of aims was made with the help of an anthology of relevant quotations culled from various educational writings. Each member of the committee was asked to indicate whether he agreed or disagreed with the ideas expressed in each of the quotations presented. The result of this survey-in-miniature was that the following two quotations found no one to agree with them at all:

Education should be completely without bias, lest the freedom of the pupil to decide the great issues for himself should be endangered: all that needs to be done is to bring his powers to the highest point and let his thoughts and ideas range where 'the wind of argument' takes them.

We must ground our young pupils so well in the Christian faith that when they eventually meet non-Christian ideas then nothing will shake them.

It so happens that both these quotations are statements coined by Rupert Davies, in his book *An Approach to Christian Education* (London: Epworth Press, 1956), for the specific purpose of arguing against them, and the fact of their unanimous rejection clearly indicated the limits of the area within which the committee felt the aims of RE to lie. On the one hand it rejected the idea that no guidance at all, no heritage of past experience, should be offered to the child; but equally it rejected the idea that the Christian educational task was in any way a process of indocrination, however beneficent in purpose that indocrination might be claimed to be.

For a positive expression of aims in RE in the secondary schools the members of the committee adopted some words of Harold Loukes (from 'The Teaching of Doubt' in *Religion in Education*, Summer 1953):

While children are small they will accept what they are told without question and are not called upon to perform anything that could fairly be described as an act of faith. But they grow up and can no longer see with borrowed light: they must look for themselves. They must, in a word, begin to doubt.

and a passage from a report of an All-Africa Conference on Christian Education held in 1964:

At the Secondary School level and above, a Christian teacher will try, where possible, to lead his pupils into a serious examination of fundamental questions in which alternative answers to the Christian ones are freely and honestly considered. In such discussions the Christian can claim no privileged position but he can bear his witness fully, not seeking too rapid an agreement with the truth he presents, but confronting his pupils with the necessity of decision.

Finally, as a general comment on the situation in the secondary-school classroom, the committee endorsed a letter published in *The Guardian* which had contained the following judgment:

A good number of the young people I meet have rejected Christianity not because of a conscious decision of will taken after weighing up both sides, but as a result of prejudices (due to the general climate of opinion) which close their mind to anything religious, deeming it not worthy even of consideration.

It must be stressed that these quotations are not being presented here as the committee's *final* consensus of views about the aims of RE, but to indicate the sort of working basis from which Survey 65 came into being. Thought and discussion springing from these quotations led to the selection of four areas of enquiry with which Survey 65 was to be concerned. These areas were the knowledge, insights, attitudes, and 'religious behaviour' of the pupils.

To examine these areas in any detail would have required a whole barrage of questionnaires, periods of observation and various other elaborate techniques. However, there were strict limitations both in the amount of time one could reasonably expect the schools to set aside for the survey, and also in the resources available for coping with evidence from such a large number of schools. It was therefore decided to concentrate on certain key topics under each of the four headings already proposed.

The most important items of *knowledge* which might be expected to have been established after ten years of RE were felt to centre around the life and teaching of Jesus. Questions were therefore drawn up to test the general level of awareness in this area (see Sections A and B of Survey 65, pp. 37–38). The most important *insights* were felt also to be concerned with the teaching of Jesus, in both its theological and its moral aspects. Tests were devised on the basis of having to find the equivalent meaning to a given statement from among a number of alternatives (see Sections C and E, pp. 38, 43). The *attitudes* of most relevance to our survey were taken to be those concerning Jesus himself, the Bible, the Church and also the religious activity of the school (RE and Assembly); these were supplemented by questions on the pupils' willingness to apply the word 'Christian' to themselves (see Sections D and F [i] and [ii]), pp. 40, 45). Finally, the *religious behaviour* of the pupils was tested through their participation in private prayer and public worship (see Section F [iii] and [iv], p. 45).

The final version of Survey 65 evolved by way of various drafts, each one of which had been emended partly in the light of experience afforded by pilot schemes, partly in the light of discussion in the small sub-committee appointed to supervise this aspect of the work and partly (I am very grateful to be able to record) in the light of comment made by Sir Ronald Gould, who most generously gave of his time to go through one of the drafts item by item with the chairman and secretary of the committee.

In March 1965 20,000 copies of Survey 65 were sent out to the schools which had agreed to take part, for completion by 'the highest ability stream' of their fourth formers. (The choice of this form and this stream was dictated by circumstances in the secondary modern schools: the best 'end results' would have come from fifth or sixth forms, but many even of the A stream pupils still leave school at the end of their fourth form.) Only thirteen of the 539 schools actually failed to have the questionnaires completed, though a further six sets failed in the end to materialize for one reason or another. This meant that by the middle of the Summer term the results from 520 schools were available for analysis and comparison, and the second stage of the survey could begin.

Each questionnaire was marked, and the scores for each section were recorded school by school. These scores were then reduced, for the purpose of analysis, to six 'mean-scores' per school:

(a) The mean-average of the individual scores for Sections A and B (knowledge)
(b) Ditto for Sections C and E (insight)
(c) Ditto for the items in Section D referring to Jesus, the Bible and the Church
(d) Ditto for those items in Section D referring to RE and Assembly
(e) Ditto for questions (i) and (ii) of Section F (reaction to term 'Christian')
(f) Ditto for questions (iii) and (iv) of Section F (religious behaviour)

Each of the scores was expressed as a percentage of the maximum score available for the relevant Section(s). These six scores were then further reduced to two, by averaging out the percentage scores for Sections AB and CE to produce an attainment score, and by similarly combining all the other percentage scores except the last to produce an attitude score. (The 'religious-behaviour' figures were ignored for the time being, as it was felt that these were likely to have been largely influenced by factors outside the control of the school.)

B

The Later Stages of the Survey

For stage two of the survey I needed to find schools which had scored comparatively well, or comparatively poorly, both in attainment and in attitude. As a first step towards this the 520 schools were stratified into twelve groups: mixed/girls/boys × large/ small × grammar/modern (i.e. each school was classified as mixed small grammar, boys' large modern, etc.). Within each of these twelve groups the seven schools with the highest overall scores (with 'attainment' and 'attitude' scores being given equal weight) were selected, as were the seven with the lowest scores. In some cases the scores of schools were so close that eight had to be chosen rather than seven, and one or two other additions to the list were felt to be necessary to maintain a proper balance between the regions, so in the end the list consisted of ninety-eight high-scoring and 102 low-scoring schools. All of these were invited to take part in stage two.

Stage two was to consist of a batch of questionnaires addressed to the headmasters/headmistresses and RE staff in each of the selected schools. The facts given in the replies to these questionnaires enabled a picture to be built up of the general life of each school, as well as of its methods and approaches, particularly in the field of RE. The questions ranged over topics such as:

The qualifications of the RE staff
The age of the RE staff, and their length of experience
The aims they held and the methods and equipment they used
The presence of RE examinations
The type of RE syllabus in use
The timetable loading of those teaching RE
The number of periods for RE on the pupils' timetables
Integration of subjects within the school
The out-of-class activities in the school
Membership of RE societies
The links between the school and the outside world
The amount of staff turnover
The employment of part-time staff
The social neighbourhood which the school served
The pattern of school Assembly

Obviously the number of questions to be filled in was considerable, and it is not surprising that just over a quarter of the 200 selected schools failed to complete and return the questionnaires. What *was* noticeable about this 29% failure, however, was that there were forty low-scoring schools who failed to make returns as opposed to only eighteen 'high-scoring' ones.[1] No school, of course, had been told which category it came into, nor even that there *were* two categories, so this could not have influenced their determination to complete the task they had accepted. One characteristic of the high-scoring schools was therefore revealed even before analysis of the returns had begun in any detail, namely, that the headmasters/headmistresses and staff were conscientious people, prepared to put themselves to considerable trouble and regarding the field of RE as of sufficient importance to devote a great deal of time to the fulfilment of demands associated with it. (Analysis of other characteristics of the high-scoring schools will be found in Chapter 5.)

The third and final stage of the survey was concerned with further investigation of the eighty high-scoring schools who had finally agreed to take part in stage two. Each school was to be visited by two members of the British Council of Churches special committee (or by other people well versed in the problems and possibilities of RE who had been invited to work with the committee on this part of the project); and then a further batch of questionnaires was to be completed, this time by the pupils who had spent longest in the school (sixth form in grammar, fifth form in modern schools), those with whom the school had had the fullest opportunity of achieving whatever 'end results' it could. In the outcome some of the schools were not able to find occasions convenient both to themselves and to the potential visitors, and twenty of them were not able to complete the fifth/sixth-form questionnaires within the period allotted. It must be remembered, however, that although sixty schools (producing approximately 1,360 completed pupil questionnaires) is not in itself a very large sample, these schools were specially selected from within an original sample of 520 schools[2] (represented by well over 15,000 pupil questionnaires).

The fifth/sixth-form questionnaire was completed almost exactly a year later than Survey 65. The appropriate title would obviously have been Survey 66, but this was in fact reserved for a subsidiary questionnaire to be used with lower streams in the fourth year[3] so

---

[1] The difference between these two figures is statistically significant, at the 0·01 level.

[2] I.e. approximately 10% of the 5350 county secondary schools operating in England and Wales at the time.

[3] The results of which have not yet been analysed.

the sixth form questionnaire became known as Survey 666 (despite the associations of Revelation 13.18!).

Most of Survey 666 was specially prepared for completion by older pupils, but nevertheless it did contain one or two sections originally used in Survey 65. These were Sections A and B, six items from Section D, and Section F.

The few very minor variations between these sections of the two questionnaires are noted on pp. 37, 45. The other sections of Survey 666 are printed in full at the end of Chapter 6. It must suffice here to note that they were concerned with the pupils' bases of moral judgment, with their prejudices and with their ability to think responsibly on certain moral and theological issues. The particular purpose of these sections was to attempt an assessment of the general *educational* effects of the RE teaching in these high-scoring schools, as an extension of the assessment of insight among the fourth-formers. There would obviously have been little advantage in the identification of factors within a school situation which produced high scores where knowledge and attitudes were concerned if these had been obtained at the expense of religious and moral insight. Therefore there was this particular concern, at the end of the whole survey, with matters such as lack of prejudice and responsibility of judgment.

The results of the different stages of the survey are set out in Chapters 2 to 6 of this report. Survey 65 is analysed in Chapters 2 and 3. The teachers' questionnaires in Chapters 4 and 5, and Survey 666 in Chapter 6. The remaining chapters attempt to spell out the significance of the findings, and make some fairly detailed suggestions for working out the pattern of RE in the future.

APPENDIX TO CHAPTER 1

1. *Survey 65 (full text of questionnaire, with scoring added)*

We are trying to discover what older secondary-school pupils think about religion. We hope you will help us in our enquiry by answering the questions in this booklet.

We are not asking you to tell us your names, but (to help us make sense of the results) we will need the following information about you:

Name of school and town $\left\{\right\}$

Class, e.g. 4A ( )   Sex, write BOY or GIRL here   ( )

Birthday   ( )   Present age, in completed years   ( )

Number of complete terms spent in your present school so far ( )

Age at which you expect to leave school   ( )

Read the instructions to each section very carefully BEFORE you start answering it.

SECTION A

Here are ten well-known sayings or quotations. Some of them come from the Gospels; some do not. Put a tick against the ones which you would find somewhere in the Gospels, spoken by Jesus.[4]

		Scoring
I am the way, and the truth, and the life.	( )	✓ = 1
All men are brothers.	( )	Blank = 1
One good turn deserves another.	( )	Blank = 1
I am the Lord your God.	( )	Blank = 1
Whoever causes one of these little ones who believe in me to sin, it would be better for him to have a great millstone fastened round his neck and to be drowned in the depth of the sea.	( )	✓ = 1
Cleave the wood and I am there.[5]	( )	Blank = 1
I am the true vine, and my father is the vine dresser.[6]	( )	✓ = 1
Blessed are the peacemakers.	( )	✓ = 1
God helps those who help themselves.	( )	Blank = 1
Your father in heaven makes his sun rise on the evil and on the good, and sends rain on the just and on the unjust.	( )	✓ = 1
		Max. 10

SECTION B

The following statements are all found in the Bible. Tick the ones which are about Jesus.[7]

[4] For Survey 666 the third sentence of the rubric ran: 'For each one put a tick in the appropriate column (using the last column if you are not sure of the answer).' The columns at the side of the sayings were headed 'From Gospels', 'Not from Gospels', 'Don't know'.

[5] In Survey 666 'Remember the Sabbath Day to keep it holy' was substituted.

[6] In Survey 666 'This is life eternal, that they might know thee the only true God' was substituted.

[7] For Survey 666 additional rubrics were added: 'Mark with a cross those which are not about him (put a question mark if you are not sure).'

The Lord said to him, 'Go from your country and
your father's house to the land that I will show you.
And I will bless those who bless you.'   ( )   Blank (×) = 1

Now he was ruddy, and had beautiful eyes and was
handsome. And the Lord said, 'Arise, anoint him for
this is he.'   ( )   Blank (×) = 1

And when he entered the temple, the chief priests and
the elders of the people came up to him as he was
teaching and said, 'By what authority are you doing
these things?'   ( )   √ = 1

Then he went up on the mountain, and the cloud
covered the mountain. The glory of the Lord settled
on Mount Sinai, and the cloud covered it six days.   ( )   Blank (×) = 1

And while they still disbelieved for joy, he said to
them, 'Have you anything here to eat?' They gave him
a piece of broiled fish, and he took it and ate before
them.   ( )   √ = 1

When they did not find him, they returned to Jerusalem, seeking him. After three days they found him in
the temple, sitting among the teachers.   ( )   √ = 1

Up to this word they listened to him; then they lifted
up their voices and said, 'Away with such a fellow
from the earth! For he ought not to live.' And as they
cried out, the tribune commanded him to be brought
into the barracks and to be examined by scourging.   ( )   Blank (×) = 1

A man came bringing twenty loaves of barley. And
he said, 'Give to the men, that they may eat.' But his
servant said, 'How am I to set this before a hundred
men?' He replied, 'Thus says the Lord, "They shall eat
and have some left".'   ( )   Blank (×) = 1

Those who had seen it told what had happened to the
demoniac and to the swine. And they began to beg
him to depart from their neighbourhood.   ( )   √ = 1

So he went and dwelt by the brook Cherith, east of
the Jordan. And the ravens brought him bread and
meat in the morning and the evening; and he drank
from the brook.   ( )   Blank (×) = 1

Max. 10

SECTION C

Here are six quotations from the Gospels, each one followed by four
sentences (a. b. c. d.) which might seem to be saying the same sort of thing
as the introductory quotation. In *each* group of sentences tick the *one*
which you think most nearly expresses what Jesus intended us to understand.

1. Jesus said, 'Look at the birds of the air: they do not sow and reap, yet your heavenly Father feeds them. You are worth more than the birds.'

Scoring

   a. A Christian has no need to work; God will provide all that money would buy.   ( ) √ = 0

   b. A Christian can spend his money how and when he likes; God will always make sure he can get some more.   ( ) √ = 0

   c. A Christian should always live in poverty.   ( ) √ = 0

   d. A Christian should not always be worrying about getting enough money; there are more important things in life than that.   ( ) √ = 1

2. Jesus taught his disciples to pray 'Thy kingdom come'.

   a. May Jesus soon come down from heaven to destroy all the wicked people.   ( ) √ = 0

   b. We believe that the world is automatically becoming a better and better place for people to live in.   ( ) √ = 0

   c. May Jesus soon come back to earth to rule in power as actual King over all the world.   ( ) √ = 0

   d. May more and more people let God be the real ruler of their lives.   ( ) √ = 1

3. Jesus said, 'Do not think that I have come to bring peace on earth; I have not come to bring peace, but a sword.'

   a. Jesus came to destroy all the wicked people on earth.   ( ) √ = 0

   b. Jesus' disciples must make all men become Christians, by force if necessary.   ( ) √ = 0

   c. Jesus' teaching asked so much of people that it could cause even friends and relations to take sides against each other.   ( ) √ = 1

   d. Jesus was hoping to lead the Jews in a rebellion against the Roman Empire.   ( ) √ = 0

4. It was not to judge the world that God sent his Son into the world, but that through him the world might be saved.

   a. God loves us all so much that he takes no notice of anything we do wrong.   ( ) √ = 0

   b. God loves his creation so much that through Jesus he did all he could to stop man from ruining himself.   ( ) √ = 1

   c. When God judges us at the end of the world, we will be quite all right as long as we tell him we are Christians.   ( ) √ = 0

   d. Since Jesus came to earth it has been impossible for men to do anything really wrong as Jesus has saved the world from sin.   ( ) √ = 0

5. Jesus said to his disciples, 'Are not sparrows two a penny?
   Yet without your Father's leave not one of them can fall
   to the ground. So have no fear; you are worth more than
   any number of sparrows.'

   a. God protects those who trust in him, and keeps them out of
      dangers and difficulty.   ( )   √ = 0

   b. Jesus' disciples must never give up their trust in God's
      love for them, whatever may happen to them.   ( )   √ = 1

   c. God has complete control over every detail of everybody's
      behaviour, and has planned it all in advance.   ( )   √ = 0

   d. Man is so precious to God, that God will always see that
      he does not get into trouble no matter how he behaves.   ( )   √ = 0

6. Jesus said, 'There will be greater joy in heaven over one
   sinner who repents than over ninety-nine righteous
   people who do not need to repent.'

   a. It is much better to sin and be sorry, than never to sin at all. ( )   √ = 0

   b. God doesn't mind you sinning, as long as you're sorry
      afterwards.   ( )   √ = 0

   c. If you sin it saddens God, but it does not make him stop
      loving you at all.   ( )   √ = 1

   d. We all ought to sin, at least a little bit, as it gives God more
      chance to show his love for us when we repent.   ( )   √ = 0

                                                                 Max. 6

SECTION D

Here are thirty-six statements about certain matters to do with religion.
For *each* one show how much you agree or disagree with it by putting *one*
tick in the appropriate column opposite it.

Scoring √ =

	I completely agree	I agree on the whole	I am not sure whether I agree or not	I disagree on the whole	I definitely disagree	Subject [8]
1. Even though the intentions of the Bible may be good, what it stands for can be obtained otherwise.	0	1	2	3	4	B
2. Going to church is a complete waste of time.	0	1	2	3	4	C

[8] B = Bible; C = Church; J = Jesus; S = School Religion.

	I completely agree	I agree on the whole	I am not sure whether I agree or not	I disagree on the whole	I definitely disagree	
3. The Church helps people to pay proper attention to the needs of others.	4	3	2	1	0	C
4. I myself believe in Jesus and enjoy learning about him.	4	3	2	1	0	J[9]
5. To me the Bible is one of the most wonderful books ever written.	4	3	2	1	0	B
6. Religion ought not to be dealt with in the classroom.	0	1	2	3	4	S
7. Jesus was sent by God to save man from gradually destroying himself.	4	3	2	1	0	J[9]
8. I find I can worship God in school Assembly just as well as in church, if not better.	Not scored					(S)
9. The Church always refuses to adapt itself to modern thinking.	0	1	2	3	4	C[9]
10. The Church is a very valuable part of our religion.	4	3	2	1	0	C
11. It is a waste of school-time learning all about Jesus and so on. The other school subjects are much more important.	0	1	2	3	4	S
12. The Church helps to strengthen people's faith.	4	3	2	1	0	C
13. Jesus may have meant well but he was misguided.	0	1	2	3	4	J
14. The Bible is the proper foundation of religious belief.	4	3	2	1	0	B
15. Church is an unpleasant way to spend a Sunday.	0	1	2	3	4	C[9]

[9] These were the only items from this section used in Survey 666.

	I completely agree	I agree on the whole	I am not sure whether I agree or not	I disagree on the whole	I definitely disagree	
16. Jesus was quite out of touch with real life.	0	1	2	3	4	J[9]
17. Reading fiction does more to help me than reading the Bible does.	0	1	2	3	4	B
18. The Church seems to me to be full of narrow-minded kill-joys.	0	1	2	3	4	C
19. Jesus' teachings were wonderful and taught men and women not to be selfish.	4	3	2	1	0	J
20. Worshipping God is a good way to start a school day.	4	3	2	1	0	S
21. The Bible is a great help when a person is in trouble.	4	3	2	1	0	B
22. Jesus must surely have been insincere in many of the things he said.	0	1	2	3	4	J
23. The New Testament contains the truest picture of God ever given to man.	4	3	2	1	0	B
24. Jesus has no importance for us today.	0	1	2	3	4	J
25. Going to church helps people to worship God.	4	3	2	1	0	C
26. The Church helps people learn what is right and what is wrong.	4	3	2	1	0	C
27. A person's education is not complete if he has not studied religion.	4	3	2	1	0	S
28. If you want to worship God, school is not the place to do it in.	0	1	2	3	4	S

	I completely agree	I agree on the whole	I am not sure whether I agree or not	I disagree on the whole	I definitely disagree	
29. Jesus often showed himself to be weak-willed.	0	1	2	3	4	J
30. Jesus was a good, wise and great teacher.	4	3	2	1	0	J
31. The Bible may help some people but it does not help me.	0	1	2	3	4	B
32. In Jesus we can see God at work.	4	3	2	1	0	J
33. I read the Bible because I feel better when I have done so.	4	3	2	1	0	B
34. The Church helps us learn how to pray better.	4	3	2	1	0	C[9]
35. The New Testament teaches us how to deal with suffering.	4	3	2	1	0	B
36. Reading the Bible helps to strengthen people's faith.	4	3	2	1	0	B

Max. (BCJ) 120; Max. (S) 20.

SECTION E

Here are five situations where conversations are taking place. One half of the conversation is given at the top of each section, and four possible replies are given underneath. For each situation tick the *one* reply which seems to you to be most right for a Christian to make.

1. Two girls on their way home from school. One says, 'I'm sorry I did that to you this morning. It was spiteful of me.' The other might reply:

Scoring

a. 'There's no need to say sorry. I'd have got over it in any case.' ( ) √ = 0

b. 'You've done this about a dozen times now and I don't believe you're sorry a bit. Go away.' ( ) √ = 0

c. 'I'll forgive you if you *prove* you're sorry by buying me some sweets.' ( ) √ = 0

    d. 'All right. Let's both try to forget what you've done, and start again.'   ( ) √ = 1

2. Two boys leaving the school grounds. One says to the other, 'Do you see Bob's been put on probation?' The other might reply:

    a. 'About time too. He's had it coming to him for some months now.'   ( ) √ = 0

    b. 'Yes, I know. And I'm glad to say my sister dropped him flat when she heard.'   ( ) √ = 0

    c. 'Poor old Bob. Who do the police think they are – always trying to get us into trouble like this!'   ( ) √ = 0

    d. 'Yes, I'm going out with him tonight just to keep him company, though Mum wasn't too keen about me getting mixed up with him after this.'   ( ) √ = 1

3. A group of boys in a youth club. Leaning on a pillar near-by is a solitary West Indian youth. One boy says to the group, 'Should we ask him to join us?' The other boys might reply:

    a. 'No. Don't encourage them. They're bad enough as it is.'   ( ) √ = 0

    b. 'Why not? He looks a bit lonely.'   ( ) √ = 1

    c. 'Yes, let's! I always think they're so exciting. I like them being different from us.'   ( ) √ = 0

    d. 'No. Leave him alone. One of his own sort'll come along in a minute.'   ( ) √ = 0

4. Boy on platform of crowded bus, with conductor right along inside. Boy says to himself, 'If I get off quickly no one will know I haven't paid the conductor.' He might then go on to say to himself:

    a. 'No, I'd better fight my way through and pay him.'   ( ) √ = 1

    b. 'And why not? If he doesn't do his job properly why should I do it for him?'   ( ) √ = 0

    c. 'No, I'd better not risk it. The inspector's on board.'   ( ) √ = 0

    d. 'After all, he's too busy to change my 10s. note. I won't bother this time.'   ( ) √ = 0

5. Two girls by a display-counter in a self-service store. One says, 'Slip this in your pocket for me and let me have it outside.' The other might reply:

    a. 'No. Do your own dirty work yourself.'   ( ) √ = 0

    b. 'No. We might get caught.'   ( ) √ = 0

    c. 'All right. I'll do it for you as you're my friend.'   ( ) √ = 0

Scoring

d. 'No. You know as well as I do that it's wrong.' ( ) √ = 1

e. 'All right, as long as you give me half.' ( ) √ = 0

Max. 5

SECTION F

(i) Do you class yourself as a Christian? Tick the answer below, which best expresses your own position.

Scoring

I definitely think of myself as a Christian.	( )	4
I think of myself as a Christian on the whole.	( )	3
I just do not know whether I am a Christian.	( )	2
I feel I am probably not a Christian	( )	1
I definitely do not call myself a Christian.	( )	0

(ii) How important to you is your answer to F (i)? Tick the sentence below, which best expresses your feelings.

This is a very important matter to me.	( )	4
It is quite important.	( )	3
It is not really important.	( )	1
It is not important at all.	( )	0

Max. 8

(iii) To what extent do you pray on your own nowadays? Tick the statement below, which best expresses your own position.

I pray regularly.	( )	4
I pray fairly often.	( )	3
I pray occasionally	( )	2
I hardly ever pray.	( )	1
I never pray at all.	( )	0

(iv) How often do you[10] attend church or chapel for worship nowadays? Tick the phrase below, which applies to you.

Once a week.	( )	4
At least once a month.	( )	3
Occasionally.	( )	2
Once or twice a year.	( )	1
Never.	( )	0

Max. 8

[10] The word 'voluntarily' was inserted into Survey 666 at this point.

N.B. The substitutes for Sections C and E in Survey 666 are printed on pp. 129–31.

2. *Sampling procedure*

To provide the required contrast-group the 293 schools on Loukes' original list were divided into 'strata' at five levels; in the first instance they were divided into grammar (72), modern (200) and comprehensive (21); then into mixed (156), girls' (88) and boys' (49); then into small (i.e. below 500 pupils) (101) and large (192); then into regional groupings (SE 104; SW 31; Mid 64; North 71; Wales 23);[11] and finally by type of Local Educational Authorities into County Council (184) and County Borough (109). Schools were then selected from a specially numbered list drawn from *The Education Authorities Directory*, using random number tables, until each stratum was equally matched (and triple-banked, for safety).

[11] The Local Educational Authorities falling within each of these groupings are shown on pp. 23 f.

2

The Overall Pattern of
Pupil Responses

THE MAIN purpose of stage one of the survey had been to collect evidence of end results from a representative sample of county secondary schools spread throughout the country, in order to select two smaller contrasting groups of high-scoring and low-scoring schools. However, the evidence which came to hand was sufficient to form the basis of a more general evaluation of end results in all 520 of the schools, though one word of warning needs to be uttered by way of prelude. Although the sample covered as many as 10% of all the county secondary schools, and although figures obtained with sample of this size respond well to tests of statistical significance, it must be remembered that such tests depend on the sample being representative, whereas 50% of the sample used for Survey 65 had been deliberately chosen on the basis of earlier recommendation. The overall results are therefore likely to show a slightly greater degree of success than might be expected from a fully random sample. There are, of course, statistical techniques by which one can compensate for bias in sampling, but there has only been time[1] to apply these in one of the cases quoted (see pp. 71–74). However, in this one case the degree of bias has been shown to be insufficiently large to have any real significance, and this fact can give us at least a 'transferred' confidence as we approach the other figures discussed in this and the following chapter.

The overall results for the 'attainment tests' (Sections A, B, C,

---

[1] The pressure of time has been a problem throughout the course of the survey, particularly once my period of secondment was finished. Had I done every statistical process I would have liked to do, the results would not be published yet!

and E of Survey 65) are shown in Figure 1. The school-mean-scores (see p. 33) are shown on the horizontal axis, grouped in intervals of 5%, and the vertical axis shows the number of schools gaining a mean-score which falls within each 5% interval. The solid line refers to modern schools, the broken line to grammar schools. For example, fifty-five grammar and 117 modern schools gained mean scores falling between 70% and 74% (inclusive). (The exact figures are given in the table below the diagram.)

Fig. 1   The distribution of attainment scores (fourth formers)

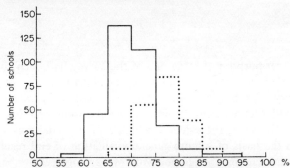

School-mean-score for attainment, expressed as percentage

%		55–59	60–64	65–69	70–74	75–79	80–84	85–89	90–94	Total
Number of schools	Grammar	0	0	8	55	80	36	5	1	185
	Modern	1	45	134	117	31	5	1	1	335

The median school-score (i.e. the score which exactly half of the schools managed to achieve or surpass), taken to the nearest whole number, was 69% for the modern schools and 76% for the grammar. This comparative success of the grammar schools is what one would expect in an attainment test, and is easy to see from the diagram above. What is not so easy to establish is the level of 'absolute' success which these results represent. Before analysing the results I had decided that 67·75% would be a reasonable pass-mark in the light of the difficulty of the questions in sections A, B, C and E. Figure 1 shows that, on this standard, nearly all the grammar schools achieved school mean scores ranking as 'passes', whereas not many more than half of the modern schools reached the required standard. (A further breakdown of the figures shows that only three grammar schools came below 68%, while 112 of the modern schools, i.e. one-third of them, 'failed' the test.) We must not, of course, forget that these school-scores are derived from the performance of the highest-ability stream in each school. This suggests that had the tests been given to the whole range of pupils the school mean scores would have been considerably reduced, and that many more (especially of the modern schools) would have failed the test.

Two further analyses can be made at this point within the overall pattern of attainment results. The first is a comparison of the contributions of the 'knowledge' test (Sections A and B) and the 'insight' test (Sections C and E); the second is a comparison of these fourth-form results (from Survey 65) with the sixth-form results (from Survey 666).

The median scores for Sections A and B were 70·4% and 62·7% (grammar and modern schools respectively), while those for Sections C and E were 81·6% and 75·0%. In other words the modern schools came slightly closer to the grammar schools on the insight tests than they did on the knowledge tests; that is to say, the modern school pupils were better at understanding than they were at remembering. This can also be seen from the fact that their median score overtopped the pre-selected pass-mark (73%) for Sections C and E by 2%, whereas in Sections A and B, where the pass mark was 62·5%, their median was only 0·2% above it. (This contrast may indicate a weakness in any form of test which seeks to judge success in RE among less academic-minded pupils purely on the basis of 'remembered-knowledge'.)

The other comparison (of fourth-form and sixth-form results) also reveals a weakness in any attempt to judge success by the amount of knowledge remembered. The inclusion of Sections A and B in both Survey 65 and 666 meant that in the thirty-two grammar schools (plus six modern schools with sixth forms) the knowledge-scores on the two surveys could be compared *within the same school.* In only three of these thirty-eight schools did the sixth formers produce better results than their corresponding fourth formers, while among the other thirty-five the average sixth-form mark was more than 10% lower than the average fourth-form mark. (In the modern schools this difference was 15%; in boys' grammar, 12·5%; in mixed grammar, 9·3%; and in girls' grammar, 7·25%.)

To put this in another way, on the basis of a 62·5% pass-mark seventeen of the sixth forms 'failed' the test, judged by their average mark; i.e. twelve out of the thirty-two grammar sixths failed, as did five out of the six modern sixths. Of the corresponding fourth forms in these thirty-eight schools, only two had failed, both of them in modern schools.

Retention of biblical knowledge is therefore *not* a feature of development in the last years at school, even in schools which reveal an overall success in RE. One must admit that it would be only a handful of sixth formers who continued biblical study with the same intensity that these fourth formers would have brought to it, many of them with O level Divinity large upon their horizons, and so this deterioration is to some extent expected. One must not forget, however, that the evidence from these thirty-eight schools comes from pupils in schools where the subject is taken with more than average serious-ness. Presumably in many schools this later deterioration in remem-bered-knowledge is even greater, which means that the picture of grammar school end-results suggested by Figure 1 is somewhat rosier than a wide-based survey of sixth formers would reveal. As for later deterioration in end-results among modern school pupils, one cannot fail to ask what happens to the great proportion of pupils who leave school altogether at the end of their fourth form. Will the new environment of their work do much to perpetuate whatever knowledge of the Bible, etc., they have managed to accumulate at school?

Attitudes

When one turns to the overall results of the attitude tests (Sections D and F [i] – [ii]) one is on firmer ground for making absolute, as opposed to comparative, evaluations. By reason of the actual construction of the attitude scales one does not have to fix 'pass-marks' subjectively. It is established from the start that a score of two out of four represents a neutral attitude, scores of one or zero represent increasingly hostile attitudes, and those of three or four reflect increasingly favourable ones. When converted into percentage scores this five-point scale appears as five areas between 1 and 100, centred round 0, 25, 50, 75 and 100, namely,

Raw score	0	1	2	3	4
% Score	0–12	13–37	38–62	63–87	88–100

Figure 2 shows the overall pattern of attitude results in percentage form. As in Figure 1 school-mean-scores are marked along the horizontal axis in 5% intervals, while the vertical axis shows the number of schools achieving mean-scores falling within each 5% interval grouping. (The exact figures are again given in the table below the diagram, and once again the solid line represents modern schools and the dotted line grammar schools.)

Fig. 2 The distribution of attitude scores (fourth formers)

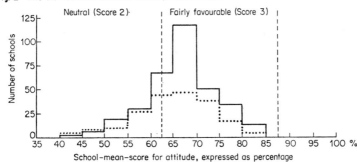

School-mean-score for attitude, expressed as percentage

%	40-44	45-49	50-54	55-59	60-64	65-69	70-74	75-79	80-84	Total
Number of schools Grammar	2	4	7	27	45	46	38	14	2	185
Modern	1	3	18	30	70	117	51	36	9	335

The median school-score for the modern schools was 67%, for the grammar schools 65%. It is clear therefore that the majority of fourth-form pupils hold an attitude towards Christianity in general which is to be described as 'fairly favourable'. Now, this conclusion is based on the amalgamated results of five different attitude tests (*re* Jesus, the Bible, the Church, School Religion, and the term 'Christian'). A breakdown of those figures into different scales will be found on pp. 62–63, but there is value at this point in studying the results relating specifically to Section F, questions (i) and (ii): 'Do you class yourself as a Christian?' and 'How important to you is your answer?' They are worth studying by themselves because the same two questions appeared in Survey 666 and the fourth- and fifth/sixth-form results can therefore be compared.

Figure 3 (*a*) shows the minimum, median and maximum school-score for these two questions (combined) from Survey 65, and Figure 3 (*b*) shows the same for Survey 666.

Various comments need to be made on this diagram, some to do

Fig. 3 The range of combined scores for questions F(i) and (ii) among (a) fourth formers and (b) fifth/sixth formers

Raw score	2	3	4	
%	38–62	63–87	88–100	
Attitude	Neutral	Fairly favourable	Definitely favourable	Number of schools
(a) Fourth formers				
Mixed Grammar	40 — [67] — 80			73
Girls' Grammar	47 — [72] — 87			63
Boys' Grammar	50 — [67] — 82			49
Mixed Modern	48 — [68] — 81			196
Girls' Modern	54 — [73] — 90			99
Boys' Modern	48 — [63] — 74			40
(b) Fifth/sixth formers				
Mixed Grammar	48 — [66] — 75			8
Girls' Grammar	56 — [69] — 85			14
Boys' Grammar	46 — [56] — 67			9
Mixed Modern	61 — [68] — 82			9
Girls' Modern	70 — [75] — 87			10
Boys' Modern	56 — [65] — 76			8

Type of school

40   50   60   70   80   90   100

School—mean—score relating to involvement with Christianity, expressed as percentage

with the study of each half separately, others to do with a comparison of the two halves.

1. The *range* of each group is obviously related in some measure to the number of schools in each group. Also one must remember that these figures refer to the mean-score of each form represented, and therefore the range is much more restricted than it would be if scores of individual pupils were being tabulated (see below).

2. It is clear that girls' schools contain the most favourable attitudes (one sees at least one girls' modern school where the school-mean-score was over 88, i.e. involvement with Christianity

is a matter of major importance to at least half of the pupils in 4A in that school).

3. The parallelism between grammar and modern schools at the fourth-form level is again apparent (cf. Figure 2), though a slight shift towards neutrality is now clear among boys' modern schools.

4. In comparing the figures in the lower part of the chart with those in the upper part it must be remembered that Survey 666 was used only in schools which had scored highly in Survey 65. It is not surprising, therefore, that the minima from the fifth/sixth forms are generally higher than those from among the fourth forms. Another point to be remembered is that the non-grammar sixth forms (and to *some* extent the fifth forms) are made up of pupils who are on the whole likely to accept 'the school line' fairly readily, and so, on this account alone, one should not be surprised to notice that there is a slight rise in median scores among the modern schools as one moves to the lower part of the diagram.

5. What one also notices, however, is that there is an actual *drop* in median scores *and* in maxima among the grammar schools, despite the fact that the lower part of the diagram only draws on the results of the schools near the top end of the scale in the upper part. This is particularly noticeable among the boys' grammar schools. When, in fact, one looks into individual school results and compares the respective fourth form and fifth/sixth form results in this part of the survey among the thirty-one grammar schools from which both sets of results are available, one finds on average an 11·5% drop from fourth to sixth form within the same school; in the girls' grammar schools this average drop was only 8·6%, in mixed grammar schools 10·25% while in the boy's grammar schools it was 17·1% (the equivalent of almost seven boys out of every ten moving down one position on the original five-point scale).

Here, then, is clear evidence that as the grammar school pupil moves through his last years at school he not only tends to *remember* less about the factual content of the Christian teaching he has received but also tends to *regard* the Christian position much less favourably.[2]

[2] E. C. Prichard's findings (*Learning for Living*, March 1967) raise the possibility that this may be to some extent due to the disappearance of RE from the timetable in the fifth and sixth forms. Of the schools (in Wales) he investigated 30% discontinued the subject after the fourth form. Figures from the British Council of Churches Survey are not so conclusive, but suggest that *at least* 11% of the schools drop the subject in either the fifth or sixth form, or both.

Although no further comparison of attitudes can be made between the fourth and fifth/sixth formers, there is nevertheless a lot of further information forthcoming from Survey 666 about the general attitude-level among senior pupils. Indeed the comparatively small numbers of pupils involved (about 1,360) made it possible to analyse their individual responses, rather than having to work with school means the whole time. Figure 4 shows the distribution of individual results from the items concerning Jesus and the Church (see pp. 41–43) on a simple three-point scale of 'unfavourable', 'neutral' and 'favourable' attitudes.

Fig. 4   The distribution of individual attitude scores regarding Jesus and the Church, expressed as percentages of the number of pupils (selected fifth/sixth formers) holding the particular kind of attitude

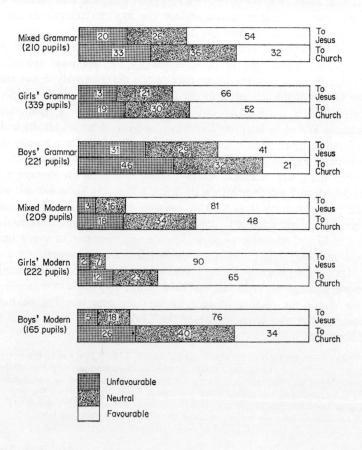

Mixed Grammar (210 pupils)
To Jesus: 20 | 26 | 54
To Church: 33 | 36 | 32

Girls' Grammar (339 pupils)
To Jesus: 13 | 21 | 66
To Church: 19 | 30 | 52

Boys' Grammar (221 pupils)
To Jesus: 31 | 29 | 41
To Church: 46 | 32 | 21

Mixed Modern (209 pupils)
To Jesus: 3 | 16 | 81
To Church: 18 | 34 | 48

Girls' Modern (222 pupils)
To Jesus: 2 | 7 | 90
To Church: 12 | 23 | 65

Boys' Modern (165 pupils)
To Jesus: 5 | 18 | 76
To Church: 26 | 40 | 34

Unfavourable
Neutral
Favourable

From these figures it is obvious that, even in these specially selected schools, the image of the Church is considerably tarnished, far more so than the image of Jesus, and the tarnishing process (with regard to both) is more advanced in grammar sixth forms than in modern fifth/sixth forms.

In an attempt to produce a rough assessment of the willingness of these fifth/sixth formers to regard Jesus as a 'saviour', the results were further analysed. It was not possible in the time available to look at the individual responses to this particular item, but each individual total for the three 'Jesus-items' was able to be used to reveal the possible range of proportions of pupils regarding Jesus as a 'saviour' within each school-group. The results were as follows:

	%
Mixed grammar	27–64
Girls' grammar	34–77
Boys' grammar	13–53
Mixed modern	30–88
Girls' modern	52–95
Boys' modern	32–81

In other words, at least half, and possibly nearly every one, of the pupils in the fifth/sixth forms in the selected girls' modern schools regarded Jesus as a saviour in some sense of the word. By contrast, in the boys' grammar schools at *most* only half of the sixth formers, and possibly as few as 13% of them, held Jesus in this regard – and this in schools which had been specially selected because of the favourable attitudes to Christianity revealed among their fourth formers.

Finally in this analysis of fifth/sixth-form attitudes, questions (i) and (ii) of Section F (see p. 45) can be looked at separately. They have already been taken in conjunction with each other to show how 'involved' the pupils were with Christianity (see Figure 3), but in view of the fairly widespread detachment from traditional Christian standpoints among these pupils, it was felt to be vital to assess the concern which they felt with the whole issue of Christianity, to assess how important they felt it was to be or, equally, *not* to be a Christian. Figure 5 shows first of all their willingness to be called Christian, and secondly their assessment of the importance of this question. (As one is dealing here with individual scores, not school means, I have classified[3] the pupils simply as fifteen/sixteen-year-

[3] For further breakdown of classification by sex, as well as age, see p. 63.

olds or seventeen/eighteen-year-olds, irrespective of whether they come from grammar or modern schools – though obviously *all* the fifteen/sixteen-year-olds will come from the latter, and most of the seventeen/eighteen-year-olds from the former.)

Fig. 5   The distribution of individual fifth and sixth formers' scores regarding (i) personal acceptance of the 'Christian label', (ii) assessment of this question as important, expressed as percentages of the number of pupils holding the particular kind of attitude

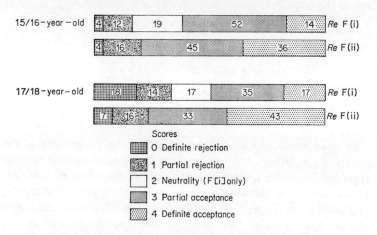

Two things are clear from this diagram – the comparatively even spread of distribution on F (i) among the older pupils (the only exception being the sharp rise at the 'partial acceptance' level); and the heavy weighting at the 'definite acceptance' end for F (ii). If one adds together those scoring 3 or 4 one finds approximately 78% of the pupils in this joint category for F (ii) (importance of the question), whereas there are only approximately 59%[4] in the same category for F (i) (acceptance of the 'Christian label'). One must remember yet again that these results are from specially selected schools, and that the national figures could well be lower on both tables, but this will not of course be likely to affect the difference *between* the tables – a difference to which we must return later.

[4] Even if one adds in half of the 'neutrals' for F (i) (there was *no* 'neutral' category offered in F (ii)) one still only finds 68%, which is significantly lower than the 78% for the same area of F (ii).

'Religious Behaviour'

The final area of investigation tackled by both Survey 65 and 666 was the question of religious behaviour, i.e. the practice of private prayer and attendance at public worship. Figure 6 shows the results of Section F, questions (iii) and (iv) (see p. 45), arranged as in Figures 1 and 2.

Fig. 6   The distribution of religious practice scores (fourth formers)

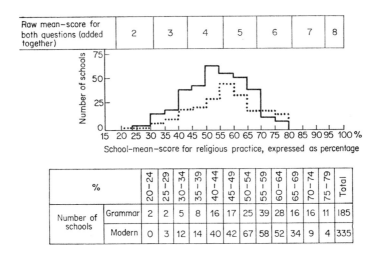

| Raw mean−score for both questions (added together) | 2 | 3 | 4 | 5 | 6 | 7 | 8 |

School-mean−score for religious practice, expressed as percentage

%		20−24	25−29	30−34	35−39	40−44	45−49	50−54	55−59	60−64	65−69	70−74	75−79	Total
Number of schools	Grammar	2	2	5	8	16	17	25	39	28	16	16	11	185
	Modern	0	3	12	14	40	42	67	58	52	34	9	4	335

The median school-score for the modern schools was 54%, and for the grammar schools it was 57% (i.e. falling in the percentage range which represents a raw score of 5, whereas the modern schools came one raw-score lower). The fact that the scores were for *both* aspects of religious behaviour makes it difficult to interpret a score in terms of actual behaviour; for example,[5] a score of 4 could be a combination of regular prayer with nil attendance at worship, or prayer 'fairly often' with worship once or twice a year, or occasional prayer and worship, or private prayer 'hardly ever' with worship at least once a month, or no private prayer at all with weekly attendance at worship. However, taken by and large, it is apparent that the great majority of the fourth formers come within the general area of 'occasional' prayer and/or worship, with a slight tendency towards

[5] See p. 45.

a little more regularity, especially among the grammar-school pupils.

The figures for the fifth/sixth formers can be presented in the same way:

Fig. 7   The distribution of religious practice scores (fifth/sixth formers)

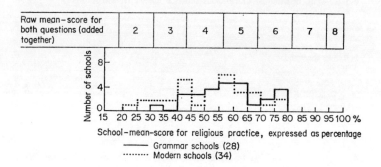

The median school-score here is 58% for the modern schools and 53% for the grammar schools, showing the same sort of shift from the fourth-form table which was noticed in comparing the two parts of Figure 3. The drop in the grammar-school median is also reflected when one looks at the results within each individual school. One finds on average a 15·8% drop in mean score from fourth to sixth form within each grammar school; among girls' grammar schools the average drop was 11·1%; in mixed grammar it was 16·4%; and in boys' grammar it was 22·9% (the equivalent of nine boys out of every ten moving down two positions on the original nine-point scale). These figures are again comparable with those on p. 52 which show the decline in 'commitment to the Christian position' between grammar-school fourth and sixth formers. It will be seen that the decline in 'religious behaviour' is even greater. The same is generally true in the modern schools as well. The overall rise in the median between Figures 6 and 7 was due almost entirely to Figure 7 being based on a highly selective sample. The results from *within* each mixed modern school show an average drop in 'religious behaviour' scores of 9·0%; in the boys' modern schools it was 6·6%. In the girls' modern schools, however, it *rose* by about 1·7%; not a very great rise, of course, but a definite one. (And this, it must be stressed, is based on a comparison between pupils in the *same* school, not just between one wide group of schools and a more select group of schools, as was being made between Figures 6 and 7.)

One of the more striking things about Figure 7 is that a shift from the centre downwards, especially among grammar schools, has led to a much wider distribution than in Figure 6. An even distribution has already been noticed when looking the individual sixth-formers' willingness to accept the label 'Christian' as applying to themselves (see p. 56). With religious behaviour, however, this evenness of distribution becomes even more apparent when the scores are analysed pupil by pupil, but at the same time it becomes clear that it is caused at least in part by the effect of opposite tendencies among boys and girls,[6] as Figure 8 reveals (see p. 60).

Once again in looking at these figures one must not forget that they come from schools chosen for high scores originally achieved in Survey 65. They therefore represent a much more favourable picture than will presumably be found among the majority of sixth forms.

Summary

To attempt at this point an evaluation of the overall findings in the survey would be premature. The most I can do for the moment is to list once again the main findings in each area, and let them speak for themselves.

The criterion of success in attainment had to be subjectively arrived at, but if this criterion is accepted, then one-third of the (335) modern schools failed the attainment tests, whereas all but three of the (185) grammar schools passed. However, there were signs of considerable later deterioration in grammar-school performance, judged on sixth-form results. (The lack of success among modern-school pupils was at least partly due to their failure to retain knowledge, rather than any failure to achieve insight into the meaning of the material handled.)

The measure of 'favourable', 'neutral' or 'unfavourable' attitudes was more objective, being built into the structure of the tests. The majority of pupils exhibited 'fairly favourable' attitudes, taken overall, though there was again strong evidence of a later shift of position among sixth formers towards a less favourable attitude.

[6] This is true to *some* extent of the 'Christian label' scores. See p. 63.

Fig. 8 The distribution of religious practice scores (selected schools only), analysed by types of school and expressed as percentages of the number of pupils holding the particular practice

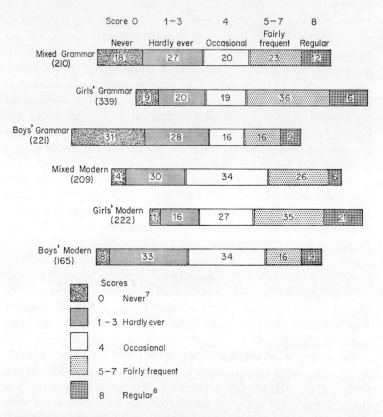

This was also the case with 'religious behaviour'. The majority of fourth formers came into the 'occasional' category, but there was a slight shift among sixth formers towards less frequent performance (especially among the boys) though the shift appears to have been from the centre downwards rather than over the whole scale.

Of the various 'areas of attitude' tested among the sixth forms the *lowest* scoring was 'attitude to the Church' (38% favourable); next

[7] 'Never' indicates that the pupils claimed they never go to church and never pray at all.

[8] 'Regular' indicates that they claimed weekly church attendance coupled with regular private prayer.

to the lowest came the ideas of Jesus as Saviour (about 40%); then came the general attitudes towards Jesus (43%); then the acceptance of the Christian 'label' (59%); and highest of all came 'the importance of the question about being a Christian' (78% accepting its importance).

APPENDIX TO CHAPTER 2

Further analyses of the attitude scores of Survey 65.

1. *Distribution of overall attitude scores (Sections D and F (i)–(ii)) analysed by school types*

% Score	40–44	45–49	50–54	55–59	60–64	65–69	70–74	75–79	80–84
Mixed grammar, large	1	3	4	11	15	10	8	1	0
Girls' grammar, large	1	0	1	1	8	10	11	6	1
Boys' grammar, large	0	1	1	4	6	8	3	1	0
Mixed grammar, small	0	0	0	0	8	7	5	0	0
Girls' grammar, small	0	0	0	4	2	5	8	4	1
Boys' grammar, small	0	0	1	7	6	6	3	2	0
Mixed modern, large	1	1	10	16	26	51	14	7	0
Girls' modern, large	0	0	0	0	10	9	14	11	2
Boys' modern, large	0	0	1	4	7	6	2	0	0
Mixed modern, small	0	1	3	5	18	29	9	5	0
Girls' modern, small	0	0	1	1	3	18	10	13	7
Boys' modern, small	0	1	3	4	6	4	2	0	0

N.B. For regional distribution, see pp. 71 f.

2. *Minima, medians and maxima expressed as percentages for B, C and J items in Section D*

Type of school	Number of schools	Minimum %	Median %	Maximum %
Mixed grammar, large	53	48	64	77
Mixed grammar, small	20	61	67	75
Girls' grammar, large	39	49	69	82
Girls' grammar, small	24	54	71	80
Boys' grammar, large	24	53	66	77
Boys' grammar, small	25	55	66	76
Mixed modern, large	126	41	65	76
Mixed modern, small	70	49	66	78
Girls' modern, large	46	58	70	83
Girls' modern, small	53	52	69	84
Boys' modern, large	20	54	64	75
Boys' modern, small	20	51	62	73

3. *Minima, medians and maxima for S items in Section D (cf. p. 65)*

Type of school	Number of schools	Minimum %	Median %	Maximum %
Mixed grammar, large	53	35	59	78
Mixed grammar, small	20	53	61	77
Girls' grammar, large	39	39	66	82
Girls' grammar, small	24	46	68	79
Boys' grammar, large	24	44	60	73
Boys' grammar, small	25	50	61	83
Mixed modern, large	126	40	63	84
Mixed modern, small	70	36	66	84
Girls' modern, large	46	57	72	86
Girls' modern, small	53	49	71	90
Boys' modern, large	20	48	61	70
Boys' modern, small	20	46	60	72

4. *Minima, medians and maxima for Section F (i)–(ii) (cf. p. 52)*

Type of school	Number of schools	Minimum %	Median %	Maximum %
Mixed grammar, large	53	40	66	80
Mixed grammar, small	20	60	69	79
Girls' grammar, large	39	47	72	87
Girls' grammar, small	24	53	73	86
Boys' grammar, large	24	50	68	82
Boys' grammar, small	25	51	66	80
Mixed modern, large	126	48	68	78
Mixed modern, small	70	51	67	81
Girls' modern, large	46	56	72	84
Girls' modern, small	53	54	73	90
Boys' modern, large	20	53	66	72
Boys' modern, small	20	48	60	74

3

Regional and other Factors

ONE TABLE of figures on its own does not tell us a great deal, even when it is centred on some 'absolute' criterion such as was incorporated into the diagrams in the preceding chapter showing the results of the attitude tests. What gives much more meaning to a table of figures is to set it in comparison with another table, so that one can see trends, correlations and so on. Inevitably, even when supposedly it was the overall situation being dealt with in the preceding chapter, internal comparisons were being constantly made, between grammar schools and modern schools, between girls and boys, between older and younger pupils, between one atttitude-area and another.

In this chapter the process will be taken even further, in an attempt to discover which of the factors directly or indirectly investigated through Survey 65 seems to have had the greatest influence on the results. Let us start with a new set of figures, not previously mentioned, the figures relating to 'school religion'. They contributed, of course, to the pattern of combined results in Figure 2, but they have not been dealt with separately before. The lowest, the highest, and the median school-scores for 'attitude to RE and Assembly' in the different types of school are set out in Figure 9.

This has the same basic pattern as Figure 3 (a), as would be expected. There is, however, an apparent shift to the left both in the minima and in the medians. This shift to the left is also apparent in comparison with the results from the other items in Section D (see p. 62). This suggests that Christianity in its school form has proved by and large not to have contributed very positively to the building up of favourable attitudes. However, if this leads anyone to suppose

Fig. 9   The range of attitude scores regarding 'school religion' (fourth formers)

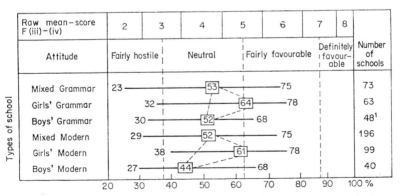

Attitude	Fairly hostile	Neutral	Fairly favourable	Definitely favourable	Number of schools
Mixed Grammar	35	[60]	78		73
Girls' Grammar	39	[67]	82		63
Boys' Grammar		44 [61]	83		49
Mixed Modern	36	[64]	84		196
Girls' Modern		49 [71]		90	99
Boys' Modern		46 [61] 72			40

30   40   50   60   70   80   90   100 %

School–mean –score showing attitude to school religion, expressed as percentage

that Christianity has been presented more effectively by the Church, then one must point to the Church-attitude figures among the fifth/sixth formers, and also to Figure 10 which shows the 'religious behaviour' figures for fourth-formers in a form easily comparable with Figure 9.

It is clear that if (and one must, of course, allow this to stand as a conditional) one's religious behaviour is a measure of the Church's impact on one's attitudes, then school-religion is a better builder of favourable attitudes than church-religion. But, as has been noted

Fig. 10   The range of religious practice scores (fourth formers)

Raw mean–score F (iii) – (iv)	2	3	4	5	6	7	8	
Attitude	Fairly hostile		Neutral		Fairly favourable		Definitely favourable	Number of schools
Mixed Grammar	23		[53]		75			73
Girls' Grammar		32		[64]	78			63
Boys' Grammar	30		[52]	68				48[1]
Mixed Modern	29		[52]		75			196
Girls' Modern		38		[61]	78			99
Boys' Modern	27		[44]	68				40

20   30   40   50   60   70   80   90   100 %

School–mean – score for religious practice, expressed as percentage

[1] One of the boys' grammar schools had a fairly large boarding house, and this over-weighted the church-attendance results, so it was ignored for this table.

C

already, there seems to be something which is considerably more effective than either in contributing to the pattern of positive attitudes shown in Figures 2 and 3. Even when a school has aroused the full loyalty and enthusiasm of its pupils by the high quality of its RE and Assembly (and there were indeed schools in our sample where this has occurred) it may still fail to register a particularly high 'general Christian attitude' score if other (and stronger) factors in the pupils' environment are tending against the formation of such attitudes.

To what source, then, can one attribute the general favour in which things Christian still seem to be held (as Figure 2 so clearly indicates)? Is this something to do with such vague, but apparently powerful, forces as 'national tradition', 'climate of ideas', etc.? Certainly, recent figures from opinion polls suggest that there is still a very strong public feeling that Christianity is somehow 'a good thing', that Britain as a country should still uphold the Christian way of life, and that our children should be brought up within the Christian faith.[2] This sort of social atmosphere is probably absorbed by the child and the adolescent, even though he may rebel against certain of its restrictions and practical applications.

The figures presented at the beginning of this chapter seem to suggest that the majority of schools are acting as media through which the general religious mood of the country is conveyed, rather than contributing anything very positive of their own. This hypothesis is strengthened when one takes a closer look at regional variations in the results of Survey 65. The experiences of the Newsom Committee had suggested that the factor of 'distance from London' might have some impact, and the sample for Survey 65 had been drawn up with this in mind (cf. p. 46). The other factors borne in mind during the construction of the sample had been size of school, status (grammar/modern), and sex distribution of pupils (mixed/girls/boys). These three factors have constantly figured in the comparisons and analyses recorded to date, but a further careful analysis was deliberately made to compare the 'strengths' of all four factors, plus the additional factor of heavily urbanized environment.

The technique of this analysis is described in some detail on pp. 70 f., but the overall results can be quite simply stated. Where the *attainment* scores were concerned the greatest difference was shown to be between grammar and modern schools (cf. Figure 1); when the

<hr>

[2] See Chapter 7.

'status factor' was isolated from all the others it made as much as 6% difference to the mean scores of the two groups. The next largest difference in attainment was between the single-sex girls' schools and the other schools (3·4% difference on mean-scores). The single-sex boys' schools were marginally higher than the mixed schools, which is not the pattern that common sense would have suggested. It would appear not only that girls produce better attainment results than boys, but that the 'academic' performance of both sexes is enhanced by their being in single-sex communities.

The difference in mean attainment scores between the regions was comparatively small (2·4% spread over all eight regions), and probably of any significance only when the two extremes are being compared. (The actual order, descending, among the regions was: North, South-east, South-west, Midlands, Midland conurbation, London conurbation, Northern conurbations, Wales.) Finally the impact of size of school on attainment results appears to be quite insignificant (less than 1·0% difference being discernible).

The impact of size on *attitude* results is even less noticeable (a difference of under 0·3%), while the impact of status in this area is also only fractional (a 0·5% difference between grammar and modern schools: the apparent difference of 2·0% shown on Figure 2 is due to the influence on the sample of *other* factors which had not been eliminated for the purposes of that particular diagram). The first factor making any real impact on attitudes would seem to be that of environment. The schools in the conurbations produced a mean-score 2·7% lower than those outside such areas.

As has been suggested by nearly every other survey in this field the sex of the pupils plays a major part in the formation of their attitudes. The difference between the mean scores of the two groups of single-sex schools was 7·4%, the girls obviously scoring more highly. The mixed schools' score fell between the two single-sex scores, but nearer to the boys rather than to the girls (from whom they differed by 5·5%).

Finally, in this review of factors affecting attitudes, one comes to the regional factor. Here the difference over the whole range (all other factors except 'urbanization' being excluded) was 8·8%, i.e. the schools in the most 'favourable' region produced a mean-attitude score 8·8% greater than that produced by the schools in the least 'favourable' region. What is particularly striking about this range of difference is its relationship with the differences caused by the 'urbanized environment' factor. As has already been mentioned, when the schools within each region were divided into 'conurbation' and 'otherwise', the range of mean-scores between the two groups was 2·7%. When the schools were divided *first* into 'conurbation' and 'otherwise', and *then* into regions, the range of mean scores over the regions was as high as 4·6% within the conurbations, and 4·4% among the other schools.[3]

The first major conclusion drawn from this must be that the region within which a school is located is probably the most important factor influencing the attitudes of its pupils, apart from the question of whether it is a girls', boys' or mixed school. And it must be stressed that the term 'region' here means what it says. This is something different from immediate environment, and also more important. The differences between the attitudes of pupils in a large city and those in a nearby rural area are likely to be less marked than the differences between the attitudes of pupils in a large city in one region and those in another large city in another region.[4]

The second major conclusion springs from the identification of which regions show the higher attitude scores and which show the lower ones. Figure 11 sets the regional mean scores out on a linear scale, centred on the average score for all 520 schools, namely, 65·8%.

This pattern, with Wales well at the top and the London conurbation even more firmly at the bottom of the scale, appears with even

Fig. 11　The range of mean attitude scores, analysed by regions (fourth formers)

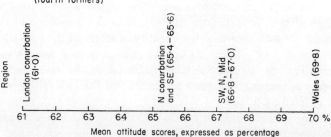

Mean attitude scores, expressed as percentage

[3] The fact that the sum of these is *more* than 8·8 % is due to the fact that the highest regional score among the conurbations overlapped with the lowest regional score among the other schools.

[4] Cf. the importance given to the 'geographic factor' in Professor Stephen Wiseman's essay in *How and Why do We Learn?* W. R. Niblett, ed. (London, Faber, 1965).

more exaggeration if one looks at the comparative regional per-
formances on the 'religious behaviour' test[5] (see Figure 12).
The final point to be made about this analysis concerns the
different impact made by RE in the different regions. As was noted

Fig. 12 The range of mean religious practice scores, analysed by regions
(fourth formers)

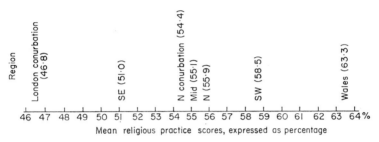

Mean religious practice scores, expressed as percentage

at the beginning of this chapter, the general level of response to
school-religion was less favourable than the general response to
Christianity (see pp. 62 and 64 f. above). However, in 193 out of the
519 schools this was not the case; within 174 of these exceptional
schools the 'RE/Assembly' score (Section Db of Survey 65) was
higher than the 'Jesus/Bible/Church' score (Section Da); in the other
nineteen the two scores were equal. When these 193 schools[6] are
sorted out on a regional basis, the following pattern emerges:

Region:	Lond. con.	N con.	Wales	SE	N	Mid	SW	
Total number of schools in the region sample	80	53	27	116	61	109	61	
Schools where Db is higher than Da	15	18	10	43	23	50	28	
These schools expressed as percentages of all schools in the region sample	19	34	37	37	38	46	46	%

[5] Some supporting evidence for this pattern is also to be found in the Confirma-
tion figures for 1958–1963 (see *Facts and Figures about the Church of England*
[London: Church Information Office, 1965]).

[6] Six of them were from the Midland conurbation, but the overall sample
from this region (twelve) was too small to be statistically significant, so it has
been omitted from all these regional diagrams.

It appears from this table that in almost half of the schools in the South-west and Midlands the RE being given is contributing something positive towards the building up of favourable attitudes towards Christianity. By contrast, in 81% of the schools in the London conurbation the fourth formers look upon the RE they receive with even less favour than their general attitude to Christianity might lead one to expect. (One must say '*even* less favour', for although the low RE scores obviously contribute something towards the lowness of the *combined* attitude scores shown on Figure 11, it is equally obvious from Figure 12 that even without the weighting of the RE scores, the general attitude scores would not be very much higher.)

The conclusion to which all this leads up, then, is that although the RE given in the South-west may well be successfully feeding on, and feeding into, the general cultural religious influences in that region of the country (and this is true of the Midlands as well, outside the conurbation area), nevertheless in the London conurbation what has been offered there by way of RE is for the most part not arousing any welcoming response whatsoever, and is probably causing a difficult situation to become even worse. The implications of this will be taken up in Chapter 8.

APPENDIX TO CHAPTER 3

1. *Re Figure 10*
The 'raw scores' shown in the top line fall into a nine-point scale (being derived from an adding together of scores for the two questions F [iii]–[iv]), whereas the 'descriptions' of attitude level in the second line apply to the five-point scale round which Section D, and Figure 9, had been built, hence the apparent non-alignment of score with description.

2. *The analysis of the sex/status/size/region/environment factors*
The schools were first of all divided into the thirty groups produced by the status-sex-region divisions $(2 \times 3 \times 5)$.[7] Within each of these thirty groups the mean attainment score was calculated, and then the mean score for the large schools and the mean score for the small schools (still working within each of the thirty groups) was also calculated. (E.g. in the twenty-five mixed grammar schools from the Midlands the mean score was 75·5%; for the eighteen large schools in this group the mean

[7] At this stage the three conurbation groups were included in their respective regions.

score was 75%, and for the seven small schools it was 77%.) The differences from the respective means (taking note of the number of schools involved) were then collected together, and the average 'difference-from-the-mean' (for both large and small schools) was calculated over the whole thirty groups. In this way the impact of size of school on attainment could be discovered, unaffected by the possible influence of any of the other three factors.

Similar analyses were made isolating status (i.e. grammar or modern), and sex. When 'region' was analysed, the schools were divided into the twelve groups produced by the status-size-sex divisions $(2 \times 2 \times 3)$, and then each group was divided into eight regions, treating the three conurbation groups as separate regions. (The dividing lines between the regions are indicated in the list of Local Education Authorities on pp. 23–24. The guidance of the Oxford Atlas was followed in classifying the conurbations – London, Birmingham and environs, Liverpool/Manchester, Bradford/Leeds, and Tyneside – but London was redefined as being 'the area within a 30-mile radius of Hyde Park Corner'.)

A similar technique was used on the attitude and religious-behaviour scores.

3. *The statistical significance of the regional variations in attitude score*

It was difficult to devise a simple statistical test to apply to the above analysis, but the 'purified' differences between the regions (see above) corresponded closely enough to the regional differences in the raw scores for it to be worth testing the standard error of the raw (observed) regional means (for the attitude scores at least).

The 'purified' difference from the overall mean for each region was: London conurbation $-4\cdot83$; South-east $-0\cdot4$; North conurbation $-0\cdot23$; Midland $+1\cdot02$; South-west $+1\cdot09$; North $+1\cdot22$; Wales $+3\cdot97$, and these form the basis of Figure 11, working from an overall mean of 65·8%. The *observed* school scores are shown in the following frequency table. (One school's figure was proved to be of no value for this table, therefore the total was 519.)

Region:	Lond. con.	SE	N con.	Mid.	SW	N	Wales	Mid. con.	All regions
School score (%)				Number of Schools					
82	1				1		3		5
81	0				1	1	0		2
80	1		3		0	0	0		4
79	0		1	1	1	2	0		5
78	1		1	4	2	1	0		9
77	1	4	1	0	4	0	1	1	12
76	0	0	0	3	3	0	1	0	7
75	0	1	1	5	2	4	0	4	17
74	3	3	0	4	1	0	1	0	12
73	2	5	1	7	2	3	2	0	22
72	0	3	1	5	1	1	1	0	12

Region:	Lond. con.	SE	N con.	Mid.	SW	N	Wales	Mid. con.	All regions
School score (%)				Number of Schools					
71	2	2	3	6	0	4	2	0	19
70	1	5	1	4	5	7	0	0	23
69	3	10	4	8	4	3	3	0	35
68	1	6	4	6	4	5	2	0	28
67	4	11	3	6	2	3	2	1	32
66	7	11	0	5	4	7	2	0	36
65	1	12	5	5	3	3	1	2	32
64	2	7	7	4	4	1	2	0	27
63	1	5	3	7	6	6	1	1	30
62	6	1	2	6	2	2	1	0	20
61	4	2	2	7	0	0	1	1	17
60	4	5	3	2	1	5	1	0	21
59	5	6	1	2	1	0		0	15
58	5	3	1	3	1	1		1	15
57	4	5	1	2	1	1		0	14
56	4	1	1	2	0	1		0	9
55	2	0	0	2	0			0	4
54	3	1	0	1	3			0	8
53	1	1	0	0	1			0	3
52	4	2	0	1	1			0	8
51	1	2	0	0				0	3
50	0	2	1	0				0	3
49	1	0	0					1	2
48	0		1	1					2
47	2	0							2
46	0	0							0
45	1	0							1
44	0	0							0
43	0		1						1
42	1								1
41	1								1
Total number of schools	80	116	53	109	61	61	27	12	519

The means (expressed as percentage) for the seven[8] regions were:

Lond.	SE	N con.	Mid.	SW	N	Wales
61·3	65·1	65·8	66·8	67·6	67·6	69·7

the overall mean being 65·8%

The standard deviation (expressed as percentage) for each region was:

Lond.	SE	N con.	Mid.	SW	N	Wales
8·3	6·055	5·487	6·393	7·226	7·503	6·104

[8] The sample for Midland conurbation in the table was too small to be of any value (the σ_m being as high as 2·49).

the overall σ being 7·167%

The standard error of the mean (expressed as percentage) for each region was:

Lond.	SE	N con.	Mid.	SW	N	Wales
0·935	0·565	1·04	0·615	0·932	0·708	1·197

the overall σ_m being 0·996%.

(To find the possible limits of the mean for any region multiply the standard error of the mean by three and move that amount in *both* directions from the mean. E.g. to find possible range of the overall mean:

$$0·996 \times 3 = 2·99$$

The sample overall mean is 65·8%. The limits of the actual overall mean are therefore 65·8% —2·99% and 65·8% +2·99%, i.e. the actual mean must lie between 62·81% and 68·79%.)

Calculations were also made to discover the statistical reliability of the differences between the regional means. Each regional mean was paired with every other regional mean in turn. The standard error of the difference of each pair of means (σ_D) was found ($= \sqrt{\sigma^2_{m1}+\sigma^2_{m2}}$) and then this was used to divide the actual difference between the means (i.e. $\dfrac{D}{\sigma_D}$). The minimum product of this calculation acceptable for 'significance' was taken as 1·96 (i.e. at the 0·05 level of probability). On this basis the following groupings and distinctions emerged:

London/SE	significantly different (at 0·01 level)
SE/N con.	not significantly different
SE/Mid.	significantly different (at 0·05 level)
SE/SW	significantly different (at 0·01 level)
SE/Wales	significantly different (at 0·01 level)
N con./SW ⎤ N con./N ⎥ Mid./SW ⎬	not significantly different
Mid./N ⎥ SW/N ⎦	
Mid./Wales	significantly different (at 0·05 level)
SW/Wales ⎤ N/Wales ⎦	not significantly different

London was clearly separate from the others, and two other (though not quite as clear-cut) divisions fell between North conurbation and Midland, and also between North and Wales (cf. Figure 11).

One further question remained. How typical was this sample of pupils' attitudes in general? There was a possibility, due to the way in which the sample had been selected, that it reflected over-favourable attitudes. A test for skewness in terms of percentiles was used

$$Sk = \frac{(P_{90}+P_{10})}{2} - P_{50}$$

giving a skewness of $-0{\cdot}17$. (This negative skewness, besides being expected, was already apparent from the fact that the median point, at 66·08, was higher than the mean, at 65·8.) But on examination this amount of skewness was shown to be not significant. The standard error of this measure of skewness is

$$\frac{(P_{90}-P_{10})\times 0{\cdot}5185}{\sqrt{N}}$$

giving 0·415. When $\dfrac{Sk}{\sigma_{Sk}}$ is calculated the product is 0·41, well under the 1·96 which is the minimum for significance to be established.[9]

4. *Regional variation in religious behaviour*

The 'purified' scores shown in Figure 12 were derived by the process described in section two of this appendix, centred on the mean of all observed school-scores, namely, 54·5%. The following frequency table gives more details of the observed school-scores, though no further calculations on them have yet been made.

Region:	Lond. con.	SE	N con.	Mid.	N	SW	Wales	All regions
School score (%)				Number of Schools				
78				1		1	1	3
77			1	1	3	1	1	7
76			0	0	0	1	0	1
75			1	0	1	1	1	4
74	1		0	3	1	0	0	5
73	1		0	0	1	0	1	3
72	0	1	1	2	1	0	1	6
71	1	2	1	0	1	1	0	6
70	0	0	0	0	1	1	1	3
69	0	0	1	1	0	1	2	5
68	0	1	0	3	1	2	2	9
67	0	1	1	4	1	1	1	9
66	2	2	2	0	2	3	1	12
65	0	4	3	3	0	2	1	13
64	0	3	1	5	2	1	1	13
63	0	3	0	3	4	4	1	15
62	1	4	2	2	3	3	1	16
61	0	4	1	6	1	2	0	14
60	2	5	2	6	2	2	1	20
59	4	6	3	2	2	3	1	21
58	3	4	0	5	3	3	0	18

[9] H. E. Garrett, *Statistics in Psychology and Education* (New York: Longmans, 1953), p. 241.

Region:	Lond. con.	SE	N con.	Mid.	N	SW	Wales	All regions
School score (%)				Number of Schools				
57	3	3	5	8	0	1	1	21
56	3	3	2	3	4	4	0	19
55	2	6	2	2	1	2	1	16
54	2	4	0	2	1	1	1	11
53	3	6	2	0	1	1	1	14
52	2	7	4	4	1	2	2	22
51	4	8	2	1	3	4	1	23
50	5	1	1	6	2	4	0	19
49	2	7	2	2	3	2	0	18
48	1	2	0	3	3	2	0	11
47	0	3	0	3	2	0	0	8
46	2	4	1	4	1	0	0	12
45	2	2	0	3	1	0	1	9
44	5	3	1	4	1	1	0	15
43	1	1	1	4	1	1	0	9
42	2	6	0	2	1	0	1	12
41	3	3	3	1	1	1		12
40	2	0	1	2	1	1		7
39	7	0	0	0	1	0		8
38	0	1	0	1	1	0		3
37	1	1	0	0	1	0		3
36	2	0	2	1		0		5
35	0	0	0	1		0		1
34	0	0	2	1		0		3
33	0	1	0	2		0		3
32	3	0	0	1		0		4
31	3	0	1	0		1		5
30	1	0	1	0				2
29	2	1		0				3
28	0	1		0				1
27	0			1				1
26	0							0
25	0							0
24	1							1
23	1							1
Total Number of Schools	80	114	53	109	61	61	27	505[10]

[10] Omitting Midland conurbation and three other schools.

4

The Teachers

STAGE TWO of the survey, as already stated in Chapter 1, was intended to provide further information to enable a more detailed comparison to be made between high-scoring and low-scoring schools. Could any distinguishing features of the two groups be identified, other than those already noted such as sex differences, status differences and regional differences?

In order to answer this question, the 142 schools who returned the staff questionnaires were divided in two ways. First they were left in their original six groupings of mixed/girls/boys × grammar/modern, and within each of these groups the schools were separated into 'high-scoring' and 'low-scoring' on the basis of their *attainment* scores. Tables were then compiled showing the comparative distribution of the different types of answer to most of the sections of the questionnaire as between 'high-scoring' and 'low-scoring' schools. The 142 schools were then redivided by sex and by *region*, grouping the regions together as suggested by the pattern of Figure 11, giving twelve groups in all (mixed/girls/boys × Wales/North+South-west+Midland/North conurbation+South-east/London conurbation). Within each of *these* groups separation was made between 'high-scoring' and 'low-scoring' schools, this time on the basis of their *attitude* scores, and another set of tables was drawn up showing the comparative distribution of answers to all sections of the questionnaire, as analysed on this basis. (For details of the composition of these attainment- and attitude-groupings see pp. 107 f.)

Although the main purpose of these tables was to draw out the distinguishing features, if any, of 'high-scoring' and low-scoring' schools, they did provide information from which a fairly reliable overall picture of 'actual practice in the schools' could be built up. The selected samples from which both tables were compiled consisted of equal numbers of 'high-scoring' and 'low-scoring' schools, their mean scores ranging from 91% to 60% on the attainment tests, and 82% to 45% on the attitude tests (cf. the distribution of scores among all 520 schools shown in Figures 1 and 2) so they were well-balanced and well-spread groups, even if somewhat hollow in the middle ranges. (In the case of those answers to the questionnaire which were analysed both on the basis of attainment and of attitude score the 'overall' figures given in this chapter are derived from a combination of the two sets of tables.)

Rather than work solemnly through all forty question analyses, I shall concentrate here on those questions which reflect the general approach to RE in the current situation, particularly those which indicate potential for the future.

Let us first look at the methods RE teachers use. Loukes, in his earlier survey, had set out a question on methods which he

Fig. 13 Classroom methods used (all schools)

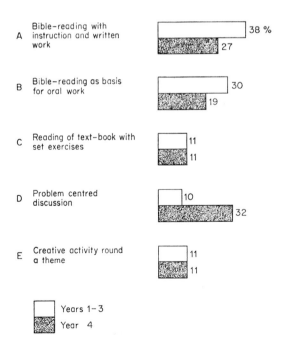

A Bible-reading with instruction and written work — 38 % / 27

B Bible-reading as basis for oral work — 30 / 19

C Reading of text-book with set exercises — 11 / 11

D Problem centred discussion — 10 / 32

E Creative activity round a theme — 11 / 11

☐ Years 1-3
▨ Year 4

generously allowed us to duplicate in our questionnaire. Figure 13 shows the response to each item in the list, which was presented under the rubric 'Which of the following lesson bases do you adopt most frequently with each of the years you teach?'

It appears from this diagram that already much work involving discussion is being tackled in the fourth form of these schools, but that Bible-centred methods still predominate in the lower forms, and further analysis shows a not unexpected exaggeration of these trends when grammar and modern schools are separated.

Fig. 14 Classroom methods used (Grammar and Modern schools contrasted)

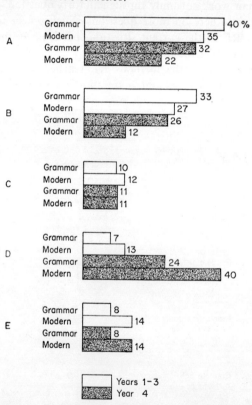

Brief mention was made in Chapter 1 of Professor Dierenfield's survey which he had carried out, during a sabbatical visit to this country, in January 1964 (twenty months or more before the parallel stage of the British Council of Churches survey).[1] Some interesting comparisons can be drawn between the two sets of findings, though the variety in formulation of question in the different questionnaires sometimes makes comparison necessarily a little rough. For example,

Fig. 15 Classroom activities used (from Dierenfield's survey)

A	Lecture-discussion	Grammar	41	32
		Modern	42	31
B	General class discussion	Grammar	33	41
		Modern	31	39
C	Reading aloud[2] by pupils	Grammar	17	37
		Modern	28	38
D	Written reports	Grammar	25	20
		Modern	38	34
E	Reading silently[3] by pupils	Grammar	18	32
		Modern	15	41
F	Lecture	Grammar	30	22
		Modern	35	18
G	Dramatization	Grammar	2	16
		Modern	5	18
H	Art and Craft Projects	Grammar	2	
		Modern	5	18

▒ Often
☐ Occasionally

('Seldom' and 'Never' not shown here)

[1] The full results, and the thesis woven round them, have been made available in mimeographed form under the title of 'The Cinderella Subject: Religion in the County Secondary Schools of England', 1965, see also p. 219.

[2] Dierenfield established elsewhere that only 57% of the grammar-school teachers used textbooks (other than the Bible) more than 'occasionally', whereas the parallel figure for modern schools was 79%.

[3] See the preceding note.

on 'methods' (or 'activities' as he called it) Dierenfield did not ask for any distinction between age-groups, and his grammar-school figures included sixth-form work, which Figures 13 and 14 did not. I have made a selection from the seventeen categories he originally used, as some of them (e.g. Field Trips and Visiting Speakers) had only minimal responses. (N.B. Dierenfield's figures would add up to 100% for each category [when the 'seldom' and 'never' groups were added], while the British Council of Churches figures total 100% [for each age range] over the whole table.)

Dierenfield is perhaps right to comment that 'classroom instruction is carried on by a somewhat narrow range of . . . academic teaching methods', particularly if he equates 'academic' with 'relying on the medium of words'. However, discussion in *some* form or another figures as largely in the overall pattern as does the 'lecture' or written work by the pupils. The teachers are obviously not un-willing to encourage discussion, though this fact alone does not tell us anything of the *subject* of this discussion. Some light on this is gained by looking at the types of syllabus in use.

The British Council of Churches staff-questionnaire included a question on this topic, which read:

Would you describe your school RI syllabus as predominantly
Bible centred (chronological)
Bible centred (biographical)
Bible centred (thematic)
Doctrine centred
Problem centred
Concerned to provide information about our contemporary religious situation?

The results, where the lower forms (i.e. first to fourth) in the schools were concerned, are given in Figure 16.

It would appear from Figure 16 that in 90% of the schools the work done in the first four years of the pupil's time is mostly 'based on' the Bible. Biblical material has been the 'organizing principle' round which the syllabus has been built.[4]

The overall 'control' exercised by the Agreed Syllabuses is of importance here. In reply to the question 'How closely have the school schemes of work been related to the Agreed Syllabus over the

[4] Cf.Harold Loukes (*New Ground in Christian Education*, London: SCM Press, 1965, p. 44): 'The syllabus itself invariably turns out to be a vast tract of biblical material.'

past year?' 12% of the schools (i.e. heads of department) replied 'Very closely'; 38% 'Fairly closely'; 41% 'Only roughly'; and 9% 'Not at all'. (Dierenfield, using different categories, found 80% of the teachers in his sample 'Did use an Agreed Syllabus as a basis

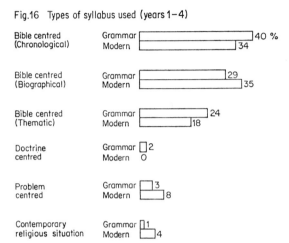

Fig.16 Types of syllabus used (years 1–4)

for their teaching'; 11% 'Did not'; and 8% used 'a modified syllabus'.)[5] This evidence of heavy reliance on Agreed Syllabuses (50% having at least 'fairly close' links; at most 11% ignoring them altogether) may seem to run counter to the impression gained at conferences and other gatherings of secondary RE teachers, but one must not forget that those who attend such gatherings are usually those who have sufficient confidence and expertise to construct their own syllabuses, and as such are not fully representative of the situation in the country as a whole.

Of course, these figures refer to the situation in 1965, and there are many signs that over the two years since this part of the survey was completed there has been increasing awareness of the limitations of the more conventional type of agreed syllabus, and consequently a decreasing reliance on them.

Changing Aims?
One sign of a parallel change of thinking among RE teachers may

[5] The British Council of Churches–National Union of Teachers Survey (see p. 87) found 'general satisfaction' with Agreed Syllabuses among 84% of the grammar schools and 71% of the modern schools investigated.

perhaps be seen in a comparison between the results of a question on 'aims' as found originally by Loukes and then later by myself.

In his earlier staff questionnaire Loukes had included the following question:

AIMS. It is acutely difficult to state the aims of religious education, except in very general terms. Tick those of the following you aim at:
1. Knowledge of biblical events.
2. Understanding of biblical doctrine.
3. Knowledge of important church history.
4. Understanding of contemporary Christian doctrine.
5. Personal Christian dedication.
6. Improvement in moral responsibility.
7. Insight into personal moral situation.
8. Insight into 'public' moral situation (e.g. war, politics, world poverty).

With his kind permission we 'borrowed' this list and included it in our own questionnaire, under this new rubric:

How many of the following 'ultimate aims of RI' do you personally subscribe to? (Please tick the ones you feel to be really important.)

The comparative results from the two surveys are shown in Figure 17. It should be remembered that fifty of the 114 schools answering this part of the British Council of Churches survey had also been covered by Loukes' inquiry, but that there was a period of from eighteen months to two years between the completion of the two questionnaires. During this time there had obviously been some changes of staff in the schools common to the two surveys, but this alone is probably not enough to account for the noticeable difference between the two sets of results, namely the change in emphasis from Loukes' item (1) to item (2). (Quite apart from other comparisons, (2) is the only item where the British Council of Churches figures show an *increase* over Loukes'.[6] The request for the 'really important' ones to be ticked obviously *reduced* the number of responses in general.)

The likelihood of this change in priorities being in some measure due to the emerging climate of thought over the past couple of years is probably strengthened by the fact that Loukes' sample consisted of ninety-one grammar and 185 modern schools, whereas the

---

[6] Could this possibly be due solely to the fact that the British Council of Churches survey substituted the term 'teaching' for Loukes' term 'doctrine' in this item?

sample for this stage of the British Council of Churches survey was more evenly balanced (fifty-four grammar, sixty modern). For it is arguable that the grammar-school tradition has always tended to set much store on knowledge 'for its own sake' (particularly when

Fig. 17   Comparison of the surveys of Loukes and the British Council of Churches on teachers' aim in RE

A. Arranged according to Loukes' order

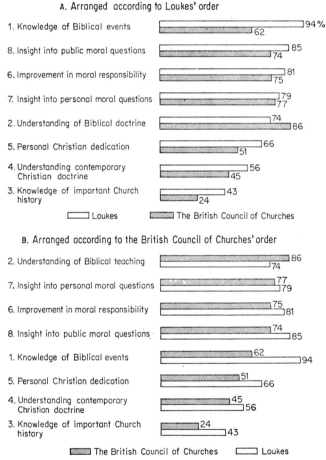

1. Knowledge of Biblical events   94% / 62

8. Insight into public moral questions   85 / 74

6. Improvement in moral responsibility   81 / 75

7. Insight into personal moral questions   79 / 77

2. Understanding of Biblical doctrine   74 / 86

5. Personal Christian dedication   66 / 51

4. Understanding contemporary Christian doctrine   56 / 45

3. Knowledge of important Church history   43 / 24

☐ Loukes   ▨ The British Council of Churches

B. Arranged according to the British Council of Churches' order

2. Understanding of Biblical teaching   86 / 74

7. Insight into personal moral questions   77 / 79

6. Improvement in moral responsibility   75 / 81

8. Insight into public moral questions   74 / 85

1. Knowledge of Biblical events   62 / 94

5. Personal Christian dedication   51 / 66

4. Understanding contemporary Christian doctrine   45 / 56

3. Knowledge of important Church history   24 / 43

▨ The British Council of Churches   ☐ Loukes

O levels are in the offing); yet despite the higher grammar-school representation in its sample, the (later) British Council of Churches survey shows that RE teachers would now rate simple 'Bible-knowledge' in the lower half of their list of aims.

On the question of teaching with the 'personal Christian dedication' of the pupils as a declared aim, opinion would now appear to be divided. One teacher wrote in the margin of the questionnaire against this item: 'This could be described as one of my *hopes*, but not one of my aims.' Many others inserted comments to this general effect. (This was in fact the item which attracted by far the most written comment in the whole questionnaire. It was obviously an issue of active concern at that moment.)

The diagram also indicates a clear recognition of the personal moral implications of RE teaching. Even though about a quarter of the teachers would still not see this as a 'really important' aim, it should be noted that it is in this area that the British Council of Churches figures stay the closest to Lukes' sample. This is particularly true of the 'insight' item, but even so 75% of the teachers are also concerned to make an impact on the actual sense of responsibility and behaviour of their pupils. (This concern finds one form of expression in the involvement of RE staff with the social service work of the schools. Exactly 75% of the schools in the sample either ran social service schemes in the surrounding community, or were engaged in money-raising to finance social work generally. In 33% of these schools the RE Department played a leading role in such schemes.)

The distribution of the figures in Figure 17 can be further compared with the results of Dierenfield's survey on this point. (His sample consisted of sixty grammar- and 156 modern-school teachers, drawn from approximately 100 schools spread throughout most of the English counties. The 114 schools used for the British Council of Churches survey [see above] produced replies from just over 175 grammar- and 150 modern-school teachers.) One of the tables he asked to be filled in was preceded by the question, 'What do you believe to be the strengths of the programme of religious knowledge instruction?', and his final findings on this are indicated in the next diagram (Figure 18).

The importance given to the 'moral' aim is again apparent here, though this is closely followed by the aim of 'spreading the Christian faith'. Unfortunately Dierenfield does not attempt to clarify what was intended by this latter phrase, whether it implied 'instruction in' or 'persuasion into' Christian faith. He does, however, quote a typical sample of ten respondents' comments, only one of which is in any way 'evangelistic' in nature, and three of which specifically reject anything which smacks of proselytism.

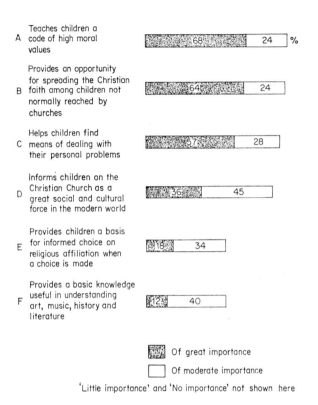

Fig.18 'Strengths of programme' in RE (from Dierenfield's survey)

A Teaches children a code of high moral values — 68 | 24 | %

B Provides an opportunity for spreading the Christian faith among children not normally reached by churches — 64 | 24

C Helps children find means of dealing with their personal problems — 57 | 28

D Informs children on the Christian Church as a great social and cultural force in the modern world — 36 | 45

E Provides children a basis for informed choice on religious affiliation when a choice is made — 18 | 34

F Provides a basic knowledge useful in understanding art, music, history and literature — 12 | 40

Of great importance

Of moderate importance

'Little importance' and 'No importance' not shown here

The 'theological loyalties' of a teacher are often suspected of influencing the extent to which he would hold 'the personal Christian dedication' of his pupils as one of his 'ultimate aims'. On the whole, it is assumed, the more evangelical the theological position, the more evangelistic the aims — though it must straightway be emphasized that a recent Inter-varsity Fellowship statement on the aims of RE does *not* support 'teaching for commitment' in the classroom.

Theological loyalties are *broadly* reflected by membership of the Christian Education Movement or the Inter-school Christian Fellowship (though quite a number of teachers are members of both). The findings from the British Council of Churches survey on membership of RE teachers' societies are shown in Figure 19.

Fig. 19 Staff membership of RE societies

Christian Education Movement
Grammar
Modern
45%
25
Inter-Schools Christian Fellowship
Grammar
Modern
13
7
Other RE societies
Grammar
Modern
2
4
No RE societies
Grammar
Modern
45
67

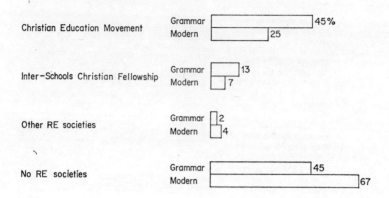

The comparatively small proportion of our sample who belonged to the Inter-school Christian Fellowship, when set against the figure of more than 50% (of teachers) endorsing Loukes' 'Aim 5', makes it reasonably clear that teaching towards personal dedication has *not* been confined to the members of the profession who are avowedly evangelical.

Fig. 20 Qualifications of RE staff

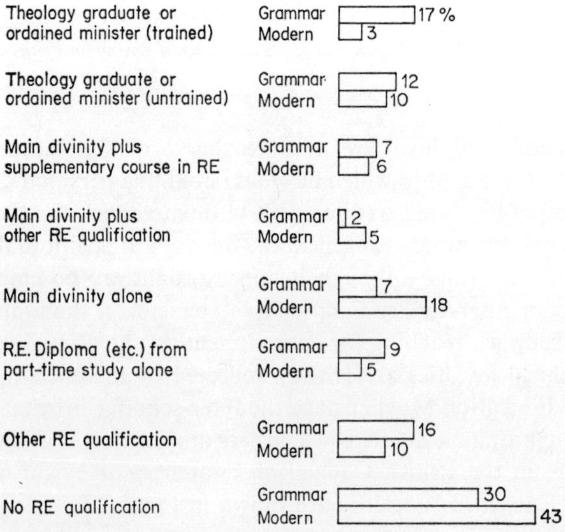

Theology graduate or ordained minister (trained)
Grammar
Modern
17 %
3
Theology graduate or ordained minister (untrained)
Grammar
Modern
12
10
Main divinity plus supplementary course in RE
Grammar
Modern
7
6
Main divinity plus other RE qualification
Grammar
Modern
2
5
Main divinity alone
Grammar
Modern
7
18
R.E. Diploma (etc.) from part-time study alone
Grammar
Modern
9
5
Other RE qualification
Grammar
Modern
16
10
No RE qualification
Grammar
Modern
30
43

Staff Qualifications

The final question to be asked in this attempt to build up an overall picture of current practice in the schools inevitably concerns the qualifications of the teachers involved. One has heard a great deal in the past about the lack of qualified teachers in the subject. What is the position revealed by our findings, and how will this affect possible developments in the future? Figure 20 records our findings on this point.

These figures refer to *all* the members of staff teaching RE in the schools covered by this part of the survey.[7] An earlier survey conducted in November 1963 by the British Council of Churches in conjunction with the National Union of Teachers had looked at the position among 135 'specialist teachers'.[8] The pattern here is shown in Figure 21.

Fig. 21 Qualifications of RE 'specialist staff' (from the British Council of Churches – National Union of Teachers survey)

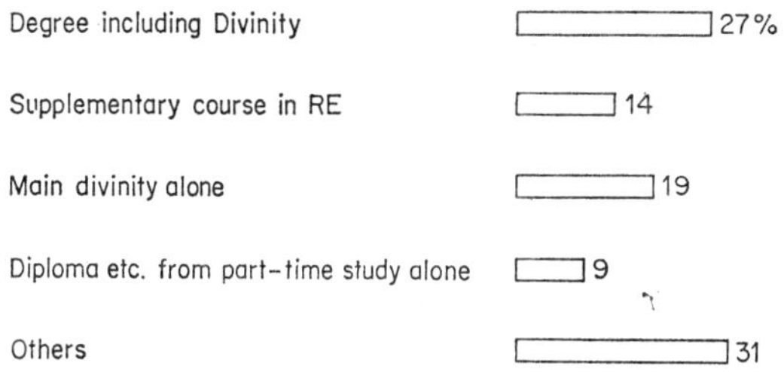

Degree including Divinity   27%

Supplementary course in RE   14

Main divinity alone   19

Diploma etc. from part–time study alone   9

Others   31

The British Council of Churches – National Union of Teachers sample consisted of 116 schools, nineteen of which were grammar, seventy-six modern, and twenty-one from other categories. A further point revealed by their survey was that three of the grammar, twenty of the modern, and five of the other schools had no 'specialist' RE teacher at all.

Dierenfield's findings in the same field were analysed under somewhat different headings, which makes detailed comparison

---

[7] The 'hollow-middle' composition of the sample was such that the percentage of 'No RE qualifications' may be a *little* above average, but not greatly so.

[8] The definition of 'specialist' was not laid down, though a contrasting category of 'non-specialist RE teacher' was also mentioned. The number of 'specialist' teachers claimed by a school varied from nought to three.

rather difficult. The following grouping of his categories, however, will reveal some parallels with the findings in Figure 20.

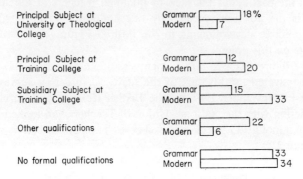

Fig. 22   Qualifications of RE staff (from Dierenfield's survey)

Dierenfield sums up his findings as follows:

> . . . (the) division of teachers on the basis of their training to handle classes of religious knowledge can be seen to fall into three rather equal groups. One-third have been well educated to deal with the problems they face in such courses. One-third have received *some* training . . . The final third must be classified as poorly trained. . . . 'These subjects (RE, English and Mathematics) have too often been handled with an amateurism[9] not accepted in other parts of the curriculum, and they have been among the least well taught.'[10] . . . 'Until there is a much better supply of skilled and knowledgeable teachers, the right to religious education at a true secondary level is bound in some schools to be little more than nominal'.[11]

Such a judgment appears to be inevitable in view of the evidence available, but the picture is not *quite* as gloomy as might at first appear. To put the present situation into context one needs to look at the situation fifteen years ago. The Institute of Christian Education enquiry (which was actually carried out between 1949 and 1953)[12] revealed that only just over 50% of the (998) grammar schools investigated then had 'specialist teachers making religious knowledge their main work', and among these 'specialists' were

[9] From a further set of figures he shows that 65% of grammar and 73% of modern school RE teachers do *not* regard RE as their 'principal subject speciality'.

[10] Quoted from Newsom Committee, *Half Our Future* (London: HMSO, 1963), p. 101.

[11] *Ibid.*, p. 169.

[12] *Religious Education in Schools* (London: SPCK, 1954), pp. 56–60.

included people whose only qualification was 'long experience in the field'. The grammar schools' total was made up by another 15% 'having one or more members of staff with some qualifications in RK teaching part-time' (i.e. devoting most of their time to other subjects); and 31% relying on teachers completely unqualified in the subject. Among the (230) modern schools only 20% had 'specialists', even allowing for the wide definition of the term quoted above. Obviously, then, the situation has improved greatly over the past fifteen years, even though it may still leave a lot to be desired when compared with the present position in other subjects.[13]

Of course, experience of the job *can* be a form of 'qualification' (as was recognized in the Institute of Christian Education report), and both Dierenfield and the British Council of Churches enquired into this factor in the situation, revealing the following patterns:

Fig. 23   Experience of RE staff in teaching RE
(from the British Council of Churches survey)

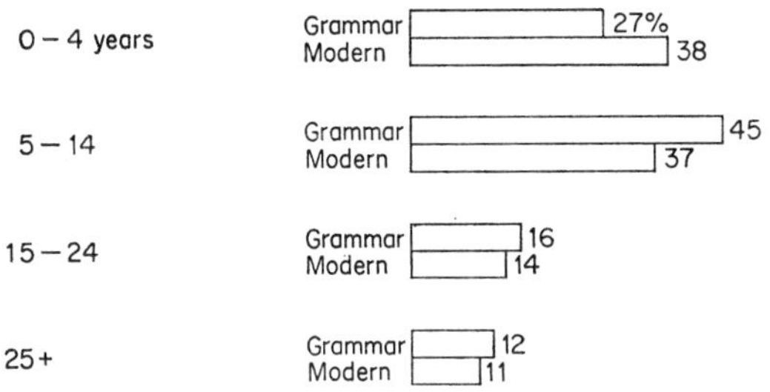

Fig. 24   Experience of RE staff in teaching RE
(from Dierenfield's survey)

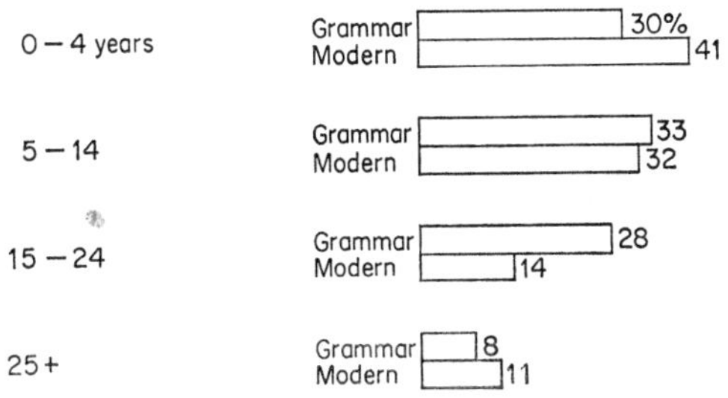

[13] See further A. G. Wedderspoon, ed., *Religious Education 1944–84* (London: Allen & Unwin, 1966), pp. 98–102.

Dierenfield notes in general terms 'the significant factor of the bulge at the lower end of the scale showing a large percentage of newcomers to the subject'. Moreover, by using a different method of analysis, he was also able to show that the median length of service for his sample was six and a half years, and that 'the lower quartile (25%) covers only two and a half years. In other words one out of every two teachers of RK from this sample has had less than $6\frac{1}{2}$ years of experience, and one out of every four has had less than $2\frac{1}{2}$.' Comparable figures from the British Council of Churches survey show almost three-quarters (72%) of those teaching RE have been doing so for less than fifteen years, and one-third have been doing so for under five years.

To produce a full picture of the level of 'qualification' of RE staff it would require an analysis of the length of experience of those teachers without 'paper' qualification, and this is not yet available. However, the general picture one gets from Figures 20 to 24 is clear enough. We are still far from having a teaching force for RE which is fully qualified either by reason of training or of length of experience.[14]

---

[14] It is relevant to note here (though whether it be cause or effect is difficult to say) that of the 100 schools replying to the section of the questionnaire regarding salaries,

  33 paid no extra allowance whatsoever to the heads of their RE Departments,
  31 paid Scale I responsibility allowances,
  21 paid Grade A or Scale II responsibility allowances,
  15 paid Grade B or C or Scale III allowances.

5

Factors within the Schools
Affecting Results

TO BUILD up an overall picture of 'current approaches and practice in schools', as has been attempted in Chapter Four, is a comparatively straightforward process. When, however, one turns to the analysis for which all this material was primarily collected then the complexities become almost insuperable.

It is simple to draw little diagrams showing the percentage of high-scoring schools having theology graduates on their staff, contrasted with the percentage of low-scoring schools having staff with these same qualifications (or whatever the point of comparison might be). It is altogether another thing to know whether such a comparison has any significance, whether it reflects a wider, 'universal' situation, or whether it is merely a chance phenomenon arising within the particular sample of schools which happened to be used for this part of the survey.

There are, of course, tests for statistical significance, and every single 'contrast table' was subjected to such a test, the X^2 test (see below) normally being used. Every point of comparison mentioned in this chapter has 'passed' such a statistical test. But the real trouble lies with those comparisons which did *not* pass such tests. It could well be that some of them are in fact very significant features of the situation (using 'significant' in its normal, non-technical sense). There are at least two simple reasons why the tables relating to them may have failed to come up to the X^2 level of acceptability: the sample may not have been large enough for any particular pattern of distribution to emerge clearly within it (and it was indeed a struggle at this stage of the survey to produce enough schools in each separate category to be within statistical safety-limits); alternatively, the 'pooling' of categories quite often demanded by the disciplines of X^2 testing (see below) may sometimes have set up the wrong 'pools' for any significance to reveal itself. And so the fact that only certain topics are dealt with in this chapter does *not* mean that none of the other factors investigated are of importance. They may well be. All one can say is that they have not been *proved* to be so as a result of this particular analysis of this particular survey. And both the reasons given above for apparent 'non-significance' of certain factors apply equally to the many apparent limitations of significant features to certain types of school or certain regions. One must not read too much meaning into 'non-significance' of any sort as this does *not* indicate negative evidence, but merely an absence of positive evidence, and an argument from silence is always open to suspicion.

Having stressed the dangerous nature of the ground ahead of us, let us nevertheless try to pick our way across it. The clearest and most positive landmark is the factor of length of service. The difference between high-scoring and low-scoring schools on this issue was shown to be statistically significant in six different analyses.

Let me illustrate both the technique and the results of such an analysis. For comparison on the basis of attitude-scores the schools had been grouped by regions and by sex-divisions, and then the seven with the highest attitude score and the seven with the lowest attitude score were chosen within each group (see pp. 107 f. for the actual composition of the groups). When *all* the schools chosen in this way as high-scoring were put together and treated as *one* group (and all those chosen as low-scoring were similarly grouped) then the pattern of length of service of the RE staff appeared as follows:

Years teaching RE	0–4	5–14	15–24	25–34	35+	Total number of staff
Number of staff in high-scoring schools	31	43	27	12	7	120
Number of staff in low-scoring schools	48	47	15	8	2	120
Total number of staff investigated	79	90	42	20	9	240

This table can easily be roughly assessed because the number of teachers in the two types of school happens to be the same. It is obvious that the centre of gravity in the high-scoring schools is further to the right as compared with the low-scoring distribution. But is it far enough to the right to be significant? One way of answering this question is to apply the X^2 test.

To do this one must first 'pool' the categories so that each 'box' contains a sufficient number of schools. Columns four and five are too sparsely populated, so they must be amalgamated with column three. It would be as well to combine one and two also at this stage, giving a new table as follows:

Years	0–14	15+	Total
High	74	46	120
Low	95	25	120
Total	169	71	240

These are the 'observed frequencies' of distribution.

Now, if one were given this hypothetical distribution table:

			Total
	w	x	120
	y	z	120
Total	169	71	240

one would *expect* w to be 84·5, x to be 35·5, y to be 84·5, z to be 35·5, which would give the required totals both vertically and horizontally. ($w = \frac{1}{2}$ of 169, or to put it into a more generally applicable form,

$$w = \frac{120}{240} \times 169, \text{ and } x = \frac{120}{240} \times 71;$$

i.e. expected frequency $= \dfrac{\text{Transverse total} \times \text{Vertical total}}{\text{Overall total}}$

The X^2 formula works from the differences between the *expected* frequencies (fe) and the *observed* frequencies (fo) $X^2 = \Sigma \dfrac{(\text{fo}-\text{fe})^2}{\text{fe}}$.)

In the case given, fo $= 74$ in the first box, while fe $= 84·5$. fo$-$fe $= -10·5$. The size of this difference, and the sign (negative or positive) are the two important features. In this particular instance, when the formula is worked right through, it produces $X^2 = 8·00$. When this figure is read off on a X^2 table it shows that such an extensive difference of distribution as our table displays could only happen *by chance* once in a hundred times, and it is therefore a highly significant set of figures.

This result encourages one to 'pool' the original figures in a more discriminating way, giving another table as follows:

Years	0–4	5–14	15+	Total
High	31	43	46	120
Low	48	47	25	120
Total	79	90	71	240

The *expected* frequencies for this table would be 39·5, 45·0 and 35·5 respectively, and therefore the observed frequencies minus the expected ones are −8·5, −2, and +10·5 for the high-scoring schools and +8·5, +2, and −10·5 for the low-scoring schools. When each of these is squared and then divided by the appropriate 'expected frequency', the sum of the six products is 6·0572. This is not merely less than the X^2 originally calculated; it is, comparatively speaking, considerably less, as this second calculation depends on *six* 'pools' as opposed to the four in the previous table, and therefore it 'ought' to be higher. Nevertheless the X^2 tables show that 6·0572 is still large enough to indicate that such a distribution as we have would only occur five times in a hundred *by chance*, and the set of figures is therefore still significant enough to be taken seriously.

Once one has tested 'significance' by this method, one then has to ask 'significant in what way?', and it is here that the positive/negative signs noted earlier in the process become important. One could

Fig. 25 The relation of experience in teaching RE to high attitude scores (all schools)

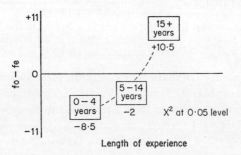

illustrate this visually, as in Figure 25, by drawing a graph of the fo–fe figures for the high-scoring schools (see above).

From this it is obvious that 'high' scores are positively associated with members of staff who have been teaching RE for fifteen years or more, and negatively associated with those teaching it for a shorter period, particularly when it is under five years.

This method of visual presentation will be used throughout this chapter – showing the amount and direction of 'deviation from the hypothetically expected frequency' among the high-scoring schools. (The deviation among the low-scoring schools is of an equal amount in the opposite direction, and it therefore need not be shown.) The symbol on the right indicates whether the pattern of deviation is at the 0·05 (5%) or 0·01 (1%) level of significance (i.e. whether it would occur, by chance, five times in a hundred, or only once in a hundred).

The same pattern appears if one looks at the schools from regional group III (North conurbation and South-east).[1]

Fig. 26 The relation of experience in teaching RE to high attitude scores (regional group III)

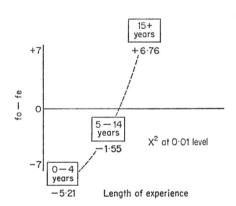

This general association between length of experience among the teachers and high-attitude scores among their pupils is confirmed in two more of the smaller groupings (mixed schools, and girls' schools, both with X^2 significant at the 0·05 level).

When one turns to the tables based on attainment-scores,[2] how-

[1] The original figures for this and the following diagrams are given on pp. 109 f.
[2] See p. 107.

ever, an interesting variation in the pattern occurs. The two statistically significant tables here are the ones for the modern schools and for all schools. The former gives the following pattern:

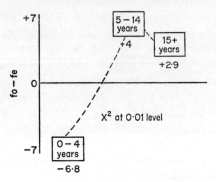

Fig. 27   The relation of experience in teaching RE to high attainment scores (modern schools)

The latter (being from a large enough sample to break into *four* 'pools') gives this refinement of it:

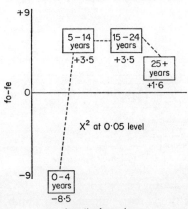

Fig. 28   The relation of experience in teaching RE to high attainment scores (all schools)

It would appear from this diagram that somewhere round about the twenty-fifth year of a teacher's period of service his efficiency (at least as a purveyor of information and cultivator of insight) begins to decline. But what is of far more importance for any

This follows the pattern already shown in Figures 25 and 26. However, the graph relating the high attitude scores to the *age* of these same RE teachers shows a different pattern:

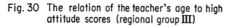

Fig. 30 The relation of the teacher's age to high attitude scores (regional group III)

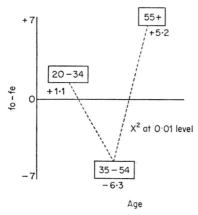

This would seem to indicate that the pattern of Figures 25 and 26 is not dependent on the age of the teachers as such, but on their maturity *in the subject* and their standing within the school.

This interpretation of the findings is strengthened when one isolates the heads of RE departments in this same group of schools and looks at their tenure of their present position:

Fig. 31 The relation of length of retention of present post by head of RE department to high attitude scores (regional group III)

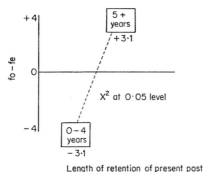

assessment of the present situation is a recognition of
for an RE teacher to have had at least five years' experi
preferably as much as ten to fifteen) before he is likely to
most effective level of performance. When one couples this
the fact that *one-third* of the present RE teaching force in
schools has had less than five years' experience (and alm
quarters of the teachers have had less than fifteen years'),
point obviously has great bearing on the overall pattern
set out in Chapter 2. It must be recognized that we are
period of growth and expansion in the staffing of RE tead
this growth, *provided* its trend and the resulting consolidati
maintained, should in itself go some way towards impr
present level of achievement.

A Matter of Status

I have spent so much time in dealing with the question
of experience' because this was the factor which stood
clearly as being associated with high-scoring on both sets
Some related evidence is also to be found in the tables r
the age of the teachers and to the length of time they hav
their present school. Figure 29 shows the 'deviation from
frequency' (among schools scoring highly on the attitud
regional group III) for the length of tenure by RE teacher
present post:

Fig. 29 The relation of length of retention of present
post by RE staff to high attitude scores
(regional group III)

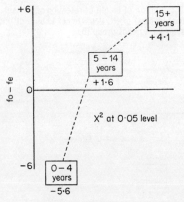

Length of retention of present post

D

The question of 'standing within the school' is also reflected in the matter of special allowances paid to RE staff. The association, and its implication, is quite obvious.

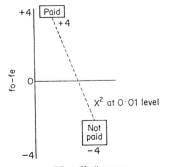

Fig.32 The relation of RE staff allowances to high attitude scores (regional group III)

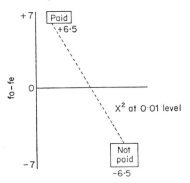

Fig.33 The relation of RE staff allowances to high attitude scores (all schools)

The character of the whole school community, as well as the standing of RE within it, seems to have some bearing on the issue, though the statistically significant evidence is a little indirect. The age of the headmaster/headmistress, for example, is related to high attitude scores in this way (possibly reflecting a certain 'stability' about the atmosphere of the school as a whole when the headmaster/headmistress is in the older group):

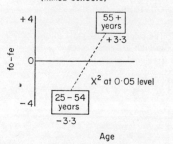

Fig. 34 The relation of the headmaster's /
         headmistress' age to high attitude scores
         (mixed schools)

But if stability is a favourable characteristic of the school community, then it would appear that a '*lively* stability' is even more
favourable. High attitude scores are associated with the number of
active school societies (of all types) in a table (drawn from all the
schools) which is *almost* statistically significant at the 0·05 level.

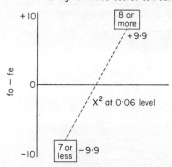

Fig. 35 The relation of the number of school societies
         to high attitude scores (all schools)

Another feature of school life associated with high attitude scores
is the involvement of the school community in schemes of social
service, particularly where the RE Department is seen to have an
active role in promoting such schemes. (See p. 111 for the relevant
figures, which are significant at the 0·01 level.)

As would be expected, the presence of a group such as the Christian
Education Movement among the school societies contributes
towards the establishment of 'pro-Christian' attitudes. The findings
from the boys' schools support this point:

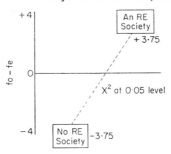

Fig. 36 The relation of the presence of RE society to high attitude scores (boys' schools)

Attempts to draw a distinction between the effects of the Christian Education Movement and the Inter-school Christian Fellowship considered separately did not prove statistically valid, which makes it all the more encouraging to learn that these two societies are now beginning to see themselves as two arms of the same enterprise,[3] rather than working in isolation, or even antagonism, as they did at one time. As one notes the positive impact an RE society can have on a school, and then notes the high proportion of schools without such a society (cf. Figure 19), there is evidently a need for joint expansion in this field.

One further analysis of the impact of RE societies on fourth-form attitudes ('fourth form' is specified because all these tables are based on the results of Survey 65) showed that the presence of a '*junior*' branch of such a society was associated with high-scoring schools:

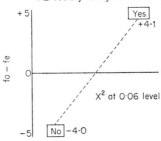

Fig. 37 The relation of the presence of a junior RE society to high attitude scores[4]

[3] See the 'Joint Statement', available from either body.

[4] This table is based on all the schools having *some* form of RE society, so 'No' indicates the presence of a senior branch without a supporting junior group.

Another source of influence over at least the attainment score of the pupils (certainly in modern schools) is the presence of external examinations.

Fig. 38 The relation of the use of external examinations to high attainment scores (modern schools) ⁓

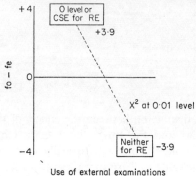

Use of external examinations

One can assume that this influence springs as much from the spur of the examination itself as from the syllabus followed prior to the examination (seeing that details of syllabus vary widely from Board to Board). On the other hand the following diagram indicates a definite relation between the *overall* syllabus a school follows and its attainment results in Survey 65.

This pattern is not really surprising, in view of the heavily biblical content of the attainment tests themselves.

Fig. 39 The relation of type of syllabus used to high attainment scores (grammar schools)

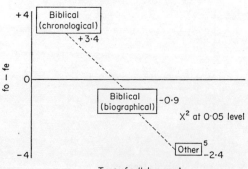

Type of syllabus used

[5] See p. 81 for details.

Methods Used

Syllabus and methods used often have some affinity, and so the pattern of the 'method' tables seems the appropriate one to turn to next. Statistically speaking the method tables were fairly significant, the girls' and modern schools producing a clear pattern on the attainment tests, and the regional group IV (London conurbation) doing the same on the attitude tests. The respective patterns were as follows (for the key to these tables, see p. 104):

Fig. 40 The relation of classroom methods used to high attainment scores (girls' schools)

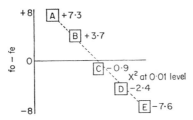

Fig. 41 The relation of classroom methods used to high attainment scores (modern schools)

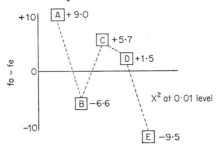

Fig. 42 The relation of classroom methods used to high attitude scores (regional group IV)

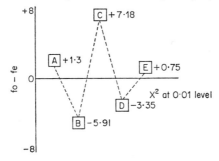

A Bible reading with instruction and written work.
B Bible reading as basis for oral work.
C Reading of textbook with set exercises.
D Problem-centred discussion.
E Creative activity round a theme.

The gradual decrease in attainment scores as one moves down the list of methods used is no real surprise. Formal methods well applied obviously lead to success as judged by formal standards. It is illuminating, though, to see that 'B' is associated with *low* attainment in the modern schools, and also with adverse attitudes. One conjures up a picture of bored classes being regaled with lengthy oral expositions of Bible texts, punctuated by an occasional question thrown at them to ensure 'class participation'!

What is even more striking, however, are the comparative positions of 'textbook' and 'discussion' in the attitude diagram. One possible explanation of this rather unexpected phenomenon might be that top-stream fourth formers like to feel they are getting somewhere, and following a textbook course gives them this feeling, whereas discussion (especially if it is not well handled) can lead frustratingly round in circles. In view of the increasing emphasis laid on discussion in the fourth year (see Figure 13) it is fervently to be hoped that the *techniques* of discussion will receive much more attention from RE staff than one fears is the case at the moment. (For further comment on the association between discussion and low-attitude scores see pp. 208–10.)

A teacher's use of equipment is one aspect of his 'methods' and a number of tables referring to aids and equipment proved to be significant, statistically at least. The 'frequent or occasional use of a tape-recorder' was associated with high attitude scores (in regional group II, X^2 at 0·01 level), but with low attainment scores (in mixed schools, X^2 at 0·05 level). Similarly, 'frequent or occasional use of visual aids' was associated with low attainment scores (in mixed schools, X^2 at 0·05 level).

Both attainment and attitude scores were *negatively* associated with use of 'The Bible and Life' programmes put out by the British Broadcasting Corporation (in mixed schools, on attainment scale, X^2 at 0·01 level; in boys' schools, on attitude scale, X^2 at 0·05 level), though this might possibly link up with the fact that the highest-scoring schools (in girls' schools and schools in regional group II, on attitude, X^2 for both at 0·05 level) were those in which no outside help was sought by the RE department by way of visits from advisers, inspectors and others. Could it be that any lack of self-confidence in the RE teacher (as manifest by reliance on other people's material and/or advice) was sensed by the pupils and the image of the subject suffered as a result? (For complete figures for the items in this and the preceding paragraph, see pp. 113–15.)

Of far wider application would be any findings I might be able to report on the effect of different qualifications, or of different aims in teaching. Unfortunately the results available here are of rather slender quality. Only one of the tables (mixed: attitude) produced any statistically significant pattern of 'qualifications', as follows:

Fig. 43   The relation of staff qualifications to high attitude scores
(mixed schools)

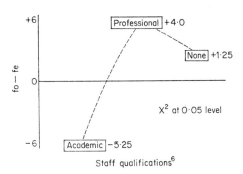

Staff qualifications[6]

This is an interesting and somewhat disturbing pattern of association, though it may not be sufficient ground in *itself* for throwing out our present 'academic' courses as completely useless, however much one may desire their reform on other grounds. Nor, on the other hand, is it sufficient ground for complacency regarding the fact that one-third of those teaching RE have no real qualifications for it (see Figures 20–22).

As for any comparison of teachers' aims and their effect on their pupils' attitudes or attainments, none of the relevant tables passed the X^2 test for significance (possibly because of wide variety in the *number* of responses from each teacher, some only endorsing one aim as being of 'real importance', others endorsing the whole list).

⁶ 'Academic' includes the first three categories on Figure 20; 'professional' includes the next four; 'none' indicates no RE qualification.

However, it was obvious from looking at the figures when converted into percentages that there were two major points of difference between the aims of the teachers in high-scoring and low-scoring schools. A test for the significance of difference between percentages was applied (see p. 115), and in both cases significance was established at the 0·05 level.

This means that one can be reasonably certain that there is a general association between pupils' high attitude scores and their teachers' desire for their 'personal Christian dedication', and also between high attainment scores and the teachers' concern with 'improvement in moral responsibility'. This is at first sight a somewhat absurd association, but it does in fact bear out a conclusion reached by Harold Loukes in his earlier survey, namely, that 'successful' teachers in general were teachers who *cared* about their pupils, and whose caring was sensed and appreciated by those they taught.

One must not lay *too* much weight on conclusions drawn from these last few sets of figures. As has already been shown earlier in the chapter the figures on which the greatest amount of reliance can be placed are those which associate an RE teacher's overall 'success' with his length of experience in teaching the subject, with his (or the subject's) 'standing' in the school and involvement with its 'social activity', and (to some extent) with the methods he employs in the classroom. These would seem to be the basic bricks with which to build 'successful RE'.

NB   Throughout this chapter and the following appendix the symbol X^2 has been used instead of the more conventional χ^2. This was due to a misunderstanding during production, and has no other significance.

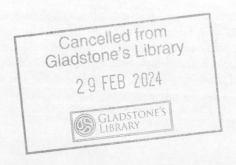

APPENDIX TO CHAPTER 5

1. *The sample for stage two of the survey*
   The schools whose results were used to build up the (stage two) tables for comparison on the basis of *attainment scores* were grouped as follows:

Basic grouping	Number of schools completing Survey 65	Mean school-score for group (%)	Number of schools completing teacher questionnaire	Number used for stage two tables	Range of Survey 65 scores among stage two schools (%)
Mixed grammar	73	74·4	22 = 13 above mean	7	79–81
			9 below „	7	68–74
Girls' grammar	58	79·6	20 = 13 above „	7	82–90
			7 below „	7	70–79·5
Boys' grammar	49	75·7	26 = 15 above „	14[7]	75–85
			11 below „	11	69–77
Mixed modern	195	68·4	24 = 13 above „	7	74–86
			11 below „	7	62·5–66·5
Girls' modern	104	71·6	25 = 15 above „	7	78–90·5
			10 below „	7	64–70
Boys' modern	40	67·6	25 = 11 above „	10	67·5–74
			14 below „	14	60–68·5

The schools whose results were used to build up the parallel tables based on *attitude scores* were grouped as follows:

I. *Wales*

		%			%
Mixed	16	68·3	3 = 1 above mean	1[8]	73
			2 below „	2	63–66
Girls'	5	76·3	2 = 2 above „	2	82
			0 below „	0	—
Boys'	6	67·5	4 = 2 above „	2	76–77
			2 below „	2	61–62

[7] Owing to a preponderance of large boys' schools among the high scoring and small boys' schools among the low scoring in the original scheme of division, the boys' schools were doubled up as far as possible (due compensation being made for this overweighting when the *overall* pattern was being considered).

[8] Owing to the small numbers here, and to a lesser extent in Group IV, there was often no point even in constructing tables, let alone testing their significance. It depended mainly on the number of teachers in each school answering a particular question.

II. *North–South-west–Midland*

Mixed	133	65·4	22 =	14 above	„	7	74–77
				8 below	„	7	48–63
Girls'	64	72·0	17 =	12 above	„	7	78–81
				5 below	„	5	57–66
Boys'	34	64·1	22 =	14 above	„	7	70–73
				8 below	„	7	52–57

III. *North conurbation–South-east–(Midland conurbation)*

Mixed	81	64·4	14 =	7 above	„	7	69–77
				7 below	„	7	47–62
Girls'	64	69·8	14 =	9 above	„	7	75–79
				5 below	„	5	51–64
Boys'	37	63·0	17 =	9 above	„	7	65–71
				8 below	„	7	51–59

IV. *London conurbation*

Mixed	38	59·2	7 =	3 above	„	3	66–73
				4 below	„	4	45–57
Girls'	29	65·2	12 =	3 above	„	3	77–82
				9 below	„	7	52–62
Boys'	12	57·6	8 =	4 above	„	4	58–63
				4 below	„	4	49–56

When groups were combined for purposes of comparison the range (and overlap) of each group was as follows:

Attainment tables

	Low scoring Number of schools	Range %	High scoring Number of schools	Range %
Mixed	14	62·5–74	14	74–86
Girls'	14	64–79·5	14	78–90
Boys'	25	60–77	24	67·5–85
Grammar	25	68–79·5	28	75–90
Modern	28	60–70	24	67·5–90·5
All	53	60–79·5	52	67·5–90·5

Attitude tables

		%		%
Mixed	20	45–66	18	66–72
Girls'	17	51–66	19	75–82
Boys'	20	49–62	20	58–77
Region I	4	61–66	5	73–82
II	19	48–66	21	70–81
III	19	47–64	21	65–79
IV	15	45–62	10	58–82
All	57	45–66	57	58–82

2. *The X^2 tables*

Re Figure 25   Experience *a*   (see pp. 92–94)
Re Figure 26   Experience *b*   (see p. 95)

	0–4	5–14	15+ years	
High fo	13	15	20	$X^2 = 11\cdot35$
fe	18·21	16·55	13·24	(df = 2)
Low fo	20	15	4	
fe	14·79	13·45	10·76	
High fo–fe	−5·21	−1·55	+6·76	

Re Mixed: attitude   Experience *c*   (cf. p. 95)

	0–14	15+ years	
High fo	35	14	$*X^2 = 5\cdot52$
fe	39·67	9·33	(df = 1)
Low fo	33	2	
fe	28·33	6·67	
High fo–fe	−4·67	+4·67	

Re Girls': attitude   Experience *d*   (cf. p. 95)

	0–14	15+ years	
High fo	16	18	$*X^2 = 4\cdot30$
fe	20·78	13·22	(df = 1)
Low fo	28	10	
fe	23·22	14·78	
High fo–fe	−4·78	+4·78	

Re Figure 27   Experience *e*   (see p. 96)

	0–4	5–14	15+ years	
High fo	11	23	14	$X^2 = 9\cdot53$
fe	17·8	19	11·1	(df = 2)
Low fo	21	11	6	
fe	14·2	15	8·9	
High fo–fe	−6·8	+4	+2·9	

Re Figure 28   Experience f (see p. 96)

	0–4	5–14	15–24	25+ years	
High fo	23	44	17	14	$X^2 = 8{\cdot}50$
fe	31·5	40·5	13·5	12·4	(df = 3)
Low fo	33	28	7	8	
fe	24·5	31·5	10·5	9·6	
High fo–fe	−8·5	+3·5	+3·5	+1·6	

Re Figure 29   Present post   (see p. 97)

	0–4	5–14	15+ years	
High fo	15	20	13	
fe	20·6	18·4	8·9	$X^2 = 8{\cdot}0$
Low fo	22	13	3	(df = 2)
fe	16·4	14·6	7·1	
High fo–fe	−5·6	+1·6	+4·1	

Re Figure 30   Age   (see p. 98)

	20–34	35–54	55+ years	
High fo	16	18	14	
fe	14·9	24·3	8·8	$X^2 = 10{\cdot}6$
Low fo	11	26	2	(df = 2)
fe	12·1	19·7	7·2	
High fo–fe	+1·1	−6·3	+5·2	

Re Figure 31   Present post   (see p. 98)

	0–4	5+ years	
High fo	2	16	
fe	5·1	12·9	$X^2 = 4{\cdot}1$
Low fo	7	7	(df = 1)
fe	3·9	10·1	
High fo–fe	−3·1	+3·1	

Re Figure 32   Allowances a (see p. 99)

	Paid	Not	
High fo	18	2	
fe	14	6	$X^2 = 6{\cdot}2$
Low fo	8	9	(df = 1)
fe	12	5	
High fo–fe	+4	−4	

Re Figure 33 Allowances *b* (see p. 99)

	Paid	Not	
High fo	40	10	
fe	33·5	16·5	$X^2 = 7·05$
Low fo	27	23	(df = 1)
fe	33·5	16·5	
High fo–fe	+6·5	−6·5	

Re Figure 34 Age of Heads (see p. 100)

	Below 55	55+ years	
High fo	6	10	
fe	9·3	6·7	$X^2 = 4·1$
Low fo	12	3	(df = 1)
fe	8·7	6·3	
High fo–fe	−3·3	+3·3	

Re Figure 35 Societies (see p. 100)

	0–7	8+	
High fo	52	52	
fe	61·9	42·1	$X^2 = 3·55$
Low fo	68	30	(df =1)
fe	58·1	39·9	
High fo–fe	−9·9	+9·9	

Re All schools: attitude Social service schemes (cf. p. 100)

	Yes RE Department	Yes Not RE Department	None	
High fo	18	22	7	
fe	11·75	23·5	11·75	$X^2 = 10·89$
Low fo	5	24	16	(df = 2)
fe	11·25	22·5	11·25	
High fo–fe	+6·25	−1·5	−4·75	

Re Figure 36 RE society (see p. 101)

	No	Yes	
High fo	3	17	
fe	6·75	13·25	$*X^2 = 4·72$
Low fo	10·5	9·5	(df = 1)
fe	6·75	13·25	
High fo–fe	−3·75	+3·75	

Re Figure 37 Junior RE society (see p. 101)

	No	Yes	
High fo	19	20	
fe	23·5	15·49	$*X^2 = 3·69$
Low fo	25	9	(df = 1)
fe	20·5	13·51	
High fo–fe	−4·5	+4·51	

Re Figure 38 External examinations (see p. 102)

	O level/CSE	No	
High fo	14	1	
fe	10·1	4·9	$*X^2 = 6·83$
Low fo	7	9	(df = 1)
fe	10·9	5·1	
High fo–fe	+3·9	−3·9	

Re Figure 39 Syllabus (see p. 102)

	Biblical chronological	Biblical biographical	Other	
High fo	11	5	3	
fe	7·6	5·9	5·4	$X^2 = 6·05$
Low fo	3	6	7	(df = 2)
fe	6·4	5·1	4·6	
High fo–fe	+3·4	−0·9	−2·4	

Re Figure 40   Methods *a*   (see p. 103)

	A[9]	B	C	D	E	
High fo	53	40	9	8	5	
fe	45·7	36·3	9·9	10·4	12·6	$X^2 = 15·21$
Low fo	30	26	9	11	18	(df = 4)
fe	37·3	29·7	8·1	8·6	10·4	
High fo–fe	+7·3	+3·7	−0·9	−2·4	−7·6	

Re Figure 41   Methods *b*   (see p. 103)

	A[10]	B	C	D	E	
High fo	77	41	33	23	23	
fe	68	47·6	27·3	21·5	32·5	$X^2 = 14·82$
Low fo	40	41	14	14	33	(df = 4)
fe	49	34·4	19·7	15·5	23·5	
High fo–fe	+9·0	−6·6	+5·7	+1·5	−9·5	

Re Figure 42   Methods *c*   (see p. 103)

	A[11]	B	C	D	E	
High fo	30	11	16	4	7	
fe	28·67	16·91	8·82	7·35	6·25	$X^2 = 15·16$
Low fo	48	35	8	16	10	(df = 4)
fe	49·33	29·09	15·18	12·65	10·75	
High fo–fe	+1·33	−5·91	+7·18	−3·35	+0·75	

Re Regional group II: attitude   Tape-recorder *a*   (cf. p. 104)

	Frequent/Occasional	Rare/Never	
High fo	18	23	
fe	12	29	$X^2 = 6·7$
Low fo	7	37	(df = 1)
fe	13	31	
High fo–fe	+6	−6	

[9] For explanation of categories see p. 77.
[10] See above, note 9.
[11] See above, note 9.

Re Mixed: attainment   Tape recorder *b*   (cf. p. 104)

	Frequent/Occasional	Rare/Never
High fo	4	8
fe	6·9	5·1
Low fo	12	4
fe	9·1	6·9
High fo–fe	−2·9	+2·9

$X^2 = 4·86$
$(df = 1)$

Re Mixed: attainment   Visual aids   (cf. p. 104)

	Frequent/Occasional	Rare/Never
High fo	4	8
fe	6·9	5·1
Low fo	12	4
fe	9·1	6·9
High fo–fe	−2·9	+2·9

$X^2 = 4·86$
$(df = 1)$

Re Mixed: attainment   The Bible and Life *a*   (cf. p. 104)

	Regular/Occasional	Never
High fo	3	40
fe	7·6	35·4
Low fo	9	16
fe	4·4	20·6
High fo–fe	−4·6	+4·6

$X^2 = 9·16$
$(df = 1)$

Re Boys': attitude   The Bible and Life *b*   (cf. p. 104)

	Regular/Occasional	Never
High fo	0	37
fe	3·5	33·5
Low fo	8	40
fe	4·5	43·5
High fo–fe	−3·5	+3·5

$X^2 = 5·0$
$(df = 1)$

Re Girls': attitude Outside advice *a* (cf. p. 104)

	Yes	No
High fo	0	14
fe	2·9	11·1
Low fo	6	9
fe	3·1	11·9
High fo–fe	−2·9	+2·9

$X^2 = 4·8$
$(df = 1)$

Re Regional group II: attitude Outside advice *b* (cf. pp. 104 f.)

	Yes	No
High fo	0	17
fe	3	14
Low fo	6	12
fe	3	15
High fo–fe	−3	+3

$X^2 = 4·7$
$(df = 1)$

Re Figure 43 Qualifications (see p. 105)

	Academic	Professional	None
High fo	7	25	17
fe	12·25	21	15·75
Low fo	14	11	10
fe	8·75	15	11·25
High fo–fe	−5·25	+4·0	+1·25

$X^2 = 7·4667$
$(df = 2)$

N.B. Yates' correction was used for 2×2 tables marked with an asterisk.

3. *Formula for significance of difference between percentages*[12]

Critical Ratio $\dfrac{D\%}{\sigma_D\%}$ must be at least 1·96, preferably 2·58.

$D\%$ = Difference between the two percentages

$\sigma_D\% = \sqrt{PQ\left(\dfrac{1}{N_1}+\dfrac{1}{N_2}\right)}$ where N_1 = raw total$_1$

N_2 = raw total$_2$ (if different)

$Q = 100-P$

$x_1\%$ = one of the two percentages

$x_2\%$ = the other of the two percentages

and $P = \dfrac{(x_1\% \times N^1)+(x_2\% \times N_2)}{N_1+N_2}$

[12] From H. E. Garrett, *Statistics in Psychology and Education*, pp. 236 f.

6

Responsible Thinking
Among Older Pupils

THE FINAL stage of the survey consisted of visits to the selected schools and the completion of the fifth/sixth form questionnaire, Survey 666. As was stated in Chapter 1, the particular purpose of this second pupil-questionnaire was to assess whether the high attitude and attainment scores achieved by these schools in Survey 65 had been obtained at the expense of real insight into religious and moral issues.

The charge of 'indoctrination' has often been flung at the RE given in our schools, 'indoctrination' which, it is claimed, produces bigoted, prejudiced people with no ability to think for themselves. In order to test how far the fifth/sixth formers in the selected schools were in fact suffering from this complaint, Survey 666 included a test of prejudice based on the well-tried technique of an 'acceptability' scale. It was felt to be important, however, not to confuse lack of prejudice with the lack of any discriminating judgment whatever, so some 'non-acceptable' characters were deliberately included on the scale (see pp. 129 f.).

The normal rubric for such a scale usually asks which of the given list of people the subject would be prepared to live next door to, join the same club as, travel in a bus with, etc. In order to keep the Survey 666 scale as simple as possible, only one such criterion was offered, and this was deliberately not couched in terms of adult concerns and situations. The relevant section of the rubric read, 'Indicate those with whom you could become close friends.' This was not a happy idea, as it turned out, as over 15% of the sixth formers refused to answer the question, on the grounds that they did not choose their friends by such considerations as were suggested. However, sufficient number *did* answer to enable three analyses to be made.[1]

The first analysis compared the sixth formers with the fifth formers. Among the sixth formers 48% were 'free of prejudice yet able to discriminate', gaining maximum marks on the scale in question, whereas this was true of only 31% of the fifth formers. This is a highly significant difference, indicating that 'the ability to discriminate without prejudice' is linked with increasing intellectual maturity.

The second analysis compared the scores of the two sexes. Among both fifth and sixth formers more girls achieved the maximum score than did boys (51% as opposed to 44% among sixth formers; 36% as opposed to 26% among the others).

The third analysis, concerned with the association between prejudice and religious belief (or lack of it) was carried out in a number of ways. The proportion of those claiming to be 'definitely Christians' who scored full marks on the 'ability to discriminate' scale was 39% among the sixth formers, and 22% among fifth formers (lower than the 'overall' percentages of those scoring full marks), which seems to indicate an above-average degree of prejudice among the Christian group. But equally, among those who claimed to be 'definitely *not* Christian' the respective percentages are 38% and 27% (*also* lower than the 48% and 31% of the overall sample). To find clear evidence of any distinction between Christian and non-Christian, correlation coefficients needed to be calculated. These coefficients proved in the event to be very small; $+0.019$ for the fifth formers and -0.093 for the older pupils. A graph will show why the first of these coefficients was so small as to be virtually non-existent. There were five positions on the 'Christian/non-Christian' scale (cf. p. 45), and one can calculate the mean score on the 'discrimination' scale gained by all those pupils holding to each of these five positions. Figure 44 shows the pattern for fifth formers, Figure 45 for sixth formers. (If there were an exact correlation between the two scales, the line on the graphs would be quite straight and would bisect the rectangle indicated by the two axes of the graph; and in such a case the coefficient of correlation would be ± 1.0.)

---

[1] The analyses of Survey 666 are of *individual* responses, *not* of school-mean-scores as with Survey 65.

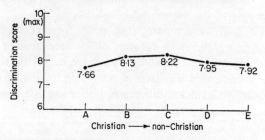

Fig. 44 The mean scores on the discrimination scale, set against the 'Christian label' scale (fifth formers)

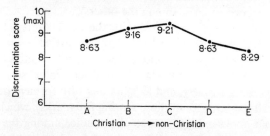

Fig. 45 The mean scores on the discrimination scale, set against the 'Christian label' scale (sixth formers)

N.B. As the discrimination score decreases so prejudice and/or lack of discrimination *in*creases.

If any conclusion can be drawn from these figures (and the -0.093 coefficient, though so small, is nevertheless statistically significant), it is that at sixth-form level prejudice and/or indiscriminate acceptance is associated with the non-Christian position rather than with the Christian.

However, the fact that the original 'acceptability scale' had deliberately sought to test both prejudice *and* lack of discrimination may well account for the general shape of the two graphs. It *could* be that it is the presence of prejudice (however slight) which lowers the score at the 'Christian' end, while the lower scores among the 'non-Christians' are due to an unwillingness to make *any* discriminating judgments, an accepting of all and sundry equally.

Authoritarianism

The above interpretation receives some support from an earlier section of Survey 666, the one dealing with bases of moral judgment.

It had asked the pupils to assess the degree of truth of certain moral assertions, which reflected an assortment of authoritative and laissez-faire positions (see pp. 130 f.). The two types of assertion were kept separate for the analysis of responses, so it was possible to correlate 'authoritarian morality' with other factors, and then to do the same with 'laissez-faire morality'.[2]

As before, the first comparison was made between fifth formers and sixth formers. Among the former 43% showed some degree of authoritarianism, compared with 26% of the latter. Large numbers of both (82%, 78% respectively) showed *some* degree of permissiveness, but as one moved further along the scale of increasing permissiveness one found an increasing preponderance of fifth formers over sixth formers. It would seem that, once again, 'intellectual maturity' makes an important contribution, and helps in establishing a balance between over-authoritarianism and over-permissiveness in one's moral judgment.

The contrast between girls and boys on this issue, however, falls into a different, but equally clear, pattern. At sixth-form level, 30% of the girls (compared with 21% of the boys) showed signs of authoritarianism; at fifth-form level the figures were 47% (girls) and 39% (boys). *Less* girls than boys, however, showed signs of laissez-faire morality – 75% at sixth-form level (as opposed to 82% among the boys), 80% at fifth form (85% boys) – and the gap between the sexes increased as one moved along the scale of permissiveness. In other words, the girls are in all respects more authoritarian, less permissive, in their judgments than the boys.

How does religious belief affect these moral judgments? Turning at once to the coefficients of correlation one finds that the correlation between adopting the 'Christian' position and making authoritarian moral judgments has a coefficient of $+0.17$ (fifth forms) and $+0.21$ (sixth forms), and with the size of samples used (565 and 793 respec-

---

[2] 'Authoritarianism' has in recent years become a common term of condemnation among psychologists. It must be strongly emphasized that in this chapter I am using the terms 'authoritarian' and 'laissez-faire' (or 'permissive') with no implied references to the classic studies of 'the authoritarian personality', but simply as a shorthand method of indicating whether a positive (authoritarian) or negative (laissez-faire/permissive) score was achieved in question III of Survey 666 (see pp. 130 f.). However, it will be clear from the arguments put forward in the following pages that an optimum position has been deemed to exist which neither depends on an uncritical application of an external, 'objective' code, nor yet assumes that all moral decisions can depend on little more than current taste or individual whim.

tively) these values are highly significant (0·001 level). Similarly the correlation between 'being Christian' and holding a 'permissive' type of morality has a coefficient of −0·2 (fifth forms) and −0·34 (sixth forms), an even greater correlation, but in a negative (*dissociated*) direction. All this can be shown visually, by adopting the same procedure as with the discrimination scale.

Fig. 46 The mean scores on the authoritarian scale, set against the 'Christian label' scale (fifth formers)

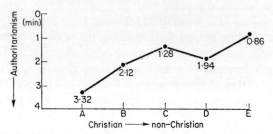

Fig. 47 The mean scores on the authoritarian scale, set against the 'Christian label' scale (sixth formers)

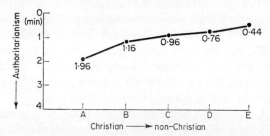

One notes that the whole sixth-form line is nearer to zero (complete *lack* of authoritarianism), and that, although more regular, it is less steep than the fifth-form line (i.e. the range of moral position between Christian and non-Christian is less in the sixth form). Again in Figures 48 and 49 the sixth-form line is nearer to zero (*lack* of permissiveness), and is less steep than the fifth-form line.

Now what comment can one make on the pattern of relationship revealed here between 'being Christian' and types of moral judgment? Are the critics of RE right? At first sight there might well appear to be evidence which suggests that marginally they are. However, a number of comments need to be made before any final judgment is passed.

Fig. 48   The mean scores on the permissive scale, set against the 'Christian label' scale (fifth formers)

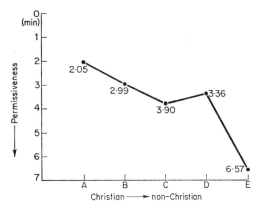

Fig. 49   The mean scores on the permissive scale, set against the 'Christian label' scale (sixth formers)

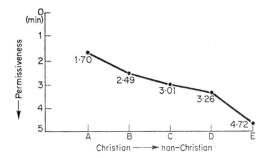

To begin with, one cannot distinguish between the effects of RE in school, and those of the other religious-attitude-forming influences in the family and in all the other relevant agencies of society. The most that one can say is that where pro-Christian attitudes and authoritarian judgments are found in association with each other among school leavers, then the school has not managed to eradicate any authoritarian trends which have been present among their pupils (and this need not by any means be a comment on the school's RE work alone but rather on its whole spirit and purpose).[3]

[3] There is also the further possibility that the authoritarian and other positions may be deeply rooted in personality characteristics, and only minimally affected by religious education, from whatever source. In this case the association between authoritarian views and pro-Christian attitudes may be due to the preference of 'authoritarian' people to identify themselves with what appears to them to be

Secondly, there is the whole question of whether one sees the shape of the graphs in this chapter as encouraging or depressing, and this will surely depend on whether one sees over-authoritarianism, or over-permissiveness, as the greater evil. At all events it is clear that a tendency towards the Christian position is associated with a greater overall responsibility of judgment, despite its authoritarian undertones. (The non-Christian is certainly more deeply stained with permissiveness than the Christian is with authoritarianism.)

Thirdly, the degree of authoritarianism shown in these graphs was disproportionately influenced by the results in just a few schools where the authoritarian score was well above average.[4] (The school mean score for one of these schools was as high as 6·08 on this scale, whereas 75% of the schools produced mean scores of under 2·0. It is noteworthy that the few schools which produced highly authoritarian pupil-scores were almost without exception schools where RE staffs held strongly authoritarian views on the subject themselves, and felt it right to encourage such views among those they taught.) In assessing the *overall* relationship between Christian commitment and authoritarianism one must not ignore the fact that of the 140 sixth formers 'definitely calling themselves Christians' seventy-eight (56%) scored zero, indicating a complete lack of authoritarianism. Therefore, despite the implication of the correlation coefficients about the general effects of present practice (whether in school, church or home), it is obvious that Christian commitment and over-authoritarianism are far from being inevitably associated.

The final comment on this issue is one which brings us right back to a question asked at the very beginning of the planning stages of the survey: 'What is the aim of RE?' If it is indeed to encourage people to be 'Christians', then *something* (however little) of the charge of 'encouraging prejudice' must be accepted in the light of our findings. However, if the aim of RE is seen in terms of encouraging people to become concerned with religious issues, then we must call in another body of findings before we pronounce judgment.

---

traditional and 'sound'. In other words, their Christianity is a vehicle of their authoritarianism, not one of its causes.

[4] E.g. if one omits the five schools with the highest school-mean-scores, then the figures for Figure 46 would be 3·2, 1·84, 1·08, 1·4 and 0·6, and for Figure 47 they would be 1·8, 1·12, 0·96, 0·76 and 0·44.

Concern with Religious Issues

One item on Survey 666 (as also on Survey 65) was 'How important to you is your answer to the last question?' ('the last question' being 'Do you class yourself as a Christian?'). Among the sixth formers (who were all in schools selected on the basis of high scores in Survey 65), 18% had definitely called themselves Christian, while 16% had taken the other extreme position; but as many as 44% indicated that, whatever the answer they had given, it was 'very important to them', and as few as 6% felt that it was 'not important at all'. (Among the fifth-formers the figures were 13% and 3%; 36% and 2% respectively.) The real success of these

Fig. 50 The mean scores on the discrimination scale, set against the scale regarding the importance of deciding for or against Christianity (fifth formers)

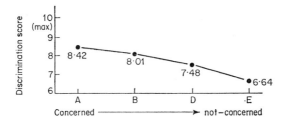

Fig. 51 The mean scores on the discrimination scale, set against the scale regarding the importance of deciding for or against Christianity (sixth formers)

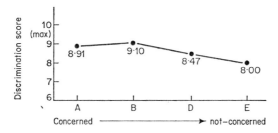

'successful' schools seems, then, to lie in having fulfilled the *second* of the two aims suggested in the last paragraph – 'encouragement towards concern with religious issues' – so perhaps it is with this question as a base, rather than the question of 'being a Christian', that one should examine correlations.

Taking this base, then, let us first look at the correlation with the discrimination scale, in Figures 50 and 51. (The 'middle' position was not offered as an alternative in this question regarding 'concern', hence the absence of 'C' on the horizontal axis.)

When one compares these two graphs with Figures 44 and 45, one notices at once that the initial 'climb-up' from the left-hand side has virtually disappeared (in fact, completely disappeared in the fifth-form graph). This indicates that success in RE, when judged on the basis of 'concern for the issues', is accompanied by a minimal risk of encouraging prejudice, and by a greater power of discrimination on the part of the pupils.

As for 'authoritarianism' and 'permissiveness', the patterns appear as shown in Figures 52 to 55.

Comparison of these four graphs[5] with Figures 46 to 49 suggests

Fig. 52 The mean scores on the authoritarian scale, set against the scale regarding the importance of deciding for or against Christianity (fifth formers)

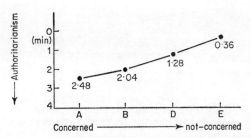

Fig. 53 The mean scores on the authoritarian scale, set against the scale regarding the importance of deciding for or against Christianity (sixth formers)

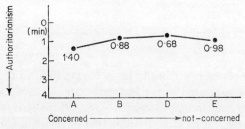

[5] The coefficients relevant to Figures 52 to 55 are +0·15, +0·13, −0·3 and −0·2 respectively.

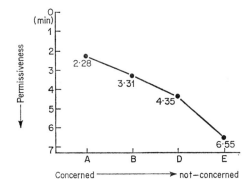

Fig. 54 The mean scores on the permissive scale, set against the scale regarding the importance of deciding for or against Christianity (fifth formers)

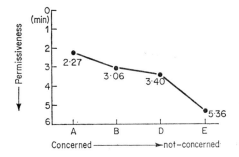

Fig. 55 The mean scores on the permissive scale, set against the scale regarding the importance of deciding for or against Christianity (sixth formers)

that when 'concern for the issues' is the aim of teaching, rather than 'Christian dedication', it lessens the risk of encouraging authoritarianism, though it could increase the risk of encouraging permissiveness. (It is interesting, incidentally, to note how the 'totally unconcerned' in Figure 53 reveal themselves as being more authoritarian in spirit than any except those to whom religious issues are '*very* important'.)

The final judgment on all this evidence must still depend on one's own attitude over the issue of authoritarianism versus permissiveness. 'Rejection of Christianity' does not produce any more responsible a moral judgment in a person, it merely establishes the ground of judgment on the other side of the fence from the 'dedicated Christian', and if anything a little further *away* from the fence than the Christian position usually is.

How 'Responsible' is their Thinking?

So far in this chapter the evidence from Survey 666 has been used for the purpose of comparing the degree of responsible thinking among Christians and non-Christians within the selected schools. It has not been used for the original purpose in gathering it, namely, an assesment of the *level* of responsible thinking in the selected schools as a whole. It has already been shown (in Chapter 2) that these schools were not 'successful' in enlarging their senior pupils' factual knowledge of the Bible, nor in encouraging them to maintain their earlier standard of religious behaviour (though, it must be admitted, their failure here may well have been less extensive than the failures of most other schools. Unfortunately, no comparable sixth-form evidence was available on this point from schools which produced *low* scores in Survey 65.) Similarly, it has been shown (in this chapter as well as in Chapter 2) that their success was greater in arousing concern with Christian issues than in producing widespread commitment to the Christian position. But of what *quality* was this concern, and how competent were the pupils in handling the issues?

In an attempt to tackle this difficult question Survey 666 asked for a number of 'paragraph-essays' on five topics, namely, the nature of the Bible, the existence of God, eternal life, divorce, and apartheid (see pp. 131–3). It must be admitted that the topics were complex and that in *some* schools time was rather limited, but one would have expected that these two considerations would merely have tended to counterbalance the fact that these were 'high-scoring' schools that were being used, and that therefore something approximating to normal distribution of grades would have occurred. This is obviously far from the actual outcome. The results are heavily inclined to the lower end of the scale (see Figure 56).

Each of the forty people who graded the essays was asked for his general comments on them, as well as for individual assessments. These are a few of the more typical comments:

> One felt that a considerable number of these children were trotting out ideas that they had heard but which they could not support by argument. . . . On the whole the same tendency to unthinking dogmatism was shown whether they were agreeing or disagreeing with the statement.

Fig. 56 The distribution of grades for the essays from Survey 666

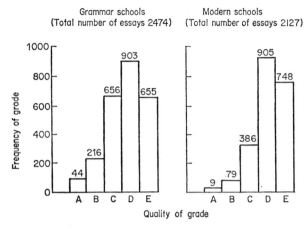

Grammar schools
(Total number of essays 2474)

Modern schools
(Total number of essays 2127)

Quality of grade

I was surprised by the number of answers that were fundamentalist. I felt that many were combating uncertainty by taking up this position of complete acceptance. Others adopted a devil-may-care attitude which only thinly covered their concern.

I think the teaching in nearly all the schools whose scripts I marked must have been pretty narrow, and there was little sign of the kind of discussion that is essential for encouraging thought. Several of the pupils were trying to think things out, but no one appeared to have helped them very much.

The worrying thing for me is that I find very little evidence of concern for truth either in those who are clearly avowed Christians or in any others. . . . Avowed 'scientists' are anything but scientific, while very few show any real capacity for logical argument.

I wonder if this question (*c*),[6] as posed, was a bit beyond the young people. Certainly there was little sign of their having given it any thought.

Almost all the candidates took the question (*d*) seriously and sought to discuss it responsibly. There were no frivolous replies . . . More impressive, however, was the tremendous ignorance among candidates of what Jesus taught. In two of the schools there appeared to have been recent teaching and discussion of the matter. In neither, however, had pupils come to an understanding of Jesus' teaching, or even to an awareness of points of view other than their own.

Even this short piece of work shows that nearly all the children feel they need a faith, but their great ignorance and shockingly fallacious opinions are stumbling blocks, if not millstones.

[6] For essay questions, see p. 131.

These children have something to say, but so many appear to use the theology of a small child.

On the whole these scripts were depressing. . . . Hardly anyone attempted analysis of the meaning of the terms. . . . Some kind of elementary training in philosophical analysis should be possible and is certainly much needed. . . . It is noteworthy that on the whole open-mindedness tends to go with an inclination towards religious belief. . . . The really dogmatic were the atheists and materialists. . . . The Christianity attacked (or sometimes defended) is always much inferior to the best expositions of it today; it is really no more than a form of deism . . . One group has a teacher who has got them to think quite a lot on the matter . . . but there was a lot of sad agnosticism on the whole.

What emerges is the surprising amount of impression, either way, that the teacher can make on the shape of opinions fashionable in the peer age group . . . In one school the youngsters were clearly used to thinking seriously and honestly.

A melancholy experience! Does this in fact represent their best efforts? Time appears to have been short, and the language of the question (*e*) is 'minority' language – middle-aged, middle-class and mid-twenties. But having said all this it is quite clear that the vast majority of scripts reflect total ignorance of the facts required to answer the question satisfactorily. (I think this could probably be said of the majority of the voting population of the United Kingdom in any case!)

I have enjoyed noting in embryo in these answers most of the philosophical positions from Hedonism to Nihilism. However, I have also been rather appalled by their attempts. . . . Inaccurate knowledge was frequent but in my opinion of far less importance than the general inability to think logically or relevantly. This cannot be laid solely at the door of poor RE teaching, but perhaps in this subject there could be the greatest opportunity to acquire good thinking skills.

When one takes these comments in conjunction with the marks shown in Figure 56 one can hardly feel complacent, despite possibly extenuating circumstances. It is relevant to recall, also, that only 48% even of the sixth formers were 'free of prejudice and able to discriminate', and only just over half (57%) of them were free of some measure of authoritarianism. And, although it is perhaps setting too high a standard to hope that sixth formers should already have found the happy medium between authoritarianism and over-permissiveness, one cannot really be happy that only 14% of them managed to achieve the optimum score of zero on *both* scales in the 'moral judgment' section.

This chapter must therefore end on a note of warning. Although there are signs, at least in our more successful county secondary schools, of a lively concern with Christian issues, fostered by staff of high standing and with a real care for their pupils' spiritual development, there are also signs of insufficient rigour in the disciplines of open and responsible thinking which should undergird any programme of religious education, particularly at sixth-form level.

APPENDIX TO CHAPTER 6

1. *The prejudice and discrimination test from Survey* 666 (*Question V*)

a. Text of Questionnaire
Here is a list of character descriptions, each one identified by a letter. Underneath is a 'scale of preference'. Enter the letters on this scale in the order that you would choose these different 'types' as friends. Then draw asterisks against those with whom you could definitely become close friends, and then draw a circle around those with whom you feel you could never become friends.

   A. An atheist whose mind is firmly closed against argument
   B. A Christian whose mind is firmly closed against argument
   C. A drug peddler
   D. A Fascist
   E. A follower of a religion to which you do not belong
   F. A member of a Christian denomination to which you do not belong
   G. A member of a different race from yourself
   H. A member of a different social class from yourself
   I. Someone of a different colour from yourself
   J. Someone with strong feelings against members of different races from himself
   K. Someone with the same general interests as yourself

Order of preference: 1 2 3 4 5 6 7 8 9 10 11
Enter 'Type' letters here:

N B Do not forget to distinguish possible '*close* friends' by drawing asterisks and also draw a circle around those with whom you could *never* become friends.

b. The scoring of this question was necessarily complex, but basically the system which was adopted marked *down* anyone giving high preference to

E

characters A B C D or J, or anyone declaring that they 'could *never* become friends' with characters E F G H I (or K). A score of 100% would therefore reveal a combination of definite standards of discrimination (in the good sense of the word) with a lack of prejudice; scores less than 100% show a falling away in one or the other (an over-readiness to accept ideas and practices no matter what their moral value is, or an irrational refusal to accept certain characteristics in other people). The method of scoring did not of course distinguish between the presence of one of these two failings or the other, but the main purpose of the question was to find the schools in which *neither* failing was present.

The school-mean-scores ranged[7] from 96·6% (a girls' grammar school) to 68·4% (a mixed modern school). In sixteen out of the thirty-two grammar schools over 50% of the pupils scored full marks, but the highest number of pupils gaining full marks in any of the modern schools was 40% (in a girls' modern school). At the other end of the scale only one grammar school (a mixed one) had more than 25% of its pupils with scores of 60% or under, whereas seven out of the twenty-eight modern schools came into this category. This is further evidence that 'discrimination without prejudice' is linked with increasing intellectual maturity (cf. p. 117).

2. *The moral judgment test from Survey* 666 (*Question III*)

The extent to which pupils agreed or disagreed with certain assertions regarding the basis of morality was taken as an indication of how far their moral judgment rested on an authoritarian, a 'responsible', or a laissez-faire basis. The assertions, and the scoring for each possible response, were as follows:

To what extent do you believe the following statements to be true? Tick the appropriate column against each one:

	Always true without exception	Usually true	Hardly ever true	Never true	Don't know (Not sure)
One should obey the law of the land	4	0	−2	−4	−1
Nothing is wrong in itself: an action can only become wrong if it is found out	−4	−3	−1	0	−2
No action is wrong in itself: the only thing to be considered is whether you enjoy it or not	−4	−3	−1	0	−2

[7] For the range of individual scores, see below, section 6.

	Always true without exception	Usually true	Hardly ever true	Never true	Don't know (Not sure)
One should not do anything that is forbidden in the New Testament	4	0	−2	−4	−1
One should not do anything that most people people feel to be wrong	4	0	−2	−4	−1

A pupil scoring zero was judged to be thinking 'responsibly', while those who accumulated a positive score erred on the over-authoritarian side, and those whose score was negative were felt to be too permissive. The greater the negative score the more anarchistic did the position become and vice versa. (The scoring allowed for a greater choice of positions, a smoother and more subtle progression, on the negative side; the positive scoring was in itself more 'black and white'.) For each school two 'final scores' were worked out, the mean average of all the positive scores, and the mean average of all the negative ones. The range of positive ('authoritarian') means was from 6·08 (a girls' modern school) to 0·20 (a boys' grammar school), out of a maximum of 12. The range of negative means was from 5·0 (mixed modern) to 0·88 (girls' grammar), out of a maximum of 20. (For range of individual scores see below, section 6.)

3. *The essay questions from Survey 666*

[The last five quarto pages (i.e. ten sides) of the questionnaire were used for the essays with the following rubric:]

State whether you agree or disagree with the statements on each of the following pages, and then write a paragraph giving the reasons for your decision.

[Each of the five pages was headed with a quotation, namely:]

(a) The Bible contains the truest picture of God ever given to man.
(b) It is only when one has rid oneself of all ideas of a 'God' that one can live life as a fully free person.
(c) One can find purpose and meaning in life only if one believes in the continuation of life after death.
(d) Easy divorce is wrong, because this does not follow the teaching of Jesus on the subject.
(e) FOR SIXTH FORMERS ONLY. The South African Government's policy of apartheid is justified by the biblical doctrine of the chosen people.

[The marking of these 'paragraph-essays' was done by assessors (some Christian, some not) drawn mainly from universities and colleges. Each essay was marked by two judges, working quite independently, and guided by a prepared scheme issued to each marker, as follows:]

Marks should be awarded or subtracted according to the general scheme set out below and also with regard to the particular scheme for each question. The final assessment should be given in the form of a letter, based on the following scale:

Marks	Letter
Below 1	E
1–1½	D
2–2½	C
3+	B
4+[8]	A

General marking

A mark should be given for each relevant fact or valid debating point which is brought into the argument.

A 'bonus' mark should be given if more than one side of an argument is represented (two 'bonus' marks being given if it is a three-sided argument, etc.).

NB 'Bonus' marks also count as marks in their own right: e.g. three 'bonuses' and none other would count as B.

A HALF mark should be subtracted for any inaccurate fact, any logical fallacy, any tendentious statement, irrelevancy or other sign of 'irresponsible thinking' or prejudice.

Marking of particular questions (additional to general marks)

(a) 'The Bible contains . . .'

A bonus mark will be given here if there is awareness of the possible validity of other religions besides Christianity, or of the 'relativity of truth' in general. Marks will be subtracted if the argument is attempted on anything other than logical or theological grounds (e.g. if the Bible's claims are attacked on the grounds of scientific inaccuracy).

(b) 'It is only when one has rid . . .'

Bonus marks should be given for attempts to discuss the use of the phrase 'a "God" ', or of the word 'free'.

(c) 'One can find purpose . . .'

Again bonus marks should be given for attempts to discuss the use of the phrases 'find purpose in life' or 'continuation after death'. A half mark should be subtracted if the discussion is conducted purely along the

---

[8] This must include at least one 'bonus' mark.

lines of the 'when you're dead, you're dead' sort of argument, or if attempts are made to 'prove' life after death purely along the lines of evidence of spiritualism, etc.

(*d*) 'Easy divorce . . .'

Bonus marks will be given if some knowledge is shown of the fact that Jesus' exact teaching on this point is not definitely known, or of the fact that there is disagreement among Christians as to the correct application of his teaching. (Any reasonable points from a 'non-religious' argument over divorce should of course be counted as 'valid debating points', though an argument which simply dismisses Jesus' teaching as entirely irrelevant will not gain any bonus marks and so cannot qualify for an A.)

(*e*) 'The South African Government's policy . . .'

For a bonus mark to be given it is essential that a clear indication of what apartheid involves should be found in the script. (This need not necessarily take the form of a *statement* as to what apartheid is, but definite knowledge of the situation in South Africa must be apparent somewhere in what is written.)

The argument should be considered 'valid' whether it works along biblical lines (e.g. 'The Old Testament doctrine, *even if* it could be taken as being transferable to the Afrikaaners, was transformed and "spiritualized" by New Testament teaching'), or whether it is conducted on a 'non-religious' basis (e.g. 'Apartheid is based on a failure to accept all men as of equal worth and therefore cannot be justified even by appeals to what is regarded as holy Scripture.').

[The grades shown on Figure 56 are derived from an averaging of the letter grades given by the two judges for each paper. The *total* number of grades shown in the diagram is obtained by multiplying the number of pupils by the number of essays (usually four or five) per pupil.]

4. *The administration of Survey 666*

[Instructions were sent to each school involved, as follows:]

This should be given to the twenty-five pupils who have been longest in the sixth form. (If there is no sixth form in the school, it should be given to twenty-five pupils who will be taking the General Certificate of Education next term. If there are less than twenty-five of them, numbers should be made up by the inclusion of Certificate of Secondary Education candidates.)

As much time as can be spared should be given to the completion of the papers. It is suggested that thirty minutes will prove to be an absolute minimum, and many sixth formers may well need a longer period to marshal their thoughts, for the last section in particular.

It should be emphasized that each paper must be filled in individually and that there should be no discussion of the topics in the questionnaire until all papers have been handed in.

Papers should be completed as soon as possible and sent to the Survey Officer, *with a note of the time taken for completion* and any other comments which are felt to be relevant.

5. *The results of questions VI (i)–(ii) of Survey* 666 (i.e. questions F (i)–(ii) of Survey 65, see p. 45)

Re VI (F) (i)

| | | Score | | | | | Total responses |
		0	1	2	3	4	
15/16– year-olds	Boys	12	34	54	127	22	249
	Girls	3	33	53	173	54	316
17/18– year-olds	Boys	79	59	53	94	57	342
	Girls	51	50	87	180	83	451

Re VI (F) (ii)

		0	1		3	4	Total responses
15/16– year-olds	Boys	11	55		122	60	248
	Girls	1	22		150	143	316
17/18– year-olds	Boys	32	64		116	127	339
	Girls	19	59		148	223	449

(Actual number of responses in each category)

N B Anyone wishing for further details from any part of the survey should write to Colin Alves, c/o 10 Eaton Gate, London, S.W.1.

6. The results of questions III and V of Survey 666 (see above Sections 2 and 1) correlated with results of VI (i)–(ii)

15/16-year-olds

'Importance' 'Christian'

	Authoritarian 0	4	8	12	—	Permissive 0	1	2	3	4	5	6	7	8	9	10	11	12	13	14	15	16	18	Prejudice 10	9	8	7	6	5	4	3	2	1	0	—	Totals
(i) 4	28	36	9	3		28	11	11	8	5	3	8	1	1										17	16	9	9	15	2	3	1	1	1	1	2	76
3	164	113	16	4	(3)	56	41	56	29	44	33	8	9	7	6	3	2	2	1	1				100	65	43	34	20	15	6	3	4	3	1	4	300
2	78	23	4	1	(1)	10	18	17	11	16	8	7	1	1	1	1								36	30	10	7	5	3	7	2		2		5	107
1	40	21	4	1	(1)	9	10	9	12	6	5	2	2	1	1	1								22	15	10	6	4	4	1				3	1	67
0	12	1	1	0	(1)	1	2	2	4	4	1	1												4	4		3			1					2	15
(ii) 4	101	80	18	3	(1)	56	31	38	20	25	16	8	2	4	1	1	4							70	54	21	22	20	4	6	2				4	203
3	158	93	14	6	(1)	41	39	50	27	40	21	16	11	12	7	2	1	4						84	59	43	27	18	12	6	5	4	1	1	7	272
2	52	20	2	0	(3)	7	1	6	11	10	11	7	1	4	1	1	1	2						24	14	7	8	4	8	3	1	2			2	77
1	10	1	0	0	(1)	1	1	1	2	1	1	2	1	1	1	1		1						1	3	1	1	1	2	2	1				1	12
0					(1)					(1)																		(1)								(1)
Total	322	194	34	9	(6)	104	80	95	60	75	49	33	14	21	10	6	3	6	1	2				179	130	72	59	44	24	17	6	8	4	8	14	565

17/18-year-olds

'Importance' 'Christian'

	Authoritarian 0	4	8	12	—	Permissive 0	1	2	3	4	5	6	7	8	9	10	11	12	13	14	15	16	18	Prejudice 10	9	8	7	6	5	4	3	2	1	0	—	Totals
(i) 4	78	56	5		(1)	54	28	17	13	17	4	2	3	8	2	2		1							55	22	9	17	9	3	2	1		1	1	22	140
3	200	66	7		(1)	65	54	49	30	30	11	13	5	7	1	3	2	1						148	47	22	13	10	6	4	1	1	1		30	274
2	108	30		1	(1)	23	32	23	16	12	9	8	1	7	3	1	1		1		1			79	10	9	10	2	1	2	1	1		1	26	140
1	88	20			(1)	18	18	19	18	16	5	5	5	5	3	4	2							49	16	18	9	2	3	2	1	1		2	21	109
0	115	14			(1)	16	11	21	7	13	8	15	6	16	4	4	3	2	1				1	50	18	12	7	4	7	2	1	2		2	23	130
(ii) 4	235	102	10		(3)	115	67	43	25	41	9	17	7	13	6	3	2	1						162	53	21	28	14	6	3	1	1		1	58	350
3	211	50	2	1		40	46	54	33	29	18	13	8	13	3	2	3	1	1		1		2	150	40	17	10	2	3	4	1	1	1		31	264
2	101	21			(1)	17	25	24	14	9	7	5	8	1	1	2	1	1	1	1		1		45	15	17	8	7	5	2	1	1	1	2	23	123
1	38	12			(1)	4	4	6	4	8	3	1	2	2	3	3	1	1	1		1		1	21	5	5	2	2	1	5	1	2		1	9	51
0	(4)	(1)				(1)	(2)	(1)		(1)			(1)											(3)	(1)			(1)							(1)	(5)
Total	589	186	12	1	(5)	176	143	129	76	88	37	43	20	36	12	10	5	5	2	1	1		3	1 · 381	113	61	48	23	12	17	6	4	1	5	122	793

PART II

7

Is it a Right and Proper
Thing to Do?

AT THE risk of being superficial, it might be as well at this point
to attempt a summary of the main findings set out in Part I, and at
the same time to make some sort of assessment of their implications.
    The overall situation as revealed by Survey 65 is that as far as
attainment (i.e. knowledge plus insight) is concerned the grammar
schools are largely successful on the criteria adopted, at least among
their fourth forms. This level of success, however, is not maintained
in the sixth forms, where 'remembered knowledge' has deteriorated
and (judging by the evidence in Survey 666) insight and rigorous
thinking on religious and moral issues are not as developed as one
might hope. Among the more successful schools at least, however,
there is a continuing concern with these issues, even though such a
concern is *not* associated with widespread commitment to the
Christian position, and is (overall) even less associated with the
performance of religious practices such as prayer and worship.
    Among the modern schools the attainment results are of a con-
siderably lower standard (as would be expected). On the whole,
attitudes towards Christianity are slightly more favourable in
modern schools than in grammar schools, particularly above the
fourth-form level, though in terms of actual 'practice' the modern
school fourth former is less 'religious' than his grammar school
contemporary.
    But it is comparisons between the sexes and between the 'cultural
settings' of schools which reveal the most significant differences.
Girls score more highly than boys, both on attainment and on
attitude tests. They are also more authoritarian and more 'dis-

criminating' than boys. The 'cultural' and 'geographical' factor, however, is only slightly less strong than the factor of sexual difference, particularly where attitudes are concerned. It is not merely a question of conurbation versus countryside; among both such groupings actual regional differences make themselves apparent, and (generally speaking) the nearer one gets to London the less favourable the attitudes towards Christianity become. It is also clear that the attitude to 'school religion' is considerably lower in the London conurbation than it is elsewhere.

What then are the implications of all this? What is the nature of the task facing those responsible for RE in the future? What is the way forward? One of the vague hopes underlying the setting up of the whole British Council of Churches' survey was almost certainly that if one could isolate those factors which make for success in the schools investigated, then one merely had to say to all the other schools in the country, 'Look, this works. If you were to do the same, you would be equally successful'. But two largely unforeseen difficulties have appeared which wreck the beautiful simplicity of such a solution. Firstly, the strength of regional differences makes it impossible to say 'This works here. It will work equally well there.' And secondly, the speed of cultural change in certain parts of the country makes it also impossible to say 'This has worked here in the past. It will continue to work in the future.' Particularly when one is faced with the situation such as one finds in the London conurbation, one has to look not merely at past, or even present, practice in the schools, but at the whole changing cultural situation itself, and the relation of the Christian gospel to such a situation. 'What is the world coming to?' need not be a cry of despair. It can, and should, be a genuine question, a necessary prelude to asking 'How can Christians continue to communicate effectively in the present and in the future?'

It was to tackle this sort of basic question that a special group (cf. pp. 218 f.) was set up fairly early in the course of the survey, and their findings will play a very important part in any assessment of the implications of the more statistical side of the investigation. (See Chapter 8.) But before we turn to the work of this group, we ought to ask another fundamental question. It would appear that a considerable effort will be required to bring the overall level of achievement in RE up to a really satisfactory standard – effort in staff-recruitment and training, effort in replanning syllabuses and in refining techniques, effort in working out underlying principles and discovering how to apply them in new situations. Is it going to be worth it? This is not the same as asking if it will *work*; it is asking whether religious education merits a place in our schools or not, and if so on what grounds.

It was pointed out in Chapter 6 that the charge of 'indoctrination' has often been brought against RE, but that the evidence of Survey 666 lends little support to the theory that 'success' in RE is nothing more nor less than the production of bigots, lacking true insight into the questions at issue. What the evidence *did* suggest was that pupils with whom RE has been successful, particularly when success is seen in terms of 'real concern with religious issues', are slightly *more* responsible in their thinking than those on whom RE has had little impact.

But it is not enough merely to refute arguments for the *removal* of RE. What is required are positive arguments for the *presence* of RE in the country's schools. It is pertinent at this point to turn to some papers specially produced for the survey committee in the early days of its deliberations. The first of these papers was written by a member of the committee itself, E. L. Clarke, and contains the following passage:

What are the motives, what is the interest of the State in insisting, in the Act of 1944, on religious worship and religious instruction in all maintained schools?

I cannot claim to have any special knowledge of the negotiations which preceded the 1944 Act;[1] my opinions are based upon the Act itself and the spirit in which it has been administered.

First, I should assume – though a communist or a cynic would disagree – that there is not a large element of 'statecraft' in this matter, in the sense of using religion as an adjunct to the police force, or as an 'opiate'. No doubt there are many politicians in whom this motive is uppermost, the same who see the Youth Service primarily as a defence against delinquency; but the Act does not seem to reflect their attitude. It is a liberal Act. It insists again and again on the welfare of the individual, seldom on the claims of the State upon the individual. In administration one has had the feeling, over many years, that the Ministry of Education has been the watchdog for the rights of the individual child and the individual parent. It seems, therefore, reasonable to assume that the clauses in question were inserted into the Act for a truly educational reason, in that they were conceived to be in the interest of the child.

[1] For comment on these negotiations see M. Cruickshank, *Church and State in English Education, 1870 to the Present Day* (London: Macmillan, 1963).

This assumption is strengthened by the Act's lack of insistence upon any particular religion. The schools are not compulsorily Christian. There are schools in which the religious instruction and worship are Jewish, and there does not seem to be any limit to the number of different faiths which could claim to have their own schools, provided their promoters could meet the financial obligations. The Established Church does not occupy a privileged position save that which it has won for itself by its educational activities in the past. The Act simply insists that religion is an essential part of education.

I think it is true to say that all children, during some period of their growth up to the age of fifteen, have needs in their emotional and spiritual development and in the field of moral education, which can be met by religion in the schools. It seems to be implicit in the Act that they cannot be met, or met so well, in any other way.

How religious education serves 'the interest of the child' is spelled out in more detail in a paper written for the committee by Dr J. W. D. Smith:[2]

Is there a real case for religious education in the State schools of today and tomorrow?

If we acknowledge frankly that the aims of a school, as a school, are 'enlightenment rather than conversion, understanding rather than discipleship' (W. R. Niblett, *Christian Education in a Secular Society* [London: Oxford University Press, 1960], p. 96), then on this view religious education can claim a place in the curriculum on educational grounds alone. This might be called the *radical* view since it acknowledges the *roots* of religion in the nature of the child. Our 'image of God' may have to go but the religious dimension of life will always remain. The dawn of self-awareness confronts man with the mystery of his own nature and destiny. As boys and girls grow towards maturity they need to be helped to become aware of those depths in human existence and to make their own personal response to the reality which confronts them in that experience.

Two stages in personal development are especially important. The first is early childhood and the second is adolescence. The human infant depends on adult care for its physical survival. The manner in which his basic physical and emotional needs are satisfied determines his earliest impressions of human existence. The first, and most enduring, patterns of individual behaviour begin to be formed in response to these impressions (cf. for example, Melanie Klein, *Our Adult World and Its Roots in Infancy* [London: Tavistock Publications Ltd, 1960], p. 4, '. . . the young infant, without being able to grasp it intellectually, feels unconsciously every discomfort as if it were inflicted on him by hostile forces. If comfort is given to him soon, in particular, warmth, the loving way he is held, the gratification of being fed – this gives rise to happier emotions. Such comfort is felt to come from good forces and, I believe, makes possible the infant's first loving relation to a person.') Knowledge of 'God' comes first

[2] Then the Principal Lecturer in RE, Jordanhill College of Education, Glasgow.

through the human environment, and the roots of the child's real religion can be traced in his first responses to that environment.

Awareness of a larger environment normally awakens before the age of five years. In one way or another the fact of death touches the child's experience and he learns the limitations of parental love and care. In this and in other ways the child begins to experience, at the emotional level, the fact of human finitude. Parental attitudes are still much more important than verbal teaching but it is at this stage that religious beliefs and practices begin to be meaningful and helpful in personal development. In the home children will naturally be introduced to parental beliefs and practices. At school it would seem appropriate to introduce them to the basic beliefs of the Christian faith – since that is the faith by which their forefathers lived and in which they died.

Adolescence brings a second period of emotional instability and insecurity. As the boy or girl adjusts to the inner and outer changes associated with adolescence the partially resolved problems of early childhood re-emerge. The basic insecurity of human existence is felt again as a deep under-current of the emotional life and it emerges at the conscious level as a problem of 'ultimate concern' which has implications for the whole of human living. The initiation rites of tribal society provide each new generation with traditional ways of resolving the adolescent problems of sexual, social and 'religious' adjustment. A secular society which refuses to acknowledge such problems is ignoring a vital educational task.

The meaning which the documents of the New Testament find in the life and death of Jesus of Nazareth offers answers to questions which are inseparable from our human situation. It is possible to reject these answers but it is impossible to escape the questions. In the words of Simone Weil, 'The danger is not lest the soul should doubt whether there is any bread but lest, by a lie, it should persuade itself that it is not hungry. It can only persuade itself of this by lying, for the reality of its hunger is not a belief, it is a certainty.' The evidence of *Teenage Religion* (by Harold Loukes) suggests that modern boys and girls are conscious of that hunger. They are aware of the questions even when they distrust or repudiate the Christian answers. The fact of that awareness is the basic justification for religious education in a secular society.

Before taking up Dr Smith's reference to the 'awareness of the questions' among modern adolescents, we should note various pronouncements from government reports, which support his general line of argument. There is first the much-quoted passage from the Spens Report (*Report of the Consultative Committee on Secondary Education with Special Reference to Grammar Schools and Technical High Schools*, 1938):

No boy or girl can be counted as properly educated unless he or she has been made aware of the fact of the existence of a religious interpretation of life.

This is taken a little further in the Crowther Report (*15 to 18* [London: HMSO, 1959]):

The teenagers with whom we are concerned need, perhaps before all else, to find a faith to live by. They will not all find precisely the same faith and some will not find any. Education can and should play some part in their search. It can assure them that there is something to search for and it can show them where to look and what other men have found (para. 66);

and again in the Newsom Report (*Half our Future*, [London: HMSO, 1963])

The nearer we got to the boys and girls on whose education we have to advise, the more it was brought home to us that Parliament gave the schools a difficult but not an impossible task when it told them to foster their spiritual and moral development. We learned that those who tried with sincerity and ability to do this found that they were not only fulfilling a statutory obligation, or discharging a social responsibility; they were meeting a felt personal need of their pupils. Most boys and girls want to be what they call 'being good' and they want to know what this really implies in the personal situations which confront them. This is difficult enough, but it is not sufficient. They want also to know what kind of animal a man is, and whether ultimately each one of them matters – and, if so, why and to whom. (para. 157.)

Comment from the Receiving End

'They were meeting a felt personal need of their pupils' (or, as para. 167 of this Report puts it: 'The best schools give their pupils something . . . which they know they need when they receive it, though they had not realized the lack before'); 'The evidence of *Teenage Religion* suggests that modern boys and girls are aware of that hunger' – how much support is lent to these claims by the findings of the British Council of Churches survey?

The position of the median scores in Figure 9 shows clearly that the majority of pupils are in favour of the continuation of the subject, and feel that their education would be incomplete without it. At the fifth/sixth-form level, at least in the specially selected schools, almost 80% of the pupils regarded the issue of Christianity as being 'very important' to them (see Figure 5).

Further evidence on this point comes from the work done by Cox, Marratt and Wright.[3] 2,276 sixth formers (from a stratified random

---

[3] See *Learning for Living*, May 1965, and Edwin Cox, *Sixth Form Religion* (London: SCM Press, 1967).

sample of schools) 'were asked whether they favoured the retention of the legal provision of R. I.'; 68% were in favour, 32% against.

Moreover, of the 736 pupils who opposed the statutory provision, at least 268 were not absolutely opposed, but criticized the administration, teachers or their methods. It would appear to justify the argument that the current objection is more to the methods than to the subject itself.

Actual examples of this sort of criticism can be found in the transcripts of the conversations which I was able to hold with groups of pupils from a wide range of schools in the early months of the survey (and which also find strong parallels in Loukes' *Teenage Religion*):

A fourth-year group of boys

Q. If Divinity was made a voluntary subject, would you go to that?
B. It all depends on the teachers, and that kind of thing. If I found the teacher interesting, I liked the things he did, the way he went about it, and that, then I think I would go. If he just sort of said 'Read that and then write a composition about it', then I wouldn't go to that.
B. I think the teacher in the class should be a bit more modern. Like Mr——, he used to say that believing in God doesn't mean going to church and then go home and kill your grandmother.
Q. But you would go if Divinity was made a voluntary lesson?
B. It depends on the teacher.
Q. But you think the subject itself is worth studying if you've got a good teacher to help you?
B. Oh yes, it is.
B.B. Yes.

A fifth-year group of boys

Q. Do you feel that religious education is an important part of a person's education, whoever does it, whether it be school, church, or parents, do you feel that it has any importance?
B. To a certain point I think it does, but otherwise no, I think people like us, fourth and fifth years, we'd think it's beginning to become a waste of time to just go in and discuss religion, well, not necessarily religion, just discuss. I think it's an utter waste of time . . .
B. Better things to do, if you see what I mean. We've got to take an examination.
Q. What sort of things do you discuss, then?
B. Sometimes it is a topic that is in the news.
Q. And you don't feel that this is important?
B. *I* think it *is*. There's nowhere else you can really express your opinion on things. There's no other lesson where you're given the chance.

B.   Ah yes, but you're talking about the free lesson we have here. Normally we wouldn't have that discussion, would we, it would be a straightforward RE lesson.

B.   But I'm talking about the RE we have now.

B.   But that's not always the case, is it? You're just talking about your own experience.

Q.   This is what I want you to do. I know that the RE in this school is perhaps freer than in many schools and I want your reaction to *this* type of RE.

B.   It's only in the fifth year and perhaps the fourth year though that it's free, but in the first and second and third years they sort of drum it into you then.

B.   I don't know about that.

B.   We did.

B.   We had a few discussions. We had more strict RE than we do now, or have had for a long time, but we did have quite a few discussions and that kind of thing.

Q.   Come back to the fourth and fifth year, which is what I'm particularly interested in. Why do you feel that it is a waste of time to discuss, for example, things that are in the news?

B.   Ah, religiously. As I said, I think we've got better things to do, we don't value it. I think we consider it's a waste of time, but when you think about it I suppose it isn't, but that's how we think about it.

Q.   You mean that the exam has such all-pressing importance on you that you can't really think about anything else at all? Is this true of all of you, do you all feel that the exam is such a bogey as this and that it directs the whole of your life and interest at this stage?

B.   It does in a way, I suppose. It's necessary; it's only for a year or two; it affects the rest of your life so you're willing to give up certain things.

A Lower-sixth group (mixed)

Q.   'Since I have come to this school I have become much more interested in religion' – would you agree or disagree with this statement?

B.G. Disagree.

Q.   Have you become less interested?

B.G. Yes.

Q.   Why is this? Because you've got older?

B.   I feel it's been poked down our throats too much. It's not been brought over in a way which will appeal to us.

G.   I think our RE lessons should take the form of discussions, and not as they say: 'Shall we read Moses', or 'Let's read the Apostles today', and they get so carried away with the Apostles, everybody sits there and hears about Peter and Paul and Mary, and how everyone did their little nuts in the days of old, and it's not very constructive towards your ideas; we should be getting ideas on religion.

B. . . . why it happens and not delve deeply in what it tells you in the Bible.

B. I think all young people are interested in religion, if it's only brought over properly.

B. To be frank, for the lesson I've just come out of, I took my library book along. I was so dead bored I just had my case up and read my book.

B.G. It's dead boring. Or else we just talk along the row. And pass sweets along. It's so boring.

B. I think the Scripture lesson would be a lot better, as they said, if it took the form of a discussion. The way we have it, it is almost like a sermon. At the moment we are studying the Sermon on the Mount and I think everyone has met the Sermon on the Mount in church, just about everyone here goes to church. . . . We go through each verse word by word. I don't feel you should read the Bible like this.

Q. Do you study English literature like this?

B.G. Yes. Yes.

Q. What do you think about the Bible itself? You've obviously had it rammed down your throats, perhaps in rather an unimaginative way, but trying to forget the way it's been treated, what do you think about the Bible? Do you think it is a book which is worth studying at all?

B.G. Yes. Yes.

G. It gives you guidance, but you don't have to take all the things so literally, because it was written by men such a long time ago. They were sincere at the time, I expect, I don't really know, but nowadays half the things they do and say don't really apply. There is a new outlook on life completely, and you have to take everything with a pinch of salt.

G. Some things are completely true.

B. Not everything.

B. I think the New Testament is the whole basis.

G. Parables, and things like that.

B. Yes, they've got a message.

An Upper-sixth group (mixed)

Q. Do you feel this is a valid subject to be taught in school? You don't feel that it is a waste of time?

B. In its present state, yes.

B. I think because religion is so important, I suppose it has to be taught in school. I don't think it should be, I don't think it is really a valid subject, no, I think there is too much importance placed on it. I don't think religion is that important to most people.

B. To some it might be.

B. I disagree with that. I should say you want to have good grounding in religion in school, find out what it's about, to sort of help you think about what you'd like to do.

B.   This is the method that's going wrong here.
Q.   At the moment I'm asking whether the subject *itself* in a general sense is one which ought to be taught in schools, not whether what you've experienced here has helped you.
B.   . . . knowledge of the contents of the Bible. Everyone should know about it.
G.   The more you know about it, the more able you are to make up your mind.
G.   Yes, I quite agree.
B.   I don't agree with this close study of the Bible. I don't think it gets anywhere. I think straightaway the classes are limp for a beginning. I think comparative religion certainly, but close study of the Bible is purposeless.

The mention of 'comparative religion' raises a further issue which must be pursued at least briefly, even if inadequately. A distinction has often been made between 'education *about* religion', and 'education *in* (or *into*) religion', and a case has been presented that RE in State schools should restrict itself entirely to the former; in fact the quotation from the Spens report (see p. 143) has been interpreted as lending support to a 'purely objective' type of 'study of religion'.

This line of argument obviously merits consideration, if only on the grounds that it must necessarily demand (and rightly so) the rejection of anything which smacks of indoctrination or proselytization. However, its weakness is that it ignores the basic fact about religion, namely, that it is one of those areas of human life which dies under dissection. A 'purely objective' (i.e. purely intellectual) approach to music, poetry or painting leaves out a vital factor in the understanding of these creative arts, for understanding must include appreciation. The same is true of religion. Deliberately to sterilize the encounter between religion and the adolescent is not to achieve 'neutrality' as some would claim; rather is it to achieve 'neuter-ality', whereby religion is presented in an emasculated form, as a possibly interesting social or psychological phenomenon. but not as a possible source of faith, power and truth.

Religious Education and Moral Education

At this point another objection may be raised and an alternative suggestion put forward, namely, if religion, to be properly understood, must in some sense be 'appreciated' as well as studied, then why not leave it out of the schools altogether and concentrate instead on moral education, which has none of the problems of religious education, and yet satisfies the felt personal needs of children in a more immediately appropriate way?

The trouble with this view is that one cannot divorce moral and religious education in this way. A recently produced humanist scheme of moral education set out as the first two areas of 'the content of moral education': '(1) experiences leading to a right evaluation of oneself and one's relationship with others; (2) experiences leading to a valid perspective on man and the universe.' These two areas are in fact areas of *religious* education, and the document was quite right to recognize that they are areas essential to any scheme of moral education. If one attempts to leave them out of such a scheme, one is implicitly assuming a *different* 'evaluation of oneself' and a *different* 'perspective on man and the universe'; one cannot, in fact, leave the issue on one side.

The same point was made in another of the papers produced[4] for the survey committee:

Here it is pertinent to raise the much debated question as to whether ethical teaching rooted in Christian belief has any distinctive virtue, or whether we should pay serious attention on educational grounds, to demands for ethical teaching 'which stands in its own right'.

We go with the humanist much of the way. A supernatural sanction for ethical conduct is not *necessarily* welcome. For example, if the Divine Will is interpreted as a series of invariant commands, evil results can ensue which range from insensitivity to the Inquisition. Again, moral action is not truly *moral* if it is motivated by thoughts of rewards and punishments after death. Nor does it appear that the *content* of right action differs much, if at all, as seen by a Christian or a humanist. A possible difference is the obligation to self-sacrifice, which a Christian might push to more extreme limits than the humanist; but this should probably be regarded as a distinction not of content but of attitude or approach. For it is in his *approach* to ethics that the Christian differs from the humanist.

First, the Christian believes that the universe, being created by God, has a moral purpose: in one word that purpose is love. He also believes that each individual, being created by God, is of paramount value. Where the humanist says that we ought to act *as if* these propositions were true, the Christian believes that they actually *are* true. Quite apart therefore from the theoretical questions (how it could be right to act consistently as if something were true which is in fact not true), a more practical consequence must also ensue, that the Christian views the course of history and of his own life from a different perspective, a fuller one even than the Marxist, namely, the *species aeternitatis*.

The Christian has also in Jesus the specification of God's purpose, the

[4] By John Dancy and Bishop Cockin.

pattern of the moral life, and the deliverer from the selfishness of sin. The life of Jesus as recorded in the gospels contains all moral lessons: that utter goodness *is possible*; that it consists not in obedience to law but in response to love; that the only unforgiveable is the unforgiving. The spirit of Jesus as known directly to the believer gives him the power to forget himself and to follow his Master.

Thirdly, the Christian has the Holy Spirit, particularly as embodied in the Church. (We are not *limiting* the Holy Spirit to the Church; but as we see it the rest of his activity is equally accessible to the humanist.) There is no need to stress the extent to which the individual Christian can receive support, courage, forgiveness, inspiration from the community of those who have committed themselves to the same way.

So the Christian has a perspective, a pattern and a power which are all his own. The detailed effects of this will vary in individual cases, but its characteristic product is a paradoxical combination of serenity and dynamism, a spirit which differs profoundly from Marxist fanaticism on the one hand and stoic (or even Buddhist?) resignation on the other. We do not, of course, claim that the spirit is either universal among Christians or exclusive to them. But most would admit that it can be seen *par excellence* in the Christian saints and martyrs; and those who know would also allow that *generically the same* spirit is met in countless simple Christian lives.

It is by considerations such as these that we believe 'religious education' (as opposed to 'simple moral education') is justified: not because of any supernatural moral sanction with which our pupils must be confronted, but because of the need to establish a perspective on life, in the light of which one can face the moral perplexities and challenges of living.

The Implications

Let us return for a moment to the comments of the pupils themselves. 'I think all young people are interested in religion, if it's only brought over properly' was a point made by one of the sixth formers. The conditional clause is, of course, vitally important, and in this review of 'support for RE' one must not become too complacent over figures such as are given in Figure 9. They *do* (as was claimed earlier in the chapter) show that the majority of pupils are in favour of RE continuing, but they *also* show (by virtue of half the medians falling below 62·5%) that this support for RE is not wildly enthusiastic. One must also remember the adverse reflection on the present practice of RE (especially in the London conurbation) provided by the figures in the table on p. 69.

This same kind of modified, or conditional, support for the continued presence of RE in the country's schools is found in a number of surveys of parental opinion conducted over the past four years. The earliest of these to be published was in *Television and*

Religion (University of London Press, 1964; see especially pp. 87–91 and 130) where the results of a Gallup Poll in the autumn of 1963 were set out. Here it was established that only 4% of the people interviewed wished to 'cut out all religion and scripture' from school (and only another 8% 'did not know' whether they wished this or not). In 1964 Cox, Marratt and Wright[5] supplemented their sixth-form enquiry by writing to the parents of the 2,276 sixth formers, asking whether they favoured the retention of the legal provision of RE in schools. 73·5% of the parents replied (which is a high response to a postal questionnaire and in itself shows the importance attached by parents to this question); once again only 4% (of the *whole* sample) were against the retention of legal provision. The particular importance to be attached to these figures is that they come from people who are thinking about their own children still at school. For the same reason, the most relevant figures from the National Opinion Poll survey (reported in *New Society*, 27 May, 1965) are the 93% of *parents of school-children* who would prefer RE to be kept on the curriculum of State secondary schools, and the 91% who felt that the present statutory position regarding RE and Assembly should continue. The most recently published survey of parental views is that undertaken in the north-east of England by May and Johnston.[6] Once again slightly over 90% of the respondents said they wanted their children to continue to have RE lessons at school.

Figures such as these must be kept in mind when one meets the occasional headline in the daily press which reads 'Parents Call for an End to School Religion' or some such phrase. Small but vocal groups who make such demands attract more notice than their numbers warrant.

This is not to say, however, that such protests should be ignored altogether. Minority interests must obviously be preserved. This is not the only consideration, however, for quite often the protests and objections are not to RE in itself but to the *type* of RE which their children are in fact receiving, or which they themselves received.

It is important to note that among the 'twenty-one to twenty-four' age-range represented in the National Opinion Poll survey only 83% wished RE to remain in the secondary school, their memories of what they themselves received there being fairly recent; it is also in

---

[5] Cf. p. 144 above.
[6] See the *Durham Research Review*, April 1967, and *Learning for Living*, March 1967.

this age-group that there is the least support (56% of the group) for the *content* of RE remaining on traditional lines.

The conclusion of this whole argument must surely be that although the educational arguments, plus the pupil and parental support, for RE provide more than enough weight to justify its continuation in our schools, we owe it to pupils and parents alike that the subject should be 'brought over properly', and that 'the teacher in the class should be a bit more modern'.

8

The New Approach Required

'Do you feel that RE is a valid subject to be taught in school? You don't feel that it is a waste of time?'

'In its present state, yes.'

INTO WHAT sort of state should RE be transformed if it is no longer to appear to this sixth former as a waste of time? This question was one of those which the small group of committee members meeting under the chairmanship of Bishop Cockin attempted to answer.

This chapter will set out the group's findings, largely in the words of various papers produced by the group, or by individual members within the group. However, for the sake of continuity and ease of reading, I have been asked to present the findings as if in my own words. But it must be firmly established at this point that this form of presentation is merely a literary device. Although I attended the meetings of the group, and fully endorse all that they say, I can claim no credit for the learned and reasoned case which I am about to argue on their behalf.

The actual starting point of discussion was a request from the full committee 'to assess the implications of what is happening in the present theological ferment for education in general and for religious education in particular'. The comments of the group members on this, and on the further questions which sprang from it, ran along the following lines.

The Theological Scene

To understand the present theological ferment one must place it in its historical context – the context of recent changes in our culture and learning in general. We have come to the end of a culture period dominated by history and archaeology. We have been projected into a period in which, for as long as we can now foresee, we are likely to be dominated by science and technology.

If this general thesis be accepted the implications for religious education are that the truth of the Incarnation must be set firmly within the realm of present-day scientific studies. Christian education, instead of being separated from the sciences, must somehow be refreshed and reformulated from within their context. Especially is this the case with the biological and psychological sciences.

But there are also inner reasons, movements of thought, within Christianity itself, which are leading to a new look and a new setting for the 'doing of theology'. Up until roughly the beginning of the nineteenth century the subject-matter of Christian teaching could be summarized as the Holy Scriptures, the Creeds, the Writings of the Fathers *for all*; the Confessions, Catechisms, and particular Orders of Worship for the respective denominations of Christendom. For expert teachers a knowledge of ancient languages was essential. For the ordinary teacher (mainly the minister) a knowledge of a system of doctrine (Luther, Calvin, Hooker, etc.) was deemed necessary. But the whole enterprise was viewed in a relatively *static* fashion. Here was a body of material to be read, learned and inwardly digested and then to be communicated to others through explanation, illustration and correlation (comparing, for example, Scripture with Scripture).

Then from the beginning of the nineteenth century came exciting discoveries of remains from the past and an intense new interest in historic development. For a long time biblical studies and instructions retained their relatively *static* character but gradually the new historical methods and criteria had to be applied to Christian standards of faith. Everything must ultimately go into the historical melting pot. Bible, Creeds, Fathers, and Liturgies must be seen against their respective *historical* backgrounds. Events of Church history must be set out in chronological order. And ultimately historic tests would need to be applied throughout: Did events really happen as recorded? If they did, what importance did they have within the total divine revelation? What is to be said about discrepancies? What is the relation of Christian history to so-called secular history? Everything is to be viewed historically and the attempt made to show the whole panorama of history being worked out according to God's design.

This *dynamic* conception of the development of Christianity began to be taught in university and theological seminary but only very gradually in pulpit and classroom. But the process could not be stayed, and ultimately the teaching of the Christian faith became virtually a part of the teaching of history. This had, it seemed, great advantages: the teaching of the faith could hold a respectable place among other disciplines; denominational teaching could be less of a barrier to common action, for if all could agree to treat the subject matter *historically*, that is, as being included in one vast historical continuity stretching from the ancient Near East to the modern West, then no serious difficulties need arise. Of course, the history must be taught *factually* with the minimum of individual interpretation. But now the more Christianity could be set in the *historical* context the better. It was therefore right to teach about the history, geography and social life of Palestine, Egypt, Greece, Babylon and Rome: to teach about the contents of other literature (apocrypha, pseudepigrapha, etc.) in biblical times, to provide background material, to compare with other cultures and to set forth the *facts* witnessed to in Scripture and Christian documents by careful historical methods – this was the enterprise in which men and women of widely different outlooks could co-operate.

But a further change has been taking place since roughly the conclusion of the first World War. It might be described in various ways, but the one common factor in all the questionings and reconsiderings is surely that of the connection between history and *meaning*. Has history as a whole any meaning? Has a particular event in history any meaning? How is meaning to be discerned? Is a naked event without meaning even conceivable? If it is, has it any right then to be called history? Has a strict chronological sequence anything to do with meaning? Can one period of history be more meaningful than another?

These questions that have been raised in regard to history in general are of vital importance in the context of Christian history. And they are bound ultimately to affect the teaching of the Christian faith as history. The urgent question is: What constitutes meaning? How in actual experience is meaning discovered? How does anything become meaningful to each individual? On the answer to these questions seems to depend the new direction in the teaching of the Christian faith.

It is therefore vital to explore the places where meaning is found in contemporary experience. In attempting 'to assess the implications of current theology for educational practice' it is also necessary to consider those aspects of the contemporary situation and climate which affect most strongly the outlook of the older boys and girls. It is to their situation that our teaching has to be directed, not only immediately in the syllabuses of upper forms, but indirectly in all that leads up to this.

The Scientific Revolution

One cannot hope in a brief report to produce any adequate treatment of a phenomenon which is affecting aspects of our culture and civilization far beyond the sphere of education. But some of the results of it are so obviously to be seen in the radical theological displacement of our time that they must at least be registered, as a necessary condition of any realistic attempt to formulate the aims of religious teaching. We note that: (1) The spectacular successes of the scientific method in discovery and demonstration have given it a prestige value which almost automatically serves to down-grade other methods of approach as being of less precision and reliability. (2) The emphasis of the scientific temper upon the continuous discovery of *new* truth tends to play down the value of truth which appears to base its claim upon its antiquity and permanence. This, of course, has a direct bearing upon the relevance of the *historical* method in the study of Christian faith and practice. (3) At the same time the increasing stringency of historical criticism as applied to the content of the Bible appears radically to reduce the residual element of what can be regarded as 'fact', even in the Gospel record. (4) The combined impact of this historical analysis, and of the linguistic examination of the 'propositional' character of religious language, tends to the adoption of an existentialist position, in which the values of 'authentic existence' and 'self-commitment' become a substitute for a historical basis of belief. (5) Closely allied to this is the view that 'religious' statements express truth only in a 'private world' inhabited by 'believers', not in the sense in which 'truth' is commonly understood in other spheres. We cannot ask whether God *is* our Father, but only what such a statement *means* to those who make it.

It is very likely that forces such as the foregoing may not impinge directly upon more than a minority either of teachers or of pupils, though at the same time their 'climatic' influence is not to be disregarded. What will undoubtedly have come home to the majority is an impact of the technological, rather than the scientific, revolution, which tends to make efficiency and tangible results the standard of valuation, rather than responsibility to God and neighbours. There is such a disease as fatty degeneration of the moral sense, which can reduce at one and the same time man's sense of dependence on any resources other than his own, and his willingness to exercise his own powers for other than immediate and measurable objectives.

Of all these characteristics of our contemporary situation the ones which affect most strongly the outlook of older boys and girls seem to be the following:

1. The expansion of knowledge – scientific, historical, archaeological, palaeontological – which appears to have reduced the framework of biblical events, on which the Christian faith is based, to a merely episodic value, if not indeed caused its rejection altogether as pious myth.

2. The dominance of scientific criteria for evaluating truth, and the relegation of poetical, artistic and imaginative insights and presentations to a departmental, peripheral, position.

3. The pressure of materialistic estimates of the 'good life' (quantitative, economic, technological) which leaves little room for any ethical criterion except perhaps hedonistic utilitarianism.

4. A one-sided and distorted valuation of human life, largely the result of the collapse of humane values since 1914, leading to the anxiety, brutality and despair which are both seen directly and mirrored in contemporary art, drama and literature.

It is not difficult to see why to many minds these trends appear to constitute a serious threat to the Christian position. And indeed there is no question that with senior boys and girls, especially those who have been mainly trained in the scientific approach, they can encourage an outlook which makes the popular understanding of traditional Christian teaching uncongenial and unconvincing.

It is not simply that this contemporary outlook makes it impossible to accept anything like a literalist interpretation of the biblical record. (That, as many of us believe, may well be a gain rather than a loss.) The challenge of the scientific outlook goes much deeper. The conception of history as the scene of operation of a divine providential ordering, the discernment of that ordering in the whole range of affairs political, economic and social, or even in the events and choices of personal experience, the identification of that ordering with the loving purpose of a personal God, all these are subjected to radical questioning.

These, then, are the major adverse factors in our developing situation which demand a reappraisal of the traditional methods and approaches of Christian education. They are some of the reasons why RE is failing to make the hoped-for impact on our secondary-school pupils, particularly in the more secularized areas of the country.

But diagnosis is not in itself a cure. An even more important task than analysing our malaise is to discover what new approaches, what new methods, what new starting-points are both demanded and made possible by the new cultural and theological situation in which we are working. One possible clue may be found in the contemporary concern with 'meaning' in history and in experience which has already been mentioned. The point which needs stressing here is that meaning always begins to take shape or, to put it in another way, gains its initial impetus *out of the experiences of the immediate present*, or *out of phenomena which are immediately apprehensible*. In other words, we cannot begin with events of a remote past and expect to find meaning in them by themselves. We must begin with events or experiences in the here-and-now and begin to build up comparisons and contrasts, continuities and discontinuities with events and experiences in the past. In the Christian context this seems to imply beginning, for example, with an actual church building or with visible objects having religious associations: or with Sunday or a festival day: or with a Bible, a book of worship, a hymn book: or with a service being enacted: to begin with them in order to start together from *a common perception* on the backward journey through time. Teacher and pupil are then united at the beginning in a common experience which can lead on to meaning as it is pursued to its origins in the historical order. The encounter with the historic past then becomes *the meeting with meaning whenever a relationship with the present experience is recognized*. To present material from the past in isolation, however skilfully and vividly it is done, can never do more than make a momentary impression unless it is related to present experience and the continuing search for meaning. Christian faith becomes real not through amassing and mastering any quantity of so-called *facts of history*, but rather through fostering the quest for meaning out of present experiences so that through the meeting life may be quickened and meaning revealed.

On the Credit Side

It is most important to recognize that the possibility of success in making this new approach with secondary-school pupils has been *enhanced* by certain features of the contemporary situation: (1) The undermining of the old certainties, while it has driven many into scepticism and even despair, has, with others, sharpened the urgency of the persistent questions. Men ask even more insistently whether life has meaning and direction, and in particular whether these are to be looked for only within the limits of the here-and-now. (Is there perhaps an interpretation of 'eternity' in terms of a dimension of 'depth' which is relevant here?) (2) The enormous expansion of knowledge and the consequent power to control environment have increased man's sense of 'fullness of life' and of responsibility for the use of his powers for the elimination of disease, poverty and suffering. (3) The realization that these powers have often been exploited for unworthy ends has helped to quicken the corporate conscience. This shows itself in a greater readiness to recognize the rights and needs of the underprivileged. The characteristic humanists' condemnation of cruelty and emphasis on the virtue of 'compassion' are significant as reflecting a criticism of sub-Christian aspects of the Church's moral standards. (4) In the sphere of religion as such, the breakdown of traditional conventions and inhibitions has opened the way for a more realistic spirit of enquiry.

It is not suggested that an awareness of all this is consciously present and operative in the minds of the majority of teachers or pupils. But we believe that all this does indirectly at least influence the attitude of many in the presentation, and even more in the reception, of religious teaching. And we should welcome this fact.

To dismiss the total effect of 'the scientific revolution' as 'secularism' is a gross over-simplification of the problem. If to some it appears as 'the shaking of the foundations', to others it seems to hold out the promise of something more like 'the New Being'. They emphasize, and rightly so, the enormous benefits which the immense enlargement of man's knowledge and power has brought in the liberation of whole areas of human life from ignorance, disease, poverty, fear, the toleration of unnecessary suffering, and most significant of all, from the superstition which has accepted, and even proclaimed, these as the will of God which it is rebellion to seek to alter. They point to the triumphs which this 'crusade of knowledge' has won as a signal illustration of the abundance of life which Jesus himself claimed to offer. They ask whether it is not dangerously near to the sin against the Holy Spirit to deny the presence and power of that Spirit in the lives of those who have made the revolution possible.

And in the sphere of religion itself many of our generation have found this same liberating experience through the explosive effects which the temper of radical questioning has produced. For them the very fact that no theological statements and claims can any longer be regarded as immune from questioning has transformed the whole business from the acceptance – or more probably the rejection – of 'dead ideas' into a living experience of enquiry and discovery. The rejection of the literalist interpretation of Scripture has given the Bible the chance to show itself in its true light as the disclosure of the heights and depths of human experience under the searchlight of the truth of God, a disclosure as relevant to the circumstances of our own day as to the originals. They find an enrichment of their idea of God in the transformation of 'Creation' into 'creativity', in the realization that his working is to be discerned in every sphere of human activity, and in the recognition of the evidence arising from scientific or historical research not as dangerous or hostile influences, against which 'religious' truth must be safeguarded, but as complementary sources of enlightenment. They are beginning to discover the true cross-fertilization of 'religious' and 'secular' study.

A New Base For Operations

Broadly speaking it would seem that the pattern on which practically all our Agreed Syllabuses have been drawn, in which straight Bible study is regarded as the foundation on which all else must be built, needs reconsideration. The Bible will indeed continue to hold a central place in the presentation of Christian faith and practice. But we shall aim at using it in a rather different way. Instead of asking the young to begin by mastering large quantities of biblical material, which they then try to 'apply' to contemporary situations and issues, we shall start from the questions which are already matters of concern to them, and then turn to the biblical insights to see what light they throw upon them.

What are 'the questions which are already matters of concern to them'? Different groups, different individuals, will find different questions to be matters of *prime* concern at different times, but there would appear to be certain 'basic questions and needs' which are present in some form in all men and which can be set out in general terms. One such formulation of these basic questions might be as follows:

1. Men seek answers to questions about the origin and nature of the universe within which their life is set. In particular they ask whether the evidence which it affords substantiates the belief that it is the outcome and expression of intelligent purpose. Moreover, what is the significance, within the whole process, of *human* development? Is it merely the story of another emerging species, or does it constitute a new and determinative factor? Is the life which man lives in time and space the sum total of the experience which is allowed to him; or is there a dimension of 'eternity', in which he is, or on certain terms may be, capable of participating?

2. The study of history and literature raises a number of further questions. What are the influences which shape the direction of human advance? Is it possible to discern the working of something like a law of moral cause and effect? When we compare different epochs of social history, or different contemporary standards as between one race and another, by what criteria do we rank one as 'higher' than another?

3. A more practical type of question naturally arises from more immediate experience, such as personal relations at home or in school or in the neighbourhood; questions seen round the next corner of life, courtship and marriage, prospective jobs, the habits and convictions of our group in society. (The newspapers and the television provide endless material.) Or some domestic event, a tragic accident, will trigger off some searching questioning about life's purpose and meaning, or about man's freedom and responsibility, whether seen in individual or collective terms. In his actual experience of his own self man has always been conscious of tension between impulses (maybe even influences or forces) which draw him in different directions; the conflict between these appears to constitute at once the glory and the misery of his existence. On the one hand there is the sum of his mental, moral and spiritual endowments. (Human history is the record of the advance made from primitive beginnings by the exercise of these powers of thought and endeavour, the advance exemplified and embodied in discovery, invention, artistic creation, social and moral enlightenment, spiritual insight.)

F

On the other hand there is the equally unmistakeable evidence of weakness, failure, sloth, cowardice, 'the traitor streak', which has so constantly betrayed his best efforts. The result of such conflict is a sense of limitation, frustration, futility, meaninglessness from which escape appears to be impossible. 'Who will deliver me?' is beyond all question one of the basic needs to which religion has claimed to provide the remedy.

The formulation of questions such as these provides the starting points from which exploration of Christian faith and practice can begin, which when rightly handled lead us directly on to examine the biblical evidence. For it is precisely these issues of ordinary life and experience which the writers and editors of the Bible were themselves seeking to illuminate.

It is perhaps questionable whether, for the kind of teaching which is here envisaged, it will be possible to produce a syllabus, as that has been understood and constructed in the past. It seems more likely that the most useful thing to do will be to provide what might be described as a 'check list', which can serve as a reminder of the main areas of Christian faith which must be included in a programme of teaching. Individual teachers will use such material in different ways according to the needs of their pupils.

Here is a rough suggestion of the kind of thing which will be needed:

1. *Nature.* Christian faith accepts the main findings of evolutionary thought. But it insists that the picture of development disclosed can only be truly interpreted when *all* the relevant evidence is given due weight. It is not enough merely to study origins; it is not enough to regard the development merely as *process*. The emergence of human life, with all that that implies in terms of human attributes, can only be evaluated as implying the working of intelligible purpose. And 'purpose' is a word which has no meaning except as the activity of intelligence which possesses, at the least, characteristics which we recognize as 'personal'. So, to the source and directive power of life there properly belongs a 'name', and for this we use the word 'God'.

2. *History.* Christian faith sees human history as the record of man's response or resistance to that 'purpose'. It looks to the realization of 'the reign of God', through man's increasing apprehension of, and obedience to, God's purpose as the clue to the right use of all his powers (intellectual, aesthetic, moral) and to the achievement of true human relationships.

3. *The impact of Jesus.* Because the nature of this purpose cannot be truly apprehended in less than personal terms, Christian faith finds the clue to its fullest expression in *a life* which it recognizes as the disclosure, the laying bare of the very mind of God. The 'Logos' is the means by which rational purpose is expressed and communicated, which is what speech in essence is. 'Here is what makes the hazardous experiment of creation and human history worth while. *This* is what it was intended to produce. *This* is God's last (and first) Word.' But the disclosure of God's purpose made in the life of Jesus is more than illumination. It is also the opening up of a channel through which, for those who will receive it, there is made available a continual experience of a re-creative and redemptive goodness. The death and resurrection of Jesus was the focal demonstration of how God deals with evil by the 'sterilizing' or 'non-conducting' power of goodness. The Christian Church is the community of those who, having thus become receptive to the influence of this goodness, can themselves become channels for its communication to others.

It need hardly be said that this highly abstract statement of Christian faith is not being offered as material suitable for direct communication in school. But on careful consideration this outline may well be seen to represent the basic essentials of Christian belief which must be included in any adequate programme of religious teaching. Of equal importance is the fact that it will be seen to correspond to some of the main questions which, as has been suggested, are already present in the mind of contemporary man, and to take account of some of the dominant trends which seem to be shaping contemporary theological thinking.

Such an approach, then, would seem to meet the demands of the present situation where the pupils are concerned, and also where the theologians are concerned. But, of course, there is another vital element in the situation, namely, the thinking and the attitudes of the teachers themselves. How far will 'a new approach' be acceptable to them?

Radical and Conservative

Here we come face to face with a problem which is familiar enough to all those concerned with religious instruction and which can be a source of real heart-searching, that is the unmistakeable divergence of outlook which is to be found within the ranks of the teachers themselves. On the one hand, there are those who by upbringing and conviction regard the authority of Scripture as the supreme principle in religious teaching, and who believe that their main task is to present the content of the Bible as the essential basis for any under-standing and acceptance of Christian faith and practice; on the other hand, there is what appears to be the growing number of those for whom this traditional method has been steadily becoming less and less convincing and usable. They do not question that central place which the Bible has held, and must continue to hold, in any Christian instruction which is to be true to the name. But they have come to feel that the way in which this central significance has been presented, through the continuous study of large sections of biblical material, particularly Old Testament material, has been calculated to defeat the very aim which religious teaching seeks to serve, and to produce a lasting alienation of many of the young from any desire to explore it further.

This contrast must not be overdrawn. Between a conservative wing at one end and a radical wing at the other, there is doubtless a large body of men and women who would hesitate to align themselves with either extreme, and who combine elements of both outlooks, perhaps in different proportions at different times, in their own teaching.

Quite clearly, as things stand, room must be found in our schools for both types. And indeed there is little doubt that our religious teaching as a whole would be the poorer, if any attempt were made to impose some kind of uniform pattern. Different boys and girls, the same boys and girls at different stages of their development, can respond to and benefit from one or the other. So long as the two schools of thought recognize each other's integrity, and make it plain in their teaching that they do so, the effect of diversity on the mental and spiritual growth of their pupils can mean gain rather than loss.

It must be accepted that for the time being at least there will be two approaches, on quite different bases, among teachers. The extent of each approach will depend on many factors, including the views of the teachers themselves, the response of their pupils, and differing sociological and environmental influences. It needs stressing, how-ever, that any future development in RE must clearly be towards the radical: if the tendencies now at work in the South-east spread to any great extent, so will the change from one approach to the other become more generally necessary.

This, then, was the general line of argument the group followed. I have tried to present their findings through a weaving together of their different papers,[1] but I must now turn to another set of papers in commentary on their final paragraphs. Throughout their deliberations the members of the group were aware of the possible seriousness of divergent theological views within the teaching profession, and so they initiated a series of discussions between two of their members and an interdenominational group of teachers 'within what could broadly be described as the evangelical section of the Church'. Arising out of these discussions came a large file of documents which have been subsequently edited and published under the title of *The Bible and the 'Open' Approach in Religious Education*.[2] (The final draft differs in a few details of wording from the draft quoted here.)

The paper opens with a caveat:

We do not pretend either to reflect all shades of evangelical opinion or to speak in the name of evangelicals. There is, as far as we understand it, no consensus of evangelical opinion on religious education, although one may be emerging. (To this end we hope our work may make a contribution.)

But they leave no doubt in the following paragraphs that they are indeed speaking from 'within the evangelical section of the Church'. This is made equally clear in their closing section, where they tackle 'Disagreement in Religious Education', but their evangelical presuppositions only serve to give added force to their conclusions.

In the wider educational field there is difficulty in discussions between those who approach religious education from the viewpoint of psychology and those who take a primarily theological standpoint. There is an even more significant type of disagreement. Twenty years ago, the difference in approach would have been between what might loosely be called 'conservatives' and 'liberals'. This difference still exists and has been highlighted by vociferous demands for a 'radical' approach from a minority of non-conservatives. We feel we have little common ground, if any at all, with those who repudiate all authority in religion save subjective inclination. Their position appears to follow inevitably from rejection of the authority of Scripture. This is why we must maintain the full and final authority of Scripture even against fellow-believers who do in some limited sense admit its force.

[1] See *Learning for Living*, January 1968, for the full text of their final report.
[2] Published by the Tyndale Press (London), 1968.

It is important not to confuse this disagreement about the whole nature of Christianity with difference of opinion about the *method* that should be adopted in religious education. The 'traditional' method is to take for granted some accepted authority (be it the Bible or the teaching of the Church or even the consensus of opinion in society) and to teach on the basis of this. The 'radical' method is to select as a point of departure the sort of question faced by young people in their existence, and to use Christian teaching simply as a viewpoint which may or may not commend itself to the individuals concerned. We would not agree that the teacher has to choose exclusively between these two, but it is clear that a teacher of orthodox beliefs might adopt a 'radical' teaching technique. And it is notorious that teachers who are very eclectic in their beliefs may be strongly 'traditional' in their teaching methods.

On the whole the writers of this paper come down on the side of 'radical' techniques. Early in their argument they define two distinct 'types of theology' as being (1) the building of a system of interior communication within a religious community (however large or small that community might be); and (2) the production of 'an objective description of a system of belief'. They then go on to examine two further 'types of theology' – 'frontier theology' and 'pre-evangelistic theology':

A third possibility is that the theologian may attempt to present the gospel in terms of a secular environment. This demands an understanding of the culture in which we live and also of the ways in which the gospel has been presented in other historical situations. Thus Aquinas provided an interpretation of the faith in terms of the dominant philosophy of his day, and Tillich has attempted to do the same for the twentieth century. The danger of this sort of approach is that it may distort biblical truth in trying to mould it to the thought-forms of the age. Yet Christians may not decline this responsibility and it will form an important part of religious education today. We must relate Christian belief to the thoughts and lives of our pupils. Secular problems – war, race, punishment, innocent suffering, personal relationships – are much discussed in schools. Neither the Christian nor the secularist can always give clear-cut answers. We must help children to work out their own response to these problems, while showing them that there is a theology which throws light on the difficulties and provides guiding principles if not ready-made solutions.

Yet there seems also to be needed in our schools today a fourth type of theology. It is worth remembering that Jesus spoke to men who already believed in God and the Law. Similarly Paul preached to Gentiles who although heathen were yet utterly convinced of the reality of the supernatural. Many – perhaps the majority – of our pupils have no such convictions, although many have a vague belief in a supernatural 'something' which is little better than superstition. Their sense of the numinous is akin to a much more generalized aesthetic experience and often almost identified with it. There are fears and a sense of need, and a concern for right and wrong. In these circumstances we may well doubt whether biblical material can have the same impact on them as on its first hearers. It appears that a good deal of our teaching will be in a sense pre-evangelistic. It will be intended to evoke a belief in a power higher than man; an attitude of awe and wonder at man's insignificance; an understanding of the need for moral values if man is to live in society; and a sense of personal responsibility for failure to live up to the values that have been individually accepted. It is important to stress that much of this preparatory work will occur incidentally through the atmosphere of the school, the attitudes of teachers, and their approaches to secular subjects, especially literature and those which are sometimes classified as 'environmental studies'. Quite often subjects raised in discussion during the limited time available for religious education may profitably be considered in other lessons.

Having made this point, the writers then turn to 'The place of the Bible in RE'. It is difficult to do justice to this section without quoting it in full, but it is far too long to be included here, so a few selected paragraphs must suffice:

We are faced with two problems here. The first is that the majority of our pupils are not simply pagans. Most regard themselves as in some sense standing with the believing community, even if they are not of it, so that they seem to require something more than the gospel, even though they are not willing to listen to the whole *heilsgeschichte* as if they were personally involved. The second problem comes when we try to decide our starting-point. In the synagogue Paul began with the story of Israel and the promise of the Messiah; but at Lystra and Athens he spoke of the Creator rather than the Redeemer. A biblical point of departure may not be the most appropriate even if the message is biblical.

For most of our pupils, and at first sight, the Bible is a dead rather than a living book. It is dead, first of all because they do not understand its thought-forms. For them, blood is a red liquid, whereas for the Hebrew it was life, crying out for vengeance when spilt, efficacious to cleanse from defilement, mysterious and sacred to God. Yet even if we can convey an intellectual understanding of biblical thought-forms, they will remain dead, because they seem so irrelevant to twentieth century western attitudes. How can the blood of Jesus Christ cleanse from sin? The whole process of religious education is thus reduced to one of antiquarian research and anthropological investigation. The 'deadness' of the living word presents us with a formidable problem.

It is pointless to try and defend incompetent handling of biblical material. Bad Bible-based teaching, it can be argued, is worse than no teaching at all, because it undermines the authority of the Scripture. When to incompetence we add the dreary repetitiveness that has characterized much Bible-based teaching we have an effective weapon for the destruction of a child's emergent faith. (This, it must be pointed out, is no more an argument for the abolition of religious education, or even of

Bible-based religious education, than is the appalling state of maths teaching an argument for the abolition of mathematics. What we need is not no teaching, but good teaching.)

We suggest there are four criteria we should use in selecting biblical material. First of all, we must use material which presents parallels between biblical experience and our pupils' experience. (The word 'parallel' is used advisedly; we realize the danger of simply equating the child's experience with that described in the Bible, and may instance the frequent understanding of the 'voice of the Lord', which children will tend to assimilate to the 'voice of my Dad', with the inevitable conclusion that 'God doesn't speak to people today'. Yet the child who has already experienced what it is to resist the pressure of conscience is in fact capable of appreciating the experience of God's demands which is part of what the Bible means by the 'voice of God'.) . . . The material selected must also be such as will help the children to see the nature and attractiveness of a God-centred life. . . . In selecting biblical material we shall also be anxious to help our pupils towards a sympathetic understanding of the purpose, nature and content of the Bible. We shall take care to select material of various types and emanating from different circles to show the variety as well as the underlying unity of the Bible . . . Above all, we shall select material that will help our pupils to understand who Jesus was, and is.

Teachers despair at the difficulty of showing pupils what believers mean when they talk about 'God'. It is difficult enough to help them see Jesus through the clouds of misunderstanding, sacred and secular, that obscure him. The answer must be to sit down before the Scripture and rediscover there the Man whom we can glimpse in the lives of his followers today.

It is obvious that there is a great deal of common ground between these three sets of quotations and the arguments which form the bulk of this chapter. It would seem to be of the utmost importance that this common ground be explored and extended as thoroughly and as widely as possible. The task facing RE teachers over the next decade is going to be formidable enough without the further complication of internal dissension. Theological differences do, and will continue to, exist. One could pretend to ignore them ('We all teach according to the Agreed Syllabus here'); one could use them as rallying points for party warfare. Alternatively, one could accept them as productive tensions within the discipline of religious education (just as there are tensions today within other disciplines), and use them creatively to forge the new techniques and approaches which our changing situation is increasingly demanding of us.

9

Examples of Current Experiments

GREAT STRESS was laid in the preceding chapter on the need for 'starting from the questions which are already matters of concern to our pupils' but the only attempt to establish what this might mean was quite deliberately done in abstract terms in an attempt to point the general lines of direction, the general area of advance. What *practical* suggestions, or actual examples from the field, can be produced?

The schools used in the sample did not provide very many striking examples of the sort of approach which has just been advocated. There was one ('high-scoring') modern school, however, which built its fourth-form syllabuses entirely around the suggestions made at the beginning of the year by the new fourth formers themselves. One such syllabus ran as follows:

Autumn term (a) Genesis 1–11
                 (b) What it means to be a Christian (discussions of practice and belief)
Spring term   (a) The colour bar
                 (b) Love and marriage
                 (c) A class outing to an old church
Summer term (a) History of the parish church
                 (b) Christian views on money and work.

The subjects were chosen (by vote) from a long list of suggestions made by various individuals in the class, and the teacher's task was to arrange them into some form of order and to decide how they should be tackled. Her comments at the end of the year were:

In retrospect, I think that this course was very successful. Although it was rather disjointed, it seemed to crystallize for many girls the teaching they had received earlier on. They made a point at the end of the year of coming to thank me together for 'the good RE lessons' they had had, and said they had found them very helpful.

Many other schools (both in the sample and outside it) have been using in their fourth forms for some time now syllabuses based on 'discussion of problems', such as Loukes advocated in *Teenage Religion*. Indeed many Certificate of Secondary Education syllabuses contain at least optional sections built round such problems. Of course, in the fourth forms the bulk of these problems and questions are concerned with personal relationships, with use of leisure time, with affluence and responsibility and so on. But lower down in the school 'problems and questions' which the pupils feel are appropriate to an RE lesson are much more likely to be biblical and doctrinal in nature. One school's syllabus which came to the notice of the survey committee has been built almost entirely round such questions. By its very nature this syllabus is a closely knit document but, as it is too long to quote in full, once again some rather disconnected extracts will have to speak for the document as a whole:

As the method to be employed involves discussion stimulated by teachers' questions and statements, only an outline programme can be given. . . . During discussion, teachers and pupils should seek their parallels and parables in their own experience and special subject, in interests and daily life; to do this is to bring a theological cast of mind to areas often marked off for 'logico-scientific' thinking. . . . Our hope, indeed our only hope, is to set our children questioning towards a systematic reflection upon the ultimate meaning of creation.

Basic Questions for First, Second and Third forms
What is the Bible? From this beginning we can elucidate (from class answers) that it is a library, and the books in it can be counted. The division of the school or public library gives a basis for classifying the Bible library into fiction and non-fiction; the next step is to ask for subject classification into History, Law, Belles-Lettres, Religion and so on, but it will quickly be found (that is, by the pupils) that there is seldom a clear-cut division in the Bible, and that the main distinction of this library is the unifying God-centredness of all the books. . . . 'The fiction element' of the Bible, lest it be dismissed as simply untrue, should be tackled firmly (*a*) by reading an extract from modern fiction with true-to-life characterisation and drawing the parallel (In what way is this episode true although invented?), or (*b*) by selecting poetic phrases of obvious intention but dubious or nonsensical *literal* meaning ('My true love has my heart, and I have his'), or (*c*) by examining the real meaning of Santa Claus, for instance, and the driving power behind St Nicholas (a knowledge of right personal relationships). From this or from the library analysis it is simple

to move to such questions as: Where do we look for scientific facts? *Is history true?* How do we know it is? Is history science? What *is* science? (A collection of verified or verifiable statements.) *What is science true about?* – or any other similar scheme of advance to the stage, How can we tell if something written is true or 'just words'? Can we examine the Bible in the same way? (We can, but children often say, 'No'.) Why not? And examine the answers in the light of what has already been agreed, and show that it is vital for a faith like Christianity to be self-critical.

A further line of approach is taken from Pilate's question 'What is truth?', but we must stay for an answer, helped by such pointers as: *How do we know things? How do we prove things? What is evidence?* (Difference between proof and evidence.) How do we know King George V lived? (Several ways), or John Bunyan? or Cleopatra? By analogy with Bunyan (or Milton, Spenser . . .) we know Paul lived, so now we turn to *Paul's hearing before Agrippa.* From a first study (Roman Law, rights of a Roman citizen, where did Paul come from? and so on) we ask, 'Why were the Jewish authorities so eager to kill Paul?' (Evidence of eagerness.) 'Were they right in what they said?' leads to a lively but *brief study of Paul's adventures and of sections of his letters,* and then, 'Why was Paul so bold?' ought to lead to the answer, 'Because of his belief'.

What is belief? is the next major question and leads to the difference between '*belief that*' (scientific, susceptible of repeated demonstration, or accepted on authority; historical, accepted on eyewitnesses' authority, or from consequences or subsequent conditions, but not repeatable; moral, accepted intuitively and very often unsuitable for experimental proof) and '*belief in*' (personal, and only demonstrable rarely and then only after acceptance).

Paul's belief IN Jesus can be shown from evidence in his letters and in his life. Our *belief* THAT *Jesus lived* is authenticated from Tacitus and other Roman historians (I. I. Bettenson, *Documents of the Christian Church* [London: Oxford University Press, 1963]) . . .

'What was Paul taking to the Gentiles?' should bring the reply the Gospel (in some formulation), and what does 'Gospel' mean? '*What is the good news?*' can lead to an estimation of life more abundant, everlasting, starting now; while '*Is it true for us?*' opens the way to study of modern men and women who follow our Lord. . . .

From time to time a session may be given over to Any Questions; the method of our Lord himself, 'You know the answer from your own experience; think!' is profitable in this context. . . .

Lest any should consider *parables* the prerogative of our Lord, two told to him (centurion and Syro-Phoenician woman) can be used to introduce an exercise in telling a parable from the ORDINARY experience of the members of the class. . . .

The bridge to Old Testament study is also provided by parables: search for parables leads us to II Sam. 12.1–7; 1 Kings 20.35–43; Isa. 5.1–6 (for instance) and opens the way for rather more emphasis than is sometimes allowed for on *the prophets* and their frequent opposition to the 'established' schools of prophets and to the priests, and their rebuking of rulers, which in those days was a dangerous undertaking. In this context the calling of a prophet can be studied. . . . All the New Testament background already gained helps us to criticize the *Old Testament in the light of Christ* and to see the Old fulfilled in the New as well as to examine the origins of N.T. thought. . . .

The fourth year

We will now be well placed to move on to further questions on matters of urgent importance in everyday life for the benefit of school-leavers: What are people for? Why shouldn't we? and the perennials of religion, morals, ethics and personal relations. . . . In this year also a whole class may ask for more detailed Bible study (New Testament or Old) or for some outline of Church history or organisation, and the political situation may be of sufficient interest to a group, especially if prodded, for a useful sequence of studies and projects, as in other subjects, to be undertaken and even to be exhibited in its final stage. . . .

The fifth form

The possibilities are very wide indeed. Starting from the base outlined above, there is a choice of closer study of the Creed, the reading and discussion of a set book (*Your God is too small* [London: Epworth Press, 1952]; *Mere Christianity* [London: Bles, 1952]; *The Young Church in Action* [London: Bles, 1956]; *Letters to Young Churches* [London: Bles, 1955]), the examination of some fresh theological or apologetic work (*Science and Christian Belief* [London: Oxford University Press, 1955]) 'potted' if need be by the teacher – all or any of these and/or a 'current affairs' approach. . . .

Lest it should be thought that in the foregoing suggestions too little definite reference is made to direct biblical texts, attention is drawn to the list of morning Assembly readings. . . . Pupils are encouraged to raise in discussion any doubts or uncertainties arising from Assemblies, and are occasionally challenged to give the theme of the day's reading, or its reference to life today.

There may well be certain criticisms which can, and should, be made of this document, and it is not presented here as 'the ideal syllabus', but it does set out an approach which has sprung directly from classroom experiences and from the questionings and difficulties which class discussion has brought to the surface.

It is encouraging to find some of the newer Agreed Syllabuses also adopting as fundamental principles approaches which have clearly emerged from specific classroom situations and experiences. The new West Riding syllabus[1] is a good example of this. The actual syllabus may at first sight seem over-formal, over-historical, but the

[1] *Suggestions for Religious Education*, available from the County Education Offices, Bond Street, Wakefield.

classroom experience from which it is born comes to the fore in 'Possible Ways of Approach' which are suggested at the beginning of each section.

For example, the first year's work is entitled 'Discovering Jesus' (and actually subtitled 'An outline of the life of Jesus drawn in the main from the Gospel according to Mark', which is as traditional-sounding as one can get), but the details of the scheme are thematic rather than chronological, and the possible ways of approach include the following suggestions:

One way of dealing with this subject is based on the question, 'What would Jesus do?'. Topics within the pupils' experience are freely and realistically discussed, with the minimum of suggestion from the teacher. The following questions are then asked, discussed, and answered: What did Jesus do? What would Jesus do today? What ought we to do? The gospel references in the list suggest possible material to be used in answering the first of these questions. Answers to the other questions should grow out of the discussion. Topics such as the following might be dealt with:

Temptation: Matt. 4.1–11
Illness: Mark 1.21–28, 40–45
Danger: Mark 4.35–41
Hunger: Mark 6.30–44
Sunday: Luke 6.1–11; 13.10–17
Exploitation: Mark 10.15–19
Greatness: Mark 10.45; John 13.1–7

Another way of dealing with the subject is based on the question, 'What would Jesus say?' The procedure is similar to the one above. Topics such as the following might be dealt with:

Forgiveness: Matt. 18.21–35
Foreigners: Luke 4.16–30; 10.25–37
Happiness: Matt. 5.3–12
Giving: Matt. 6.2–4; Mark 12.41–44
Prayer: Matt. 6.5–15; Luke 11.1–13
Worry: Matt. 6.25–34
Criticism: Matt. 7.1–5
Hospitality: Luke 7.36–50; 14.7–14
Greatness: Mark 9.33–37
Money: Mark 10.23–31

The lists are formal, but the topics should be introduced informally to promote free discussion using the current vocabulary of young people today.

Following on 'Discovering Jesus' comes 'Discovering the Christian Community'. Again the treatment in the syllabus is thematic ('The

Church Grows', 'The Church Faces Opposition', 'The Church Serves the World' – each one of which spans the period from New Testament times to the twentieth century), and the possible ways of approach include:

1. Studying at depth a particular period, a special activity or a leading personality.
2. Carrying out projects and surveys, e.g. about the Church overseas or about local churches, their history and present activities.
3. Correlation with other subjects such as social studies, history and literature.
4. Taking a backward look from the churches of today to their origins and early history.
5. Comparing the work of the Church in recent times with that of the early Church, e.g. modern missionaries and those of the first century; churches in our towns and those in Jerusalem, Antioch and Rome in the first century.

The next section of the syllabus carries the following introduction:

Themes and Activities for Middle Adolescence (13–16 *years*)
   (i) Christian Worship and Practice
  (ii) Personal Relationships: Discovering Oneself
 (iii) Christianity in the Modern World

It is not suggested that each of these themes should be regarded as a year's work. It is intended that teachers should select from this material, possibly using some sections from all three themes, in each year, as the basis of their work with adolescent pupils. The suggested ways of approach are manifold:

(i) Christian Worship and Practice:
Visit churches of various traditions and discuss with clergy and ministers the various forms of worship. Use films and filmstrips, e.g. on the Parish Church, The Mass, New Churches.

Collect and arrange an exhibition of photographs of churches and their activities.

Consider how churches have shared and are sharing their traditions, e.g. the hymns which all Christians sing, written by members of different denominations.

Discuss such questions as:

(*a*) Can Christian worship become too set in its forms?
(*b*) How does Christian worship differ from Jewish and Moslem worship?
(*c*) What kind of public worship is best suited to the needs of ordinary people?
(*d*) Can worship be too divorced from everyday experience?
(*e*) What steps have been taken to make united acts of worship possible?

Compare passages in new translations of the New Testament which attempt to express the faith in contemporary language.

Consider the attempts by modern artists to express the faith, and the use of modern art as an aid to worship. Visit if possible some new churches or collect photographs of them. Consider the relationship between architecture and worship.

Plan services for various school occasions and for the Christian Festivals. Study some modern illustrations of Worship and Prayer.

(ii) Discovering Oneself [this is subtitled 'Personal Relationships in terms of Responsibility to myself and to others' and covers Honesty, Work, Leisure, Possessions, Family, Friendship, Marriage, Class and Race, Forgiveness, etc.].

1. The biblical passages suggested in the syllabus could be explored to enable young people to discover some of the unique qualities of love in the New Testament sense. In the light of this exploration definitions of love might be written and discussed.
2. The Problem Approach through planned discussion: Start with a familiar experience or a situation. Attempt to analyse the problem and discover a Christian judgment upon it. Finally attempt to solve the problem and to apply the solution practically.[2]

(iii) Christianity in the Modern World:
[Here the suggestions are incorporated into the syllabus itself, but they are mainly of the 'discover and discuss' type. The overall purpose of this section is defined as being 'to help young people in their search for meaning and to enable them to discover what the Lordship of Christ means in the twentieth century', and the material is set out under the following headings:]

A   The Search for Meaning
    (*a*) The Bible
    (*b*) Jesus Christ
    (*c*) God
    (*d*) Man
    (*e*) Sin and Forgiveness
    (*f*) Suffering and Disasters
    (*g*) Prayer
    (*h*) The Church
    (*i*) Science and Religion
    (*j*) Miracles

B   Facing World Problems
    (*a*) Mass Media
    (*b*) World Hunger
    (*c*) Work and Leisure
    (*d*) Politics
    (*e*) Gambling

[2] See Harold Loukes, *Teenage Religion*, Chapters 4 and 5.

(*f*) Alcohol and Drugs
(*g*) The Colour Problem
(*h*) War
(*i*) Refugees
(*j*) Illiteracy
(*k*) World Religions

The material in the later stages of this five-year syllabus will be familiar to many people teaching fourth and fifth formers, and the sixth-form material which follows it is also fairly normal to current practice. What is different about the West Riding syllabus is that instead of preceding 'life-centred discussion' by conventional, though condensed, study of Old and New Testament material (as so often happens), it encourages the use of familiar experience as the starting-point of study throughout the *whole* age range.

Another example of a syllabus which does this is the new Wiltshire Secondary Schools Syllabus (Preliminary Draft).

FIRST YEAR
Term
1. Study of Books and their Uses; including the Bible – contents, growth, authorship, accuracy.
2. Questions children ask about God.
3. Growth of Personal Relationships (showing the need for right personal relationships and the right use of leisure).

SECOND YEAR
1. Character of God.
2. Questions about Faith and Life.
3. Development of Personal Relationships (questions on love, sex, marriage and leisure).

THIRD YEAR
1. Christianity in Wiltshire.
2. Life of Jesus (topic approach, or through questions children ask).
3. Further development of Personal Relationships.
   A. Getting to Know Yourself.
   B. Man's Relationship with God.

FOURTH YEAR (Leavers' Course)
1. Projects on Modern Christians. Leading to suggestions for jobs and vocations.
2. Social and *Practical* Service. (Within and without the school time-table.)
3. Teenage Topics. (Christian Education Movement wall charts.)

FOURTH YEAR (Alternative)
1. Problems of Christian Living.

2. Study of John's Gospel.
3. Social and Practical Service. (Or term 1 [Leavers' Course] above, Vocation.)

ADDITIONAL FIFTH- AND SIXTH-YEAR MATERIAL
1. Science and Religion.
2. World Religions.
3. Faith of the Creeds.
4. Twentieth-century Church.
5. Modern Missionary Movement.
6. Pattern of Christian Society.
7. Humanism and Marxism.
8. Christianity in Action now (Project Work).

In this form the syllabus looks alarmingly full of abstract ideas, but in the actual working out of these topics in the classroom familiar experience readily finds its place. For example, one development of 'Man's relationship with God' started from a series of studies on 'Man finds God through . . .', where the children's own reactions to music, art, nature, the universe, the Bible, worship and prayer, etc., served as the points of departure.

The school in which these particular studies were carried out formed part of the subject of an article ('Recent Experiments in Religious Education') in *Learning for Living*, September 1966, in which actual classroom methods were described. An extract from this article will show how 'experience-centred' the whole of the RE work in this school was:

Last year I visited[3] a school where the RE work had been completely adapted to the problem-centred approach. This involved not merely the reorganization of the syllabus, not merely the discovery of new methods of working, but even the refurnishing of the RE classroom. Gone were all the desks (but for a few around the walls). The chairs were grouped in fives or sixes in different parts of the room. Walls and sidetables were covered with displays and 'resource material', some obviously produced by the pupils themselves. On one wall was a large cardboard letterbox. The far corner of the room looked particularly out of the ordinary, with a television set, a couple of easy chairs, a small table and a mock fireplace.

From the age of eleven upwards, children in this school tackle all their RE work mainly through research and discussion. Each group or each pupil is given a task card to work through during the course of a lesson, knowing that a written or spoken report will have to be produced for later study by the whole class. The work cards are built round a cutting from a

[3] By kind permission of the Chief Education Officer for Wiltshire, and of the Headmaster of the School, Mr A. W. King.

newspaper, from a teenage comic, from the advice column of a woman's magazine, and carefully graded questions are set out for discussion. Sometimes the work cards start from a biblical incident or saying; but more often than not, biblical material is introduced by being incorporated into the questions themselves.

Occasionally, for the sake of variety, the starting point of discussion is a film strip, or rather a picture strip, made by older pupils and displayed, by means of a simple system of rollers, through the screen of the television set (which turns out on closer inspection, of course, to be empty of works). This television set, though, has another function to perform when some of the older classes are using the room. Returned to its place in the corner, along with the easy chairs and mock fireplace, it becomes part of the 'living-room' setting for the free drama work and role play, through which the older pupils are encouraged to explore the problems set before them.

From time to time the chairs are moved out of the smaller circles and put round in one big circle, and it is then that the staff take their turn in answering questions put to them by the pupils, rather than the other way round. These questions can arise from the group reports from a previous lesson, or, more usually, will have come from individual children, who will have placed them anonymously in the letter box on the wall. (Each class has its own box, which is brought out whenever they have a lesson.)

Next to the letter box is a large-scale map of the area immediately surrounding the school, with coloured pins stuck into certain of the houses or streets. This is a record of the school's social work in the area. A class of school leavers have one afternoon a week timetabled for the organization and execution of these social responsibilities.

These are just a few of the approaches in syllabus and method which can arise when RE teachers take seriously the need to 'start from the questions which are already matters of concern to our pupils'. But one must not forget that RE, if seen as a separate discipline, does not have the monopoly of such questions. The more attention one pays to the pupils' 'questions of concern', the more artificial the barriers surrounding RE come to appear. One is therefore not surprised to learn of RE teachers seeming to trespass in other fields.

Theological discussion with a sixth form arising out of an extract from a 'non-theological' book is of course nothing new (though one could hardly claim that it is a universal practice, even so!). *A Kind of Loving, Brave New World, The Plague* will be therefore recognized by many sixth-form teachers as typical of a whole range of literature which is likely to spark off discussion on man and the forces and pressures impinging on him, on the worthwhileness of man's struggle for personal existence, on width of responsibility, etc. But how many RE teachers have tried a similar approach from literature further down the school? (Their English colleagues could tell them of the tremendous possibilities here, possibilities which they themselves have not always got time to make full use of.) In one school when fourth formers were also presented with *The Plague* the discussion may not have been as penetrating as it had been in the sixth form, but it was just as effective at its own level. Again, great profit was extracted from the situation which arose when *Lady Chatterley's Lover* had been confiscated from a third-former (in another lesson altogether), and the class questioned this: 'What sort of man was D. H. Lawrence, then?' And how much more exciting and challenging the reading and discussion of *The Lord of the Flies* with the first formers proved to be than yet another 'straight' study of 'Jesus' Ministry and Teaching' would have been at this point in their school career.

It was interesting to discover the same teacher who had provided the Survey committee with this information about her use of 'secular literature' in RE, later writing an article for *Learning for Living*[4] in which she described a scheme she was just embarking on which was similar in spirit to the one described on pp. 170–2. She would appear to have 'gone back to the Bible', but with a new facility in her use of biblical material, treating 'the Bible as literature' in the deepest and the only worthwhile sense of that phrase:

> With the First Year we have studied Joshua, Judges and 1 Samuel in two terms, talking freely about oral tradition, interpretation within the accounts, what the story discloses about the people for whom it was important, their ideas about and attitudes towards God. I can scarcely think of a lesson when the discussion has not been contemporary, since what arises always seems to relate to how human beings behave and react, and the class are discovering (and giving increasing support from observation) that there are some aspects of the human situation which basically remain the same but can be interpreted in a different light. They are also realizing that religious belief is to do with seeing life and interpreting it in a certain way. . . . I am planning my new scheme of work on the assumption that I need never abandon the Bible in favour of Life as an alternative, since this is a false either/or with these classes.

There are, of course, other teachers who have come to a similar realization that there is no antithesis between the Bible and Life, but nevertheless have chosen to 'start with Life' as it is in the context of actual contemporary life that their pupils find 'questions of

[4] Brenda Mawby, 'Danger, Children Thinking', *Learning for Living*, January 1967.

concern' really pressing in on them. These teachers would presumably welcome recent experiments in the form of team teaching and integrated syllabuses. The thinking behind such experiments has been cogently set out in the Schools Council's Working Paper No. 2 on *Raising the School Leaving Age* (1965):

> There is wide agreement that a man's understanding of himself, and of Man, is of the first importance in the education of ordinary pupils. To quote from the Newsom Report: 'The field in which it is most important that ordinary boys and girls should learn to exercise a common sense judgment quickened by imaginative insight is that of personal relations. Their greatest service to the community, and there is none greater, will be as men and women who can be relied on to make a success of their own lives and by the quality of their living to bring up their children to do the same. This is not something that can be taken for granted or left to traditional methods of indoctrination. In a contracting world, where all men are neighbours but by no means necessarily friends, everybody needs an education of the imagination and the will to enlarge the area of his concern and acceptance of responsibility.' (Para. 315.)
>
> It is therefore basic to the ideas put forward in this Working Paper that some understanding is needed, however limited, of human nature and conduct, and of the means which men use in developing concepts of value, and in using the physical world for valued human purposes. . . . There is traditionally a large area of the curriculum which has to do with understanding man and his place on this earth – history, geography, English and religious education. . . .
>
> When one looks at the present position in schools, it is obvious that much is already being attempted. Not only have there been experiments in the teaching of history, geography, English and religious education as such, but there are also many experiments which do not fall neatly under a traditional 'subject' heading – social studies, civics, citizenship, social science, careers work, environmental studies. . . .
>
> It is clear that the matters treated by these subjects cross many traditional subject boundaries, whilst still requiring, in any given area, the exercise of many of the traditional subject disciplines. The task facing the schools is to work out the large purposes for the curriculum as a whole, and then to probe by experiments of many different kinds – the improvement of content and treatment within traditional subject areas, team teaching over a number of subject areas, the introduction of new topics or even subjects – how best to give the teaching relevance to the students' experience so far, and to human needs and purposes in the adult world which they will soon be joining.

Working Paper No. 2 was followed by Working Paper No. 11, *Society and the Young School Leaver* (1967), which includes some detailed descriptions of integrated syllabuses already being put into practice in different secondary schools. One of the schemes described there started from 'a personal assignment for each pupil – a personal meditation on themselves'. From here they moved to class assignments on heredity, then back to individual assignments on 'My family tree'. The subject of 'The Family' was then taken up in detail – its organization, the growth of children (physically, educationally, mentally, spiritually), the relation between the family and the community, building a home, building a community. Then 'the community as a family' became the theme, and this was worked out over communities of different size and complexity – for example, school, church, local government area, geographical region, parliamentary community, commonwealth, internationalism.

This is very similar in general outline and direction to *Man in Society: An Integrated Course* compiled by a group of teachers from different schools, working under the patronage of the Congregational Church, and published by the Independent Press (London), 1967.

These two courses quoted do have the great merit of being truly integrated, of dealing with the real religious issues as they naturally arise. The same cannot be said of all the schemes reported or suggested in *Society and the Young School Leaver*. In more than one of them 'religion' is dragged in by the back-hair; in others it is ignored altogether. A great deal of real theological understanding will have to be brought to the production of schemes of this type to ensure that they do not become the occasion of RE being made to appear even more remote and artificial than when it was safely in its own little separate subject niche. A certain amount of watchfulness may also be needed to guard against the adoption of an integrated syllabus becoming a covert method of dropping RE altogether from the curriculum.[5] It must constantly be stressed that there will be a continuing (and increasing) need for teachers in every school who have been properly equipped to make a theological contribution to the preparation and execution of the overall syllabus. No one must be allowed to forget that 'a team is made of skilled members in co-operation, not of all-purpose people with no special knowledge'. With these provisos, however, integrated syllabuses are surely to be

[5] One such syllabus has already come my way. In its preamble it states, 'This course will operate in the periods formerly allotted to History, Geography, English Literature and RE. It will be organized and staffed by members of the History, Geography and English departments.'

welcomed as possible expressions of the principles laid down in the preceding chapter.

Of course, one of the great advantages of the integrated-syllabus system is the flexibility of time-tabling which it provides. When one puts together, let us say, all the periods normally allotted to History, Geography, RE and English, and so becomes able to take whole mornings or afternoons at a time, this does provide elbow-room for all kinds of variety in organization. And it is this setting-aside of occasional long periods of time, rather than the twice-weekly (or once-weekly) nibble, which is the hallmark of another approach to RE currently being tried out. The following account was written by Gordon Benfield, the RE Adviser to the Hampshire Education Authority, who was responsible for initiating the scheme.

Experimental Residential Courses for Less Able School Leavers

The Hampshire Education Committee has recently organized a series of residential courses for groups of secondary children from non-academic streams. The courses were undertaken in full co-operation with the Heads of schools concerned. The detailed planning and leadership of the courses has been shared by the RE Adviser, the Rev. Michael Beesley (youth worker in the parish of Eastleigh and formerly Assistant Youth Chaplain in Winchester Diocese), and the Warden of Calshot Activities Centre where the courses have been held.

The Newsom Report comments on the need of these pupils to have 'access to the countryside, the experience of living together in civilized and beautiful surroundings, and a chance to respond to the challenge of adventure' and also their need 'to begin to arrive at some code of moral and social behaviour'. These courses are designed to meet these needs in a limited way.

Recruitment for the courses is in the hands of the Heads of the schools who are invited to send a mixed party of thirty children who, in their opinion, would most benefit from the course. Parents are informed that the course is a preparation for leaving school and for life in an adult community and that fifty per cent of the cost of the course will be met by the local authority. At least one member of the school staff accompanies the children and is, under the Warden of the Centre, responsible for discipline and shares in the running of the course. Some form of physical activity appropriate to the time of year is organized by the Centre staff and integrated into the course programme.

The main theme of the course is to give the young people an opportunity to ask questions about being a person in terms of other people; many of them have had no previous experience of living in a community, if indeed they have previously lived away from home at all. This theme is first introduced by a suitable film or film extract on the first evening when the young people are invited to observe the film and note the reaction of the ordinary people in ordinary human situations. This leads into a simple discussion of de-personalisation in the modern world and the difficulties of being a real person under contemporary social pressures. This is followed throughout the four days by sessions on the following topics:

1. 'Me' – What does it mean to be an individual – people we like and don't like – qualities that attract us to other people or make us dislike them. This includes simple group work such as listing qualities we like or don't like in other people and leads to self-analysis.
2. 'Me and the Folks' – based on role play of situations in family life – relationships with parents and the strain of these relationships for the young adult – attempts to understand the parents' point of view.
3. 'Me and the Boss' – usually led by a person from industry who is concerned with the problems of young entrants – an attempt to give the children an understanding of the other side of their problems before they meet them – difference in attitude to persons in the world of work.
4. 'Me and Him/Her' – boy/girl relationships and the implications of these in terms of respect for other people – trained Marriage Guidance Counsellors with educational experience are invited to lead these sessions.

Throughout the four days of the conference the young people undertake simple projects. These include an analysis of current newspapers with emphasis on reading the news in an attempt to understand the human situations with the general theme of 'People in the News'; a group administer an opinionnaire to the rest of the members discovering their attitudes to a wide range of subjects from pop music to God and the church; a group prepares and plans for a more formal meal on the final evening and discusses the social value of the exercise; another group expresses some of the main themes of the conference, especially feelings and attitudes to others, through a variety of art media. The afternoons are devoted to some physical activity such as orienteering and, if possible, preparations for a night under canvas or a strenuous walk in the New Forest which again provides material for discussion on understanding ourselves and the way that we face challenges in life. Each day begins with an experimental form of worship using role play and records of folk or pop music to stimulate awareness of the needs of people in the contemporary scene and using simple forms of prayer. Evening sessions are devoted to discussions about music, film and literature with an attempt to deepen the young peoples' understanding of these as a means of entering into thoughts and deeper feelings of ordinary people.

Seven of these courses have so far been arranged and the reaction of Heads and pupils have given encouraging indication of their value.

Such residential courses are, of course, not being planned as a *substitute* for the RE on the schools' time-tabled curriculum, but work of this type may increasingly come to be seen as a necessary complement to what may be achieved in the classroom (and the availability of such courses may in turn effect what is actually attempted in the classroom).

A comparatively long period of concentration on themes and projects such as have been outlined here not merely provides an opportunity for tackling more fully 'questions which are already matters of concern to the pupils'; it also produces the sort of atmosphere in which completely new concerns may arise, and whole new perspectives may open up. As Tillich wrote, in his classic essay on 'A Theology of Education', there is a twofold task facing us, to answer questions, and to arouse questions (remembering always the need for these to be *real* questions):

> Every religious educator must try to find the existentially important questions which are alive in the minds and hearts of the pupils. We must make the pupil aware of the questions which he already has.[6]

Further ways of pursuing this task will be explored in the following chapter.

[6] Paul Tillich, 'A Theology of Education' in *Theology of Culture* (New York: Oxford University Press, 1964), p. 154.

IO

Freedom to Choose and Freedom to Grow

BY TAKING up the issue of 'integrated syllabuses' the argument has tended to move away from the question of RE as such to a consideration of the religious element in all education, and it is right that this should have happened. The effectiveness of RE, its ability to arouse concern for religious issues, depends not simply on the skills and convictions of the RE staff, but far more on the whole atmosphere of 'concern' in the school and indeed in the surrounding society as a whole.

The question of whether RE should be 'allowed' to take place, of whether it is damaging to the pupils' moral and intellectual responsibility, has been dealt with and answered in Chapter 6. But is there much point in merely 'allowing' RE to occur? Is not the real question how far a school community should throw its support behind the specific RE work going on in its midst by showing its own concern for 'religious issues', 'fundamental questions', wherever and whenever they arise (as they most assuredly could do at any time)? In current terminology: How far can a State school be 'committed' on religious and moral issues? Has it not got to remain entirely 'open'?

One really needs to approach this question through the even wider question of how far a State school can be 'committed' on anything, serving as it does a society of widely mixed views, opinions and beliefs. Let us take, for example, the question of a school's 'commitment' over musical taste.[1] Even accepting the dictum that a music teacher should *not* play 'nothing but the classics' in musical

[1] Cf. p. 195.

appreciation lessons, and that he should encourage comparison and discussion of Beethoven versus the Beatles, Stravinsky versus the Stones, fugue versus folk, and so on, there still remains the question of 'the school line' on music. Is it to remain entirely impartial as a community, and perform anything and everything at assemblies, speech days and the like, or is it justified in 'commending the best' by using only 'the best' on such occasions? Surely it *is* justified in doing so, and would be failing its pupils if it did not do so. The only, but essential, condition is that the school's 'commendation' shall be fully open to challenge and discussion by the pupils, and this shall be acknowledged and accepted by the whole school community.

The same must be true of a school's religious position. It need not try to be religiously neutral in order to be 'open' – indeed it cannot succeed even if it were to try. It has to adopt either a position of 'commendation' or of 'dismissal'. Either position (providing it were truly 'open') would be theoretically justifiable. The position in England and Wales today, however, is such that society clearly wishes the schools still to 'commend' Christianity by their general life and teaching. It is in this sense that a school will be basically committed to the Christian position, even though the RE work in its classrooms and even the act of worship in its assemblies, is of an 'open' character.

It was not idle chance that produced the phrase 'the RE work in its classrooms' rather than 'the work in its RE classrooms'. As has already been said, effective RE cannot be isolated from the work of other subject disciplines, for they too (it is to be hoped) meet the pupils' 'questions of concern'. Some subjects do, however, raise more fundamental issues than others, and this is why RE has particularly close links with the 'social' studies (such as history, geography, and the newer subjects in this field), with the study of literature, and with science (in its interpretative aspects). We have already looked in detail at some of the new 'Humanities' courses, or similar integrated-syllabus work, being experimented with in the schools at the moment (see pp. 180–1). There is a major problem here which we have not touched on, however, namely, the problem of the 'conscience clauses' and their application to such combined courses. How can one in fact 'withdraw' from RE when it is interwoven with all these other subjects? Does one have to withdraw from the whole course?

Some people are apparently afraid that the whole future of these courses may be wrecked on this one question, and so rather want to play the question down. I personally welcome the question, as it has at last brought out into the open something which has been forgotten, or ignored, for far too long – the absurdity of the fact that the 'conscience clauses' are quite specifically restricted to work done under the label of RE. Possibly RE may be (even ought to be) the subject in which controversial issues lie most closely under the surface, but it is quite ludicrous to pretend that such issues are entirely absent from all other subjects, and this *is* the implication of the present working of the conscience clauses.

Just how ludicrous such a pretence is can be illustrated from the experience of one family I know of who belong to an ultra-conservative sect. The son was allowed to attend RE lessons at his school until he came home one day with ideas on evolution which did not square with his parents' interpretation of Gen. 1–3. He was immediately withdrawn from all RE. However, he was *not* withdrawn from his science lessons, where the offending theory of evolution is presumably still being firmly and constantly pumped into him.

Or again, it seems strange that a Marxist atheist has the right to withdraw his children from lessons about the life of Jesus or the work of the Christian Church, whereas a Christian parent has no right (short of changing schools) of withdrawing his children from history lessons which are subtly (or overtly) tinged with Marxist dogma, or from literature lessons which 'commend' to the children standards and values that are far from Christian. I am not saying that these latter situations are to be found at all frequently. I *am* saying, however, that given the possibility of such a situation arising, the conscience clauses as they stand would not be applicable. (As one of the survey-committee members has pointed out in a letter to me, 'The Cowper-Temple clauses sprang from the conflict between the establishment and the free churches and referred to denominational teaching and "body snatching" rather than to any deeper philosophical conflict'.)

Either, it would seem to me, the right of withdrawal from the classroom has to be *extended*, or (and this is surely preferable) it has to be reduced, *with the proviso that* all controversial issues, wherever, and whenever they appear, shall be treated in a fully 'open' way. The great merit of the new integrated courses is that they are almost bound to partake of this open character in the treatment of their material.

They are 'almost bound' but admittedly not quite. There will have to be safeguards of some sort, to meet the consciences of both 'sides'. It is to be hoped that such safeguards can be arranged without constant recourse to legal sanctions, though the law itself must obviously continue to preserve (in some form or other) the right of the taught to be protected from indoctrination by the teacher, and the right of the teacher to be protected from having to subscribe to that which he does not believe.

Before leaving this question of 'combined courses' we must have a brief look at another form of 'cross-subject teaching' which is attracting greater attention these days, namely, 'moral education'. Again, in the past, this has been something far too often linked closely, almost exclusively, with RE. Various attempts have been made in some schools, however, to work out in practice the belief that *all* the staff are equally responsible for the moral education of the pupils, and one or two actual written schemes have been produced showing how the different subjects should contribute to a child's moral development, quite apart from the influence of the staff on their pupils simply as people.

More recently some Local Education Authorities have put such teaching on a slightly different basis, by introducing into their schools carefully organized 'courses in personal relationships' in which moral (and particularly sexual) problems are tackled in specially time-tabled periods. Sometimes these are run by an RE teacher, sometimes by a biologist, sometimes by neither. (One survey visitor reported from a school where such a course was being run: 'Much of their open-minded enquiring attitude is attributable to the influence of their mathematics master who was responsible for their "personal relationships" course. They said that they could discuss anything with him.' In this particular school six RE periods in the fifth form were 'taken over' by the course, even though the RE staff had nothing to do with it; in other years it was fitted into a different part of the time-table.) This sort of scheme must surely be welcomed, enabling as it does the RE staff to make some sort of contribution to moral education without thrusting upon them the sole responsibility in the school for 'making the kids good'.

The Provision of Options

Changes in time-tabling and in organization of a slightly different sort can also make a significant contribution to the 'openness' of RE in a school. A few hints have already been dropped (in the quotations from conversations I had with some fifth formers: pp. 145–6) as to one of the chief complaints the pupils have against the subject. It is not only that it often seems irrelevant; it nearly always seems imposed. (That is, the *subject* itself was imposed, however 'open' the treatment of the issues within the subject.) The full force of this objection has become increasingly apparent in discussions I have held over recent years with college of education students. Their complaint was not that they had wanted to withdraw from RE on conscientious grounds, but that they had resented the subject as being the only one to be forced on them with monolithic inevitability (bar English Language in some cases) once they had entered the world of options and specialization in the fourth form and upwards. The only 'option' they had ever been given in RE was whether to do it for an external examination, or to do it *not* for an external examination.

A few schools have for some time been working optional alternatives into their sixth-form RE work, particularly where this forms part of a general studies course. Presumably within integrated courses lower down the school some system of alternative assignments could introduce a similar opportunity for real choice. However, one does not have to go as far as to mount an integrated course simply to achieve the possibility of alternative options within the RE course. A little care with time-tabling can produce the same result.

In the larger schools, which look like becoming more and more frequent in the future, the inevitable size of the RE Department will enable *setting* in RE to become a normal feature of a secondary school. If one were to assume that in an eight-stream entry school there were three members of the RE Department available at any one time, then three streams could be given RE on the time-table at one and the same time, the advantage of this being that these three streams could then be treated as one unit and redivided into sets on the basis of pupil-options, with each set doing a different course. These courses would last for a term and then the groups would be reset for the next batch of courses. In this way a 'key course' could be made to appear in different terms so that everyone would have the opportunity of doing that one, yet at the same time having a real choice of 'supplementary-courses'. One could, for example, introduce sections of the new West Riding syllabus in this way:

Year 4	Set I	Set II	Set III
Term 1	A Worship in the Old and New Testaments	B Personal Relationships	C The Christian Year
Term 2	B Personal Relationships	D Christian worship today	E The Bible and Christian belief
Term 3	F The Church today – what it does	G World hunger and Refugees	B Personal Relationships

Assuming that B was the constant 'key course' then each pupil would have the free choice of courses ABF, ABG, ADB, AEB, BDF, BDG, BEF, BEG, CBF, CBG, CDB or CEB, though certain safeguards would have to be made to ensure a *roughly* equal division of numbers between the sets. Another type of condition might be that if, let us say, course E were also to appear in Year 5, then this would *have* to be taken either there or here.

Besides giving the pupils more freedom of choice, this system also gives greater freedom to the staff to 'specialize' in the areas where they are most proficient, or at any rate to avoid those where they are least knowledgeable.

In an eight-stream school with this set up one would, of course, have to work on the basis of a three-stream group plus another three-stream group plus a two-stream group, and the last group would have a more restricted choice (unless one made their courses run for half-a-term only).

A similar result *can* be achieved in a much smaller school by the use of subject-pools. The following scheme is in operation in a school with only a three-stream entry, where about half the pupils are Jews.[2] The need for different courses in RE in the upper part of the school is met by creating sets for the subject (RE x, RE y, and RE z), and working these sets in conjunction with one of the pools of O-level subjects (which happens in this case to consist of French, Geography, Mathematics, Woodwork and Domestic Science).

[2] I am most grateful to the headmaster, W. Maynard Potts, for providing all this information.

In these O-level years all pupils *not* doing Woodwork or Domestic Science have a choice of joining either RE x (Christian-based) or RE y (Jewish-based). In the second of the two years Woodwork/ Domestic Science takes up a whole morning, and those not doing these two subjects go first to French, Geography, or Mathematics, then to RE x or RE y and then to Physical Education. Those who *do* do Woodwork/Domestic Science fall automatically into RE z (and PE z) which they have later in the week when everyone else is doing French, Geography or Mathematics. (This does mean, of course, that this particular group do *not* have a free choice of which RE set they belong to, but this is an unvoidable drawback within a smaller school.) In the first O-level year, the RE is time-tabled in *three* separate periods, set against the other pool-subjects, or against Physical Education, or Music (which are also divided on the basis of the pupils' choice in RE). The whole scheme works out like this:

	Fourth year		Fifth year	
	x/y	z	x/y	z
Mon 1 }	Fr. or Geog. {	PE		
2 }	or Maths {	RE		
5	PE x RE y	Mus		
Tues 1 }			Fr. or Geog.	Woodwork/DS
2 }			or Maths	
3			RE x RE y	Woodwork/DS
4			PE	
Wed 1 }	Fr. or Geog.	Woodwork/DS		
2 }	or Maths			
3	RE x Mus y	Woodwork/DS		
4	Mus x PE y			
Fri 6			} Fr. or Geog. {	RE
7			} or Maths {	PE

The great advantage of such a scheme is that it could be worked even by a school which had just the one RE specialist (assisted by someone teaching RE for one or two periods only) and yet offers a clear and free choice between RE courses for at least two-thirds of its pupils.

Whichever technique is employed, it is obviously quite practicable to offer pupils a choice within the subject; possibly a choice between a 'Bible-centred' study, and an 'ethics and philosophy' type of course (a choice between two different *tables d'hôtes*, as it were), or choice within a variety of short termly courses (a full *à la carte* system).[3]

These, then, are some of the possibilities and some of the difficulties in reconciling the 'committed' position of the school as a whole with RE work of an 'open' nature in its classrooms. But what of the communal act of worship? How can this reflect the school's 'commitment' and yet be 'open' in character?

'Open' School Worship

Harold Loukes tells of a conversation between a headmistress and some senior pupils who said to her, 'You have no right to make us pray.' 'But I don't,' she replied, 'nobody can *make* you pray.' 'But you try to,' they countered, 'you say, "Let us pray".' Loukes comments that this is not just a quibble over words, for the form of school worship seems always to imply not merely a *statement* of commitment by the community as a whole, but a *call* to commitment on the part of each individual pupil.

The same point was taken up by the small group of survey committee members working with Bishop Cockin, in a paper[4] they were asked to produce on 'Worship':

A good divinity lesson will provide opportunity for open expression of differing points of view: it will leave elbow-room for a measure of doubt, even scepticism, which is an essential ingredient in healthy growth in religious understanding: while it may stress the necessity for 'commitment', it will not try to impose it before it can honestly be made. The mental integrity of the pupil is not prejudiced by the process, since he remains free to accept or reject what is offered. By contrast the atmosphere of Assembly subtly heightens the element of implicit pressure to conform. To be present at it seems to imply a measure of initial acceptance which may not actually be forthcoming in a given individual, and the unwilling participant has no means of escape except that of interior withdrawal and resentment.

Two reservations to this statement are called for immediately. Firstly, the objections which the majority of pupils voice regarding Assembly are directed at aspects of it which appear unconnected with these questions of commitment and integrity (see below, pp. 196, 199). Secondly, there is a 'means of escape' by *physical* withdrawal, a clearly established right in the provisions of the 1944 Act.

---

[3] I am indebted to David Ayerst for these phrases as well as for the incentive to explore the possibilities of such schemes.

[4] Published in full in *Learning for Living*, March 1968.

But some later comments from the same paper, on the position of members of staff, may well also apply to the more senior pupils (those who would be most likely to consider the possibility of 'withdrawal' for reasons of integrity):

> We can assume, as common ground with all those who are concerned for the deepening of the sense of solidarity and mutual responsibility in the school community, agreement that the regular gathering together of its members has its own value as both a symbolic and an efficacious act.

It is, of course, impossible as things stand to withdraw from 'School Worship' and yet be present at 'Assembly' (unless one is prepared to dignify with that name the session of notice-reading, for which those who *have* withdrawn from the service are usually summoned into the hall), and it could well be that many staff and senior pupils tolerate the act of worship in order to support the act of community. Certainly, the number of those who do physically withdraw is very small.

The survey questionnaire to teachers asked for each school to indicate whether there were 'any self-styled non-Christians on the staff'. Only fifty-nine schools replied to this question (whether this question was applicable or not depended on an affirmative answer to an earlier question) but of these 66% replied 'Yes'. (Among the schools in the South-east the proportion was up to 80%.) On the other hand, of the 101 schools who answered 'How many of your full-time teaching staff asked to be excused attendance at assembly last year on grounds of conscience?' 64% replied 'None', 31% gave 'one or two', and only 6% gave 'three or more'.[5] This indicates that many staff who would not accept the label 'Christian' have none the less not chosen to withdraw themselves from Assembly (at least, not officially).

Concerning the pupils, I was only able to collect figures for actual withdrawals. (No question on the 'religious allegiance' of the pupils was included in the staff questionnaire.) Of the ninety-six schools which replied 24% reported 'no withdrawals from assembly', and another 54% reported withdrawals of '3% or less' of their pupils. The actual overall proportion of pupils withdrawn was just under 2% (909

[5] For the fifty-seven schools answering from the South-east the figures were: 58%, 33% and 9% respectively. To put it in another way, of the six (out of 101) schools where 'three or more' withdrew, five were in the South-east. ('South-east', here and above, *includes* the London conurbation.)

G

out of 46,375). As for the reasons for withdrawal, they were almost entirely of a denominational character.

Roman Catholics	699
Jehovah's Witnesses	92
Jews	38
Hindus	21
Atheist-Agnostic	12
Muslims	9
Buddhists	7
Others	31
Total	909

As with the question of parental objections to RE in the classroom, we cannot avoid the conclusion that the 'problem of withdrawal' is, numerically speaking, far less of a major issue than certain critics would have us believe. But again, as with the earlier question, we cannot ignore the existence of the minority group, however small, for it must be admitted that the gathering of the school for an act of Christian worship can (and does) create a potentially divisive situation in the life of the school community. It was with this consideration, among others, in mind that the paper on 'Worship' already quoted had these comments to make:[6]

> In the face of such a situation it is imperative that those who claim to speak in the name of the churches should ask themselves very seriously indeed what they believe to be the aim and value of a daily corporate act of worship in the actual context of the life of our schools today.
> Beneath all the diversities of form which worship may take in the range of Christian traditions, and indeed of the great religions, there would appear to be certain constants. One of these is unquestionably the element of self-offering, the response of the worshipper to the worshipful. Participation in the act of worship has two complementary effects. It brings vividly before the worshipper the dimension of depth in the object of worship: it makes God more real. And it enhances the quality of his response, by deepening his sense of awe or of need, by suggesting ways in which his desire to give himself more fully may be translated into forms of action which embrace his relationship not only to his God but also to his fellow men. In all this the effectiveness of the experience clearly depends upon the presence in the souls of the worshippers of a real measure of corporate faith and involvement.
> But we must not ignore the possibility, and indeed the fact, that a true act of worship can have a real and valuable influence upon the outsider who may be brought into it.

[6] For another helpful examination of the issues involved see E. C. D. Stanford, *Education in Focus* (London: Religious Education Press, 1965), pp. 82–87.

In other words, participation in worship involves a two-way activity: the worshipper *does* something, and has something *done* to him: he acts, and learns from his activity. The latter aspect of this two-way process had for some inexplicable reason been considerably played down by the Newsom Committee in *Half Our Future*:

Corporate worship is not to be thought of as an instrument of education – though it is that – but as a time in which pupils and teachers seek help in prayer, express awe and gratitude and joy, and pause to recollect the presence of God. (Para. 174.)

A more realistic, and more defensible, definition of school worship (pressing Loukes' words from *New Ground*, p. 131, into the Newsom mould) would be:

School assembly is not to be thought of merely as a time of self-offering, a declaration of commitment by the committed – though it is that – but also as an educative instrument, a means to insight, an evocation of vision.

In a lecture published in a symposium on *School Worship* (Leeds University Institute of Education, 1964) Canon R. Cant put it this way:

Worship is both expressive and impressive. It expresses the beliefs and attitudes of the worshippers towards the ultimate horizon of their experience, God. It impresses them, through the words, music and actions employed, and that indefinable thing, atmosphere, with the sense of the reality of God. . . . The teacher of music or art is aware that his pupils are going to face all sorts of shoddiness in the world; nevertheless he continues to commend the best, and he does see some reward for his efforts. There is a similar case for the schools continuing to set before their members the worthiness of God by beginning the day with an act of worship. This may not be preparation for the world as it is – how many shops or factories begin the day's work with worship? – but it is an affirmation of the true meaning of the world, and of the true end of man and of all his activity. . . . Such an act of worship can be deeply and powerfully educative.

Comments from the pupils themselves seem to support the view that the function of school worship is 'an evocation of vision'. In the early stages of the survey I asked some fourth formers:

Q. If School Assembly was suddenly made voluntary would you still go?
G. No.
Q. Why not?
G. I'm not very much a believer in God anyway.
Q. And so you only go now because you have to, not because you want to. What about the rest of you?

B.   If it was worth going to I'd go. It just depends what was going on.
Q.   What would make it worth going to?
B.   Something interesting. Interesting reading or something like that.
Q.   Just the reading?
B.   You know, the general Assembly.
Q.   Have you had any interesting Assemblies recently?
B.   It's nearly always the same.
B.   It's different when we came here in the first year in the lower school, but we got to know the pattern of the school, and it gets boring after a while.
Q.   But if Assembly was changed and made more interesting you would still come, even if it was voluntary?
B.G. Yes.

There was a similar reaction from the other groups with whom I raised this question, and Loukes has recorded a further significant remark from a fourteen-year-old:

Instead of the old, incomprehensible prayers we want more newer prayers concerning subjects of our time, in naturally phrased language which will make people think.

'Prayers to make you think' will seem to some churchmen to be an entirely false understanding of prayer, but it is a major clue to the way older secondary pupils (and, incidentally, college students) regard assembly, and a guide as to how assembly could both be made more effective, and also partake of a more 'open' character.

The paper from the group of committee members has certain specific suggestions along these lines:

What are the principles upon which Christians ought to stand in stating the case for the maintenance of an act of worship as an integral part of the life of the school? Clearly there are certain claims which cannot be surrendered without selling the pass to a secularist view of education. Equally we shall do no service to the Christian position by trying to insist on a position of privilege which reasonable opinion within, and outside, the teaching profession is no longer willing to accord.

If we are realistic, we shall recognize that the motive and purpose of assembly will be differently understood both among members of the staff and among pupils. And we shall do well, as has been wisely insisted upon in the discussion of services of reunification in schemes of reunion, to make a completely frank acknowledgement of this diversity of intention, as an essential condition of individual integrity and mutual trust. We shall make it plain that, on the Christian view, any act of commitment of this kind implies the recognition that God knows and respects the honest intention of all those taking part in it.

We shall therefore seek to draw into the planning and conduct of the assembly as many as possible of those who genuinely desire to make a contribution to the moral and spiritual vitality of school life. This must, of course, be done *not* by the bogus attempt to devise forms which no one can object to, but by providing opportunity for the explicit offering of the best that a given individual or group can contribute.

We should make it clear beyond all question that we believe that there is a place in such co-operative search for those who, while not prepared to call themselves Christian, are concerned for the moral and spiritual health of the school community. (We believe that these suggestions might do a good deal to *relax psychological tension* among both staff and pupils. The 'closed shop' atmosphere is not a healthy educational one.)

This in itself implies the constant search for forms of expression in acts of worship, readings, music, simple dramatic presentation, which will both give scope to insights already reached by senior and junior members of the school, *and* bring before them, from the Bible, from the masters of the spiritual life, from great literature, biography, poetry and music, fresh insights and incentives. (Schools will be wise to avail themselves of the experience and skill of broadcasting in devising such forms.)

Equally it implies a constant attempt to relate the content of the worship to the actual life of the school and the world. Michel Quoist's *Prayers of Life* (Dublin: Gill, 1963) is a classic example of the livingness of meditation, confession and intercession, which spring directly from reflection upon entirely ordinary incidents and experience in the course of every day.[7] The life of the school, or the daily papers will serve to provide ample material.

The whole question of the attitude of the young to prayer calls for careful consideration. The classical tradition of language in prayer is that of the direct address to God ('Thou'). Even when modified to 'You', this presents real difficulties to those whose direct apprehension of God as personal is hesitant. But there is also a classical tradition of *meditation* in which concentrated reflection upon some aspect of God's nature (as illustrated for instance in a passage of Scripture or a great poem or picture) can most certainly promote devotion. We fancy that this is often a more congenial line of approach for many today.

Is it possible, without robbing prayer and worship of their essential character, to carry this modification of traditional form still further? As one member of our group put it: 'Can worship ever be an intransitive verb?' In an age in which the dominance of scientific and sociological thinking tends to eradicate the sense of the numinous there is, we believe, real value in fostering any method of approach which helps to restore the balance by giving opportunities for the exercise of faculties other than the critical and analytical. It is, for instance, widely recognized that for large numbers of young people the activity most stimulating and creative of response is that of making or listening to music. It is probably the nearest that many of them get to a specifically 'religious' experience. In our

---

[7] Cf. also Malcolm Boyd, *Are You Running with Me, Jesus?* (London: SCM Press, 1967).

judgment anything which helps to foster sensitivity, receptiveness, appreciation, contemplation is to be welcomed as a contribution, not dismissed as a substitute. No one can say at what point in such an exposure of the spirit to aesthetic values the authentic religious recognition may break in.

No one can study sympathetically the comments on school worship, so plentifully gathered in recent surveys and questionnaires, without becoming aware of the major sources of dissatisfaction here: insincerity, formalism, constant repetition of the same material, lack of relevance to the needs and interests of those for whom the worship is provided. To lay stress on them is not to deny or underestimate the value of association with familiar classical forms of devotion. It is to insist that this can never be made an excuse for allowing an unexacting reliance on routine to take the place of imagination and sensitivity.

All Together and Every Day?

Those nine paragraphs formed the section of their paper that its authors particularly wished to stress. Nevertheless, there were other problems and difficulties which they felt had to be examined, ones arising directly from the regulations of the 1944 Act:

> The school day in every county school shall begin with collective worship on the part of all pupils in attendance at the school, and the arrangements made therefor shall provide for a single act of worship attended by all such pupils (unless . . . the school premises are such as to make it impracticable to assemble them for that purpose). . . . The collective worship shall not be distinctive of any particular religious denomination.

The intentions here were obviously good. The possibility of two 'rival' assemblies being held was specifically ruled out, and the 'common act' was itself to be of a 'neutral' character. All sources of division within the community were to be eradicated. The only exception was to be the possibility of excusal, at the parents' request, of the very small number who might wish to take no part in such a ceremony, however 'undenominational'.

In practice, however, certain difficulties have arisen. In a few schools (particularly in some Jewish or strongly Roman Catholic areas) the number of 'withdrawals' has bid fair to exceed the number of 'attenders'. But a more widespread difficulty has arisen around the interpretation of the phrase 'impracticable to assemble them for that purpose'. For *what* purpose? Most schools have felt that as long as they could cram all their pupils into the one hall (even though it may have been built for a school of half the size) then they were not justified, by the wording of the Act, in arranging for two parallel assemblies. If one was to insist that the proper interpretation of the

Act was that the premises had to be suitable for the assembled school to meet in an atmosphere conducive to worship, then the vast majority of schools would *have* to change to split, or parallel, assemblies. 'The assembly we attended was pleasant and dignified – every person attending had a chair' is a rare sort of comment among all the reports the survey visitors sent in. Far more typical were descriptions of children having to sit on the none-too-clean floor, and one sympathizes very strongly with the fourth former who told Loukes 'It's more like a PE lesson, up and down, up and down', or the one whose only reaction when I asked him what he felt about assembly was 'It's stuffy. They can't get the windows open.'

It was not surprising, therefore, that the survey visitors came across some schools who had deliberately turned their back on the common interpretation of the Act on this point, and had abandoned any attempt to assemble the whole school every day, even in parallel assemblies.

A School Assembly is only held once a week in this school. On other days Form Prayers are held in the Form Rooms.

Owing to the large numbers, classes attend Assembly in the Hall once a week only. On the other four days class teachers are free to make their own use of this time. On the day of our visit boys who were receiving remedial help in all years came to the Assembly. The atmosphere was one of worship and involvement. . . . Occasionally in fine weather the whole school would have a service of worship in the playground – these occasions were reverent and moving.

Each school which filled in the staff questionnaire was asked how frequently the whole school did *not* meet together for assembly, and in 50% of the schools this happened at least once a week. Some of these schools, moreover, split their assemblies on the grounds not of inadequate accommodation, but of excessive age-range. The practice of holding separate sixth-form assemblies, for example, has grown over the past few years, and even in schools catering only for a four-year range 'upper' and 'lower' assemblies are sometimes to be found. One of the survey visitors reported pupils' reactions to this:

The fourth formers' attitude to Assembly reflected the usual warnings about dullness. The trouble was that several times a week they had to assemble with the whole school. This they thought, meant that the staff had to please the younger people and made it dull for the older ones. On the other hand, they have a segregated assembly twice a week, and they approve of this.

The committee paper on 'Worship' suggests that even though such experiments might be felt to be against the letter of the 1944 Act they are not against its spirit, for these schools were trying to make the morning act of worship a significant act for those who took part, and any dividing up of the school community which might have become necessary to achieve this result was not along denominational lines, and so was not introducing 'religious divisions' into the community. For this reason such experiments were to be welcomed.

In the very large schools (which seem likely to increase in number) it is often physically impossible to provide for a single Assembly, at any rate, under conditions which make participation in it conducive to an atmosphere of reflective meditation or worship. In a number of cases experiment has shown that smaller gatherings (with some possibility of age-segregation) provide a far better opportunity to meet the need.

But there is another outcome of the literal interpretation of the Act's requirements which also needs questioning:

Further genuine doubts are felt as to whether the demand for a *daily* exercise of this kind is not imposing an undue strain alike upon the receptive capacity of children and young people and upon the liturgical and devotional resources of those responsible for its conduct. A more carefully chosen selection of occasions might help to eliminate some of the only too well-known dangers of repetition and formalism.

In discussion on this point great emphasis was laid on the difference between primary and secondary children. The timescale of the primary child is such that the 'dailiness' of a routine adds force to the educational impact of such a routine; with the secondary school pupil the opposite is true. Presumably the major intention of the Act here is that the life of the school should be set in a religious context, and in a primary school this is best achieved by ensuring that 'the school day . . . shall begin with collective worship'. However, in a secondary school the 'religious marks' within the life of the community may well be more effective if they are seen not to be a matter of 'mere daily routine'.

The group of committee members did not feel competent to make any positive recommendations on this, but nevertheless felt that the issue needed to be raised. In this they echoed the authors of an earlier pamphlet on *Religious and Moral Education*.[8] Although this

[8] Privately published in 1965. Copies may still be available from Howard Marratt, Borough Road College, Isleworth, Middlesex.

pamphlet did put forward the suggestion that on one or two days in the week there might be no Assembly at all, or an Assembly solely for notices and talks, nevertheless their final comment was that 'these thoughts on Assembly are put forward to stimulate comment and criticism'.

The relation between 'notices and talks' and an act of worship has already been examined very thoroughly by Loukes (*New Ground*, pp. 133–5). The British Council of Churches survey attempted to find the views of headmasters/headmistresses on this, as reflected by their actual practice. To the question 'How would you describe the morning Assembly in your school – (*a*) entirely an act of worship, (*b*) mainly an act of worship, (*c*) a roughly equal balance between worship and administration?' 24% replied 'entirely worship', 40% 'mainly worship', 36% 'roughly equal'. (One indicated that on four days a week Assembly was 'entirely an act of worship', but on the other day it was 'entirely administrative'.) There is, however, no way of telling from these figures the exact manner of 'relating' worship and administration, and it is here that the committee paper echoed Loukes' general line of argument.

Everybody knows how disastrous the use of the Daily Assembly for 'school business' can be when done without thought or imagination. But it needs to be remembered that in a school which is seeking to be a Christian community, many items of administration and discipline can be seen and presented in a way which immediately relates them to the faith by which the school tries to live.

When administrative matters appear to clash with the 'worship-element' in Assembly, it is not the principle of conjunction which is at fault, but the practical mechanics of the occasion:

Careful planning, a skilful use of a variety of voices, a short interval between the two elements, can make the whole difference between real moral insight, and bathos – or worse.

The remaining two points on which this paper makes comment concern those individual members of the school community who feel that the act of worship in Assembly is either (*a*) 'too religious for them' or (*b*) 'not really religious enough'.

The first of these points obviously raises the question of withdrawal once again. One would hope that if the suggestions made earlier in this chapter were adopted, then desire to withdraw would be considerably lessened, but this is definitely *not* to suggest that the right of the individual to withdraw should be removed. Quite the reverse. The group's comment here sprang from 'an examination of the element of compulsion in the Butler Act':

> Clearly there are two elements here which need to be distinguished.
>
> (a) There is the explicit compulsion which the Act imposes upon the school as such.
>
> (b) There is the implicit compulsion which (despite the existence of the conscience and withdrawal clauses) the school tends to impose upon its members.

It seems to us that there is room for some more imaginative thinking about possible relaxations of this conformity imposed on *all* pupils. It may well be that at the lower-age range parental wishes and school discipline should have the final voice. But there is such a thing as growth in maturity of thinking and capacity to make responsible choices. And it may well be that by the time the sixth form is reached pupils should be allowed, and indeed encouraged, to make some judgment of their own in this matter. It is worth while remembering (as *they* pretty certainly will) that their contemporaries in Technical Colleges are not subjected to any such regulation.

And what is going to be the practice in Sixth Form Colleges? Could it perhaps be recommended that boys and girls staying on at school after the statutory minimum leaving-age should enjoy a greater measure of freedom?

Once again, this is a suggestion put forward 'for consideration'. Obviously there would be difficulties, not the least of which would be the possible equation of 'growing up' with 'dropping Assembly', so that attendance at Assembly came to appear as a burden unwillingly carried by the younger members of the school, the 'kids' who had not yet reached the age of discretion, nor had yet been granted the privilege of dispensing with childish activity of this sort. There easily could develop a 'convention of non-attendance' in some schools which would be as difficult for older pupils to resist as the 'implicit compulsion to attend' has been in the past. Nevertheless it is surely worth while exploring the possibilities of some form of pupil's request for withdrawal (even if only for a specified period and only after careful discussion between pupil, parents and staff) as opposed to the present position where officially the request should be acted on only if it comes from the parents.

The other aspect of this problem to be considered is the clear compulsion upon the schools to 'provide' an act of worship. While this reflects the wishes of the majority of parents,[9] and also safe-

[9] Cf. p. 151. The polls showed similar support for the retention of school worship.

guards the rights of the pupil to be educated in the deepest and widest sense, it nevertheless has created difficulties among non-Christian members of staff, and particularly among non-Christian potential headmasters/headmistresses, who sometimes feel that promotion is dependent upon willingness to conduct an act of worship to which they personally cannot subscribe. It must first be stressed that the compulsion to provide an act of worship is laid upon the school, not upon the head personally, though one must agree with E. C. D. Stanford[10] that 'there is a strong English tradition that the head conducts Assembly and "takes prayers" '. With the advent of large schools and the increase of 'split Assemblies', however, this tradition is beginning to be broken, and if some of the suggestions made earlier in this chapter (about a more 'open' type of worship and about a more flexible pattern of 'worship Assemblies' and 'administrative Assemblies') should be adopted, then the strains on the integrity of non-Christian heads should be considerably reduced in the process.

The Needs of the Committed

Now what of the pupils and staff who find the present type of assembly 'not really religious enough'? The group felt that this could be a very real problem in some cases:

> Our emphasis up to this point has fallen largely on the side of the more 'liberal', 'comprehensive', 'open' approach to the interpretation and shaping of the School Assembly. We have pleaded for the widest possible inclusion, as active participants, of all those members of the community who desire to contribute to the enrichment of moral and spiritual life: we have urged the use of any kind of experiment which may serve to introduce freshness and variety into corporate worship.
>
> But there is another aspect of the situation which equally deserves attention. Sixty years ago it might perhaps have been a case of pleading that the needs of a small minority of genuine agnostics should not be disregarded in providing for the normal doctrinal needs of the main body of 'conformists'. Today it would hardly be an exaggeration to suggest that the position is reversed. There is almost a danger of being so preoccupied with searching for the ninety and nine which have strayed that we forget to provide sustenance for the one left in the fold. It is essential not to ignore the very real need for special care of the convinced and practising Christians in our schools, who may well be finding the maintenance of their faith a real struggle against the pressure of the world around them.
>
> Earlier in this essay we commended the value of small groups as wor-

---

10 *Education in Focus*, p. 83.

shipping units. This does *not* mean (repeat *not*) that we want to see Christian boys and girls hived off from the rest of the school, least of all extracted from the general Assembly for private devotional exercises of their own. But we would very definitely suggest that in the climate of our time some thought needs to be given to ensuring that they receive, in whatever form is felt to be appropriate, the special instruction and pastoral care which it is no longer safe to assume that either home or Church is giving them.

Some experimental work along these lines has already been tried. The 'out-of-school societies' such as the Inter-school Christian Fellowship and Christian Education Movement have, of course, provided such opportunities for many years now, but more recently some schools have themselves taken the initiative by providing facilities for 'small-group worship' of one form or another – the 'quiet-rooms' in some Leicestershire schools,[11] the Crypt Room serving a number of schools in Leicester itself, or the 'focus rooms' currently being considered by another Local Education Authority. A paper setting out the ideas behind this latter project was unfortunately produced too late for the survey committee members to discuss and comment on, but these extracts from the paper will speak for themselves.

A 'focus room' is not a chapel. The idea of a chapel tends to suggest a 'place apart' to which one retires for renewal through prayer and certain spiritual exercises. Its existence in an institution as a meaningful centre in the life of a community assumes certain pre-suppositions which cannot be made about the cross-section of young society which will spend only a small part of its formative years within the school. There will be those who through the combined influence of the school and other agencies, home and church particularly, will feel the need, given opportunity, to 'stand aside' and turn their thoughts to the things of the spirit. Others, probably the majority, may find the traditional setting for devotional activity more an embarrassment than an aid to higher thought. The conception of a 'focus room' is an attempt to create a setting where the majority can feel at ease and be stimulated to deeper thought about the basic and fundamental questions concerning man's existence, purpose and destiny.

The 'focus room' idea is not intended to be a compromise. It assumes that the school has the duty to present clearly, and in terms of the Christian revelation, an answer to the questions referred to above. The design of the room and its suggested use does, however, recognize that there are many ways in which young people can be brought face to face with these questions and that *traditional* experiences of the Christian Faith are not the only way through which they can find a way to living life in depth.

[11] See G. V. Stratford, *The Devotional Rooms in Leicestershire Secondary Schools* (Leicestershire Education Committee).

The room will be the focal centre of 'higher' or 'deeper' thought. It will be the place where the academic and creative life of the school can be brought into focus, viewed objectively and fitted into the framework of 'Life' with a capital 'L' which it is the school's task to construct. All that is best in the life and work of the school can be lifted in the room above the level of the work bench and the classroom desk. For some the room will be a place of consecration and dedication: for others it will be a place to stand aside and *enjoy*, rather than create or analyse. For all it could become a place of deeper questioning and richer experience.

The central feature of the room is a symbolically designed focal point in the shape of a cross. It implies, and could be interpreted as, an altar but is also usuable for display purposes, or as a lectern or prayer desk. A school-designed mobile surmounting the central feature will also incorporate Christian symbolism. The chairs and tables are contemporary and comfortable. Wall panels, display boards and shelving provide space for representative art and craft, and piano and record player are included.

Activities which would fit the idea of the room being the 'centre of thought' might include:

1. Worship on special occasions for small groups – Christian societies, clubs and organizations.
2. Recitals of verse, literature and music.
3. Exhibitions of art and craft and discussions based on them.
4. Groups of lessons at the culmination of courses of study in any subject when the implication of new knowledge in terms of 'Life' can be discussed in a fresh setting.
5. Group thought and discussion leading to Christian service in the community.
6. Set times for quiet thought, reading and devotion with suitable material always at hand.

These are only a few advance suggestions and many other uses should evolve. The full purpose of such a Focus Room must necessarily grow from the life of the School and its uses will depend very much on the attitude and approach of the leading staff. It seems reasonable to assert that any endeavour which may bring young people to encounter something of the 'Beyond in the midst of Life' is something which might seriously be undertaken.

Here, it would seem to me, is a scheme which is potentially able to provide a much needed complement to the 'collective act of worship' required by the Act, yet at the same time preserves the 'open' and 'life-centred' approach which one would hope will permeate *every* act of worship organized in our schools in the years to come.

II

Looking to the Future

THE SUBSTANCE of the second part of this volume has concerned itself mainly with 'the needs of religious education'. Any final recommendations arising out of this report must clearly be more than my own personal opinions and predilections, and the inferences drawn by the whole committee are in fact set out in the opening pages of the book. There may still be room, however, for a few final personal reflections both on 'the state of RE' and on its 'needs' for the future.

Looking back over the summary with which this second part opened the first point which seems to call for comment is the comparative success of 'religious' education almost as opposed to 'Christian' education, and certainly as opposed to 'ecclesiastical' education.

Gone are the days, if they ever existed, when RE in State schools could be thought of in terms of Britannia nurturing her children in the family faith, preparing them to take their places in the family church. This may appear to some as an admission of total failure, and a cause of deep concern for the future. Others may see it as evidence that the rising generation are saying in their own way what some elder (and not so elder) statesmen within the Church itself are also beginning to say, namely, that the form and style of the Church in western society today is no longer a form and style appropriate to the needs of that society. What does seem to be clear, when all the relevant considerations are brought together, is that the Church needs seriously to lay to heart its overall failure to make fruitful contact with young people at school, but that whatever steps she takes to rectify this it should be done more in the spirit of 'presence' rather than of 'mission' (as traditionally conceived). The

Church must not look on the schools simply as if they were places where she has right of entry in order to win new recruits for her diminished ranks. She has no such right. Nevertheless she has a real ministry to perform. Any Christian teacher who sees himself as performing a major part of that ministry is fully justified in holding such a picture of his role. But no field-worker can remain effective for long if the lines of communication and support become blocked or cut. The Church *as a whole* must surely find ways of providing more support for what the teachers themselves are doing both in the RE classroom and in the general life of the school.

The second point calling for comment is on quite a different tack altogether. One of the factors strongly affecting the attitude scores has been shown to be the region in which a school is situated. It is obviously important to discover *why* this is so, and not be content simply to note that it *is* so. However, this task was not one which the survey set itself to fulfil, so the most that can be done at this stage is to put up a few hypotheses which it is hoped later work will be able to destroy or confirm.

It could be that these regional differences are somehow inbred, that a northerner or a westerner (shadows of the Celtic fringe?) has always been more religiously minded than his fellow countrymen in the South-east. Even if this *were* true, of course, it would not be a very illuminating analysis as there would then remain the task of discovering how this came about in the first place. But, in any case, even assuming it *has* been true in the past, the country has become much more mixed in population than it used to be; there has been a considerable amount of mobility between the regions, particularly since the Second World War.

This fact in itself *may* be the clue we are seeking. Although the official analysis of the figures in the 1961 census indicates that there is *not* an overall drift to the South-east after all, it *does* indicate that there is greater mobility within this region than in any other. More people move in and out; more people move around from place to place within it. In other words, the regions where the most favourable attitudes to Christianity are found are the regions which are most stable, where community influence is deeper-rooted and more pervasive.

Another possible cause may be more directly economic. The regional survey of incomes made recently by Rawstron and Coates[1]

[1] See *The Guardian*, 12–13 April, 1967.

clearly shows that the level of affluence in the Greater London area and most of the Home Counties is considerably higher than in the rest of England, and that the level in Wales is generally lower than in England. Is it that as men feel themselves becoming *economically* more secure, they feel less need for security of a more spiritual kind and so their concern with religion drops away? (It must be stressed that this is being offered as a possible hypothesis, not being asserted as a proven fact.)

To move to another, though related, point – the factors within the schools most firmly linked with high scores on the attitude tests were the teachers' length of experience in teaching the subject, the subject's standing in the school, and (to a lesser extent) the methods employed in the classroom. The pattern of association among the latter showed that the use of discussion produced *low* attitude scores, at least in regional group IV (the only group where the figures were statistically valid, see pp. 103 f.). It was suggested in Chapter 5 that this could be due to bad discussion-technique, but that there *might* be a different reason.

What is somewhat surprising about the poor showing of discussion on this table is that its position conflicts with the expressed desire of so many pupils for *more* discussion. One would have expected schools providing discussion to have gained higher scores on the 'attitude to school religion' scale, which was one of the contributors to the *overall* attitude scores. Unfortunately no correlations based solely on the 'attitude to school religion' scale were possible in the time available. One therefore has to rely on conjecture at this point. But it is surely a reasonable conjecture that any higher score gained by schools where discussion is widely used (and welcomed by the pupils) could be offset by a breaking down of conventional, traditionalist attitudes among those who are beginning to discuss things for themselves, resulting in a *reduction* in the overall attitude-score, seeing that a major contribution to this overall score came from the 'Jesus/Bible/Church' scale which was itself based on fairly traditionalist positions.

This last point may also account for the unease expressed by *some* of the survey visitors. Many of them reported in terms such as the following:

The high scores of the pupils in the 'insight and understanding' sections of the questionnaire were not a fluke or the result of a statistical accident. I was most impressed by the alertness, interest, and open-minded and intelligent approach to religious problems which I found in all the groups to which I talked.

Or (in a covering letter from another visitor to another school):

> I had a most enjoyable and profitable visit. It was a tonic to see what could be achieved of real worth with these boys. Never mind their academic knowledge. They had learned to think and make decisions.

There were, however, others who felt impelled to make comment along lines such as this:

> Discussions with groups and observations of lessons would suggest that the high score achieved in 'Survey 65' did *not* reflect good religious education or any vital interest in the subject on the part of the pupils. It reflected only the extent to which they had been indoctrinated with 'religious *knowledge*' and conditioned to expressing the 'right' attitudes.[2]

One cannot help being reminded of Hyde's comment on his own tests – 'This proved to be a test of religious orthodoxy, not a true test of religious concepts'[3] – nor help wondering how far the attitude scale of Survey 65 was no more than a test of the pupil's willingness to endorse orthodox positions. If this were indeed so, then it would account for the further phenomenon that discussion seems to be associated with high scores in regional group II (see p. 108), despite its association with low scores in regional group IV (cf. p. 103). In other words, the discussion method tends to open up the pupils' thinking and make them less likely to adopt 'orthodox' positions in an attitude test, unless the school community itself is deeply imbued with such orthodox, traditional attitudes – as, for example, in the more stable areas of the country. In these more settled, traditionalist communities ideas can be examined and discussed without the basic community attitudes being affected; but where this settled background is missing, then the *absence* of discussion can be a sort of defence against the lack of traditional attitudes in the community at large, and when discussion methods are introduced then the barriers come down and 'orthodoxy' gets swept on one side. One must surely ask, what do we want – orthodoxy at all costs, or an honest expression and examination of basic community attitudes? If we choose the former, then it would seem

---

[2] All three of the remarks quoted here come from College of Education lecturers.

[3] See K. E. Hyde, *Religious Learning in Adolescence* (London: Oliver and Boyd, 1965), p. 42.

that discussion must be avoided whenever possible; if we choose the latter, then discussion becomes an essential tool of the RE teacher's trade.

This has, of course, thrust us firmly back into the question of 'aims', but because this is so fundamental I want to clear one or two other points out of the way first.

In April 1965 a study conference was held under the auspices of the Institute of Education at London University[4] which produced a number of recommendations. The findings of the British Council of Churches survey have underlined the urgency of many of these recommendations, and I therefore feel it is appropriate to set them out again here, with brief comments. (The numbers refer to the original list of recommendations.)

3. Research findings since 1944 have repeatedly stressed the shortage of qualified religious education teachers. An acute staffing crisis now exists. A joint executive body requires to be set up without delay to examine and act upon this as a matter of urgency. This body should be representative of the schools, the churches, the Department of Education and Science, and the Teacher Training Institutions. It must be representative enough to ensure respect and small enough to ensure action. It is idle to suppose that religious education can effectively continue as a live option in the schools unless this staffing crisis is resolved. The Conference agreed that this was the one most obvious practical need for Religious Education in Britain in the foreseeable future.

[Little needs to be added by way of comment here, other than by referring back to the figures given on pp. 87–90.]

6. Teachers of Religious Education in the Primary school require more adequate and relevant theological preparation.

8. Immediate examination is required of what constitutes a 'Theological Qualification' for those who intend to become teachers. The contents of many University and Training College courses in theology were criticized as excessively historical and linguistic and unrelated to contemporary intellectual concerns.

9. A serious failure of communication exists between the work of theologians in Universities and the work of Religious Education teachers in schools. The University Institutes of Education, Extra-Mural Departments, Local Education Authorities, and the Christian Education Movement, are urged to provide regular courses to preserve contact between these two groups of teachers whose work is in many ways inter-related.

One wonders why number 6 of these recommendations was confined to 'the Primary school'. When members of the British Council of

[4] See A. G. Wedderspoon, ed., *Religious Education 1944–1984* (London: Allen and Unwin, 1966).

Churches survey committee were asked for their personal comments on the whole issue of qualifications and training, their concern was apparent over the whole age range:

An increase in communication between theologians and RE teachers seems to me to be quite central. As I see it, very many of those teaching religion in schools at present have no idea what recent theological developments have been. The 'communication' at the moment seems to be between the religious psychologist and the teacher. Is it possible to popularize courses which will get over the new theological emphases?

I believe that we need first of all consultations to identify the points of distance between the work of academic theologians and the theological outlook of teachers of RE, and then a whole series of 'teach-ins', conferences, etc.

Possibly the first step would be the provision of reading lists which could be made available to teachers. An extension of this should be organized reading parties, possibly for as long as a week or a fortnight. Theologians could be available to give advice and to conduct tutorials and seminars. (One has to remember, incidentally, that such reading must not stop at Robinson, Tillich, Bultmann & Co. There are others who have much to contribute.)

There must be much more effort to bring theologians and teachers together, particularly the more 'solid' sort of theologian. In the past it has been only the biblical scholars who have succeeded in making real contact; just recently the 'new theologians' have made themselves heard to some extent. But it is important that teachers should be made aware of the work of others besides the *avant garde*, and even though it may mean a great deal of effort to bring teachers and theologians together, it would be of very great advantage (to *both* sides).

One suggestion which has been put forward with great vigour is that the churches should attempt to bridge this gap at its root, as it were, by bringing together teacher-training and theological-training on to the same 'campus'. In this way the ordinands could take advantage of the wide facilities of the colleges of education (though retaining their identity as a separate community within, or even quite distinct from, the college), and the college students, particularly in the RE department, would have not only the possibility of attending lectures by the theologians, but would also have a heightened awareness of current theological issues, simply through the greater presence of theological discussion within the college unit.

But what is going on in the present structure of the colleges, and what are the needs here? Again, personal comments from some of the committee members were quite forthright:

The training of RE teachers needs to be a great deal more subtle in respect of enabling people to think theologically (and to be able to help others to think theologically) about life.

The Universities have for too long continued to teach from a static point of view and tend to produce an arid field of enquiry which is detached from the real problems of communication. Some Colleges of Education are now experimenting with broadly based courses, including attendance at Marriage Guidance Clinics, Juvenile Courts and working with Welfare Officers. This forms the basis for discussion of moral issues as well as educational techniques.

In this connection it is encouraging that a working party set up recently by the Council of the Church Colleges of Education should have been 'delighted to find in some colleges an imaginative use of art forms, music and mime as media for the teaching of RE' and that they should also have been 'excited by the courses where the Divinity Departments combine with other departments and in which the immediacy and relevance of Christianity can be seen in its contact with, for instance, modern sociological and biological studies'. About some of the Main Divinity work currently being done, however, they 'felt some misgivings, wondering whether the content and presentation of the Main Divinity Courses were perhaps leading these specialist students into some small private world, happy in its own interests and in its own vocabulary, but progressively more and more out of touch with the world in which other students lived'.

Two further aspects of the problem were touched on by two other members of the British Council of Churches survey committee:

An adequate supply of good teachers pre-supposes a supply of well-trained lecturers. Could not a university, or universities, offer special courses (or at least refresher courses) to help supply this need?

Great care must be exercised in the selection of students for training as RE teachers, to ensure that they are suitable for the job as *people*, not simply judged by academic qualification.

Clearly it is here, in the personalities and the training of the RE teachers, and in their adequate supply, that the crux of the whole matter lies (assuming, that is, that the 'basic community attitudes' of the school are already providing clear and full support for the subject. This is a vital prerequisite.)

But the right teachers will demand the freedom to work from the right syllabuses. The London Conference had this to say on the subject:

Agreed Syllabuses of religious instruction are necessary and should be retained. The majority of Agreed Syllabuses in use require revision in form and content. The Standing Advisory Council on Religious Education in each Local Authority should examine the Syllabus currently in use by that Authority. If no action has been taken in the recent past, immediate steps should be taken to revise the Syllabus in the light of contemporary scholarship and educational practice. Action should also be taken to ensure that the Syllabus is kept under regular review.

Most of the Agreed Syllabuses still in use were drawn up with 'Britannia nurturing her children in the family faith' as the dominant picture of what RE was all about. They obviously need changing, yet *some* form of syllabus would still appear to be necessary. (Many schools are not yet ready for launching out entirely on their own, even if one felt this to be the ideal development for the future.) But there are signs that not only the syllabuses themselves need changing, but the system by which they are produced. The views of individual members of the survey committee seemed agreed on this point, though not on the practical outworkings of it.

The idea of syllabuses agreed locally seems to me to be out of court altogether. I should think that the most one could expect would be a general document of guidance from a body got together nationally and very familiar with the needs of children.

I think that the day may have arrived for regional Syllabuses, especially in areas where there are a large number of Local Educational Authorities. It would have to be by voluntary agreement, however.

A nationally devised syllabus should be available, but not compulsory, and regionally devised syllabuses should be reasonably in consonance with this.

I strongly oppose the idea of a national syllabus. We've fought against central dictatorship for generations. However, panels of teachers set up for Certificate of Secondary Education syllabus preparation could form area groups linked with Local Educational Authorities and clergy, to formulate experimental syllabuses. From this work a regional syllabus might emerge.

Can it be ensured that some real theologians and some good educational psychologists should be present on every syllabus-drafting committee in the future, as well as the present 'agreeing' parties? (The Universities and Colleges of Education would surely be interested if approached.)

I feel that a syllabus ought to be a loose leaf affair in order to make it possible to alter the syllabus easily from time to time as sections proved to be unworkable or out of touch with modern trends. And there is, of course, a great need for courses for teachers to help them understand the new trends, and in all this work a vital role will be played by an RE Adviser, working with an Advisory Committee (as envisaged in the 1944 Act).

The beneficial impact of the appointment of such an adviser can be vouched for by the few Local Education Authorities who have so far taken this step, and it is really rather surprising that this development has been such a recent one. After all, it is widely accepted in the classroom that textbooks alone cannot teach the children; 'people' (i.e. the teachers) are needed as well. Similarly, it is not enough to provide just 'a book' for the teachers. The 'personal' guidance and stimulus of an adviser is needed as well as a syllabus, as a possible source of confidence and support to those actually doing the job in the classrooms.

The failure of the printed word alone, particularly in times of change and reorientation, can be illustrated firstly by the use made of one of the earlier Agreed Syllabuses; secondly by the history so far of the Certificate of Secondary Education RE Syllabuses. The Agreed Syllabus in question was produced in 1951, and contains what for those days was the unusual feature of alternative syllabuses both within the primary and within the secondary section. One of the alternatives for the secondary school was very much in line with the type of syllabus recommended in Chapter 8 with many starting-points found in the pupils' own experience. However, despite the fact that this alternative was presented on equal terms with the other (more traditional) form of syllabus, enquiries made through the Chief Education Officer for the county in question suggest that not a single school over the last fifteen years has adopted it. Similarly, despite the freedom given to schools in the recently evolved CSE system, only 14% of the pupils examined in the first couple of years came from schools presenting their own RE syllabuses for examination. The actual percentage of *schools* doing this seems to be well under 10%, and even some of these have produced their own syllabus because their 'official' syllabus seemed to them to be too revolutionary for their usual way of working (despite the fact that many of the 'official' syllabuses have been a source of deep disappointment to many people, who have felt that this opportunity for a new approach to the subject has been too timorously handled). Obviously, where teachers are presented with alternative courses, many of them will need a good deal of personal encouragement to see the possibilities in the more unfamiliar material suggested for their use, and this is where an adviser becomes a virtually necessary adjunct to any syllabus revision.

The London Conference also advocated such appointments, but they also realized that there are still other sources of influence over the content of work done in the schools. Not only do Agreed Syllabuses and Certificate of Secondary Education Syllabuses and the personal advice of Advisers, etc., leave their mark; so (of course) do General Certificate of Education syllabuses, and so do publishers of religious textbooks. And so, I would add, may the local syllabus development centres which the Schools Council have urged should be set up in connection with integrated-syllabus work. All these sources of influence will need 'feeding' with the right ideas if the desired changes are to occur over the whole field of RE, rather than be limited to a few scattered pockets.

But why is change necessary at all? Here let me pick up the question of 'aims' which I shelved a few pages ago. The question, as posed there, was 'Do we want orthodoxy at all costs?' This is a crude formulation of the question, with a very obvious answer. The London Conference in fact stated as their very first principle that 'The aims of RE in the County School under the 1944 Act are fundamentally educational', that is, aimed at fulfilling educational needs, not at imposing doctrinal norms.

But this statement forces us to put the question in a different form. It was obvious from visitors' reports and from staff-questionnaires alike that there are two interpretations of 'children's educational needs' where religion is concerned. One interpretation sees a need to *protect* the pupils against the world, 'to keep them as young and unsophisticated as possible', to encourage a general receptivity to school influences rather than foster a critical spirit towards anything. (It is feared that such a critical spirit might turn and bite the hand that fed it, and so become a barrier to the effective working of any and every influence for good.) The other interpretation sees a need to *challenge* the pupils to think for themselves and to make their own decisions in full responsibility; and to encourage the pupils to face up to the standards and values of their environment and to be critical where criticism is needed, whatever the risk.

When the question of 'aims' is couched in the form of these alternatives, the right alternative may not seem to be *quite* so obvious, but faced with such a choice I personally would have little hesitation in

choosing the latter. The reason for this choice would come very near
to the ideas in the following condensed passage from Tillich's essay
on 'The Struggle between Time and Space':

> Time and space stand in a tension with each other which is the most
> fundamental tension of history. The power of space is great; it is the basis
> of the desire of any group of human beings to have a place of their own,
> a place which gives them reality, presence, power of living. The turning
> point in the struggle between space and time is the prophetic message –
> The God of time is the God of history. History has a direction, something
> new is to be created in it and through it. The gods of space who are strong
> in every human soul, in every race and nation, are afraid of the Lord of
> time and history. The Church is always in danger of losing its prophetic
> spirit and of identifying herself with the static gods of space and of failing
> to challenge their works of injustice and sectional arrogance. Ours is an
> age in which the gods of space more than ever show their power over souls
> and nations. The Church should be steadfast in the struggle against them
> and for the God of time.[5]

There has been a tendency over the past few centuries for the
Church to use architectural metaphors of itself and of its teaching –
the basis (or 'foundations') of belief, the structure of doctrine, etc.,
as if God was to be known primarily as a static entity; but just
recently metaphors of movement have been heard once more, and
the Church has begun to see herself again as an instrument of the
dynamic power that is God.

Many of the institutions and practices of RE are, however, still
tied to what is predominantly a static view of the Church and her
message. Hence the need for changes. But this new (or rather,
revived) concept which the Church has of her role is possibly symp-
tomatic of an even more fundamental movement in our time. Dare
we take seriously these words of Teilhard de Chardin?

> In every epoch man has thought himself at a 'turning-point of history'.
> And to a certain extent, if he be thought to be on a mounting spiral, he
> has not been wrong. But there are moments when this impression of
> transformation becomes accentuated and is thus particularly justified.
> And we are certainly not exaggerating the importance of our contemporary
> existences in estimating that, pivoted upon them, a turn of profound
> importance is taking place in the world which may even crush them.
> When did this turn begin? It is naturally impossible to say exactly. Like
> a great ship, the human mass only changes its course gradually, so much
> so that we can put far back– at least as far as the Renaissance – the first
> vibrations which indicate the change of route. It is clear, at any rate, that

[5] Paul Tillich, *Theology of Culture* (New York: Oxford University Press, 1964),
pp. 30–39.

at the end of the eighteenth century the course had been changed in the West. Since then, in spite of our occasional obstinacy in pretending that we are the same, we have in fact entered a different world.

What we are up against is the heavy swell of an unknown sea which we are just entering from behind the cape that protected us. What is troubling us intellectually, politically and even spiritually is something quite simple. With his customary acute intuition, Henri Breuil said to me one day: 'We have only just cast off the last moorings which held us to the Neolithic age.' The formula is paradoxical but illuminating.

We are, at this very moment, passing through an age of transition.

The age of industry; the age of oil, electricity and the atom; the age of the machine, of huge collectivities and of science – the future will decide what is the best name to describe the era we are entering. The word matters little. What does matter is that we should be told that, at the cost of what we are enduring, life is taking a step, and a decisive step, in us and in our environment. After the long maturation that has been steadily going on during the apparent immobility of the agricultural centuries, the hour has come at last, characterised by the birth pangs inevitable in another change of state.[6]

If we can accept even a morsel of truth in this vision then our work in religious education cannot remain unaffected. Teilhard sees the great danger lying ahead of humanity as one of a failure of faith in its own future, for

. . . *without the taste for life* mankind, even under the spur of immediate fear or desire, would soon cease from work it knew to be doomed in advance. And stricken at the very source of the impetus which sustains it, it would disintegrate from nausea or revolt and crumble into dust. . . . Between the two alternatives of absolute optimism or absolute pessimism there is no middle way. On neither side is there any tangible evidence to produce. Only, in support of hope, there are rational invitations to an act of faith.[7]

This is the measure of our responsibility and of our task.

[6] P. Teilhard de Chardin, *The Phenomenon of Man* (London: Collins, 1959), pp. 213–14.
[7] *Ibid.*, pp. 232–34.

MEMBERS OF THE SURVEY COMMITTEE

Ayerst, Mr D. G. O. (Chairman) — Formerly Senior Staff Inspector for Religious Knowledge, Department of Education and Science.

Arundale, Mr R. L. — Formerly Headmaster, Horbury Secondary Modern School, Yorkshire.

Bliss, Dr Kathleen — then General Secretary, Church of England Board of Education.

Clarke, Mr E. L. — Director of Education, Westmorland.

*Cockin, The Rt Rev. F. A. — Formerly Bishop of Bristol.

Dale, The Rev. A. T. — then Head of RE Department, Dudley College of Education.

*Dancy, Mr J. C. — The Master of Marlborough College.

*Davies, The Rev. R. E. — Principal, Wesley College, Bristol.

*Dillistone, The Very Rev. F. W. — Fellow of Oriel College, Oxford.

Goldman, Dr R. J. — Principal, Didsbury College of Education.

Harding, Miss J. — then Field Officer, Church of England Children's Council.

Herbert, The Rev. Prof. A. S. — Selly Oak Colleges, Birmingham.

Hewitt, The Rev. G. B. — Youth and Education Secretary, Church of Scotland (Corresponding member).

Hilliard, Dr F. H. — then Reader in RE in the University of London.

Hough, Mr J. E. T. — Baptist Union of Great Britain and Ireland.

Howard, The Rev. H. B.	Education Secretary, Free Church Federal Council.
Hubery, The Rev. D. S.	General Secretary, Methodist Youth Department.
*Lace, Miss O. J.	then Senior Lecturer and Tutor at William Temple College, Rugby.
Lee-Woolf, The Rev. J. P.	General Secretary, Christian Education Movement.
MacWilliam, The Rev. Dr A. G.	Head of Divinity Department, Trinity College, Carmarthen.
Mathews, Dr H. F.	Principal, Summerfield College of Education, Kidderminster.
*Niblett, Professor W. R.	Dean of the Institute of Education, University of London.
Osborn, The Rev. G. R.	Secretary, Methodist Education Committee.
Price, Mr T. R. Newell	then General Secretary, SCM in Schools.
Rapp, Mr J. B.	Formerly H.M.I.
Stanford, The Rev. E. C. D.	Education Secretary, Congregational Church.
Trillo, The Rt Rev. J.	Bishop of Bedford.
Venables, Mr F. I.	then Director, Institute of Christian Education.
*Wainwright, The Rev. J. A. (Secretary)	then Secretary of the Education Department, B.C.C.
Clark, Miss D., H.M.I. *Assessor*	Senior Staff Inspector for Religious Knowledge, Department of Education and Science.
Whigham-Price, The Rev. A.	Lecturer in English, Bede College, Durham.

* Also member of the Sub-committee mentioned in Chapters 7, 8 and 10.

BIBLIOGRAPHY

A *Accounts of research (readily accessible)*

ABERDARE, LORD, *et al.*, 'The teaching of religion in schools', *Hansard* 286 : 8 (15th November), HMSO, 1967

BIELBY, A. R., *Sixth Form Worship*, SCM Press, 1968

CHURCH OF ENGLAND BOARD OF EDUCATION, *The communication of the Christian Faith* (CA 1654), Church Information Office, 1967

COX, E., *Sixth Form Religion*, SCM Press, 1967

DAINES, J. W., *An Enquiry into the Methods and Effects of RE in Sixth Forms*, University of Nottingham Institute of Education, 1962

    Abstracts of Unpublished Theses in RE (Part I: 1918–1957. Part II: 1958–1963), University of Nottingham Institute of Education, 1963–4

    Meaning or Muddle?, University of Nottingham Institute of Education, 1966

DIERENFIELD, R. B., 'The Cinderella Subject', *Religious Education* (New Haven, Conn.), LXII, 1 (1967)

GALLUP POLL LTD, *Television and Religion*, ULP, 1964

GOLDMAN, R. J., *Religious Thinking from Childhood to Adolescence*, Routledge and Kegan Paul, 1964

    'Do We Want Our Children Taught About God?', *New Society* (27 May 1965)

GORER, G., *Exploring English Character*, Cresset Press, 1955

HEBRON, M. E., 'The Research into the Teaching of RK', *Studies in Education*, University of Hull (1957)

HILLIARD, F. H., 'The Influence of RE upon the Development of Children's Moral Ideas', *British Journal of Educational Psychology*, 29 (1959)

    'Ideas of God among Secondary School Children', *Religion in Education*, XXVII, 1 (1959)

HYDE, K. E., *Religious Learning in Adolescence*, Oliver & Boyd, 1965

JAHODA, G., 'Development of Unfavourable Attitudes towards Religion', *British Psychological Society Quarterly Bulletin*, 2 (1951).

KENWRICK, J. G., *The Religious Quest*, SPCK, 1955

LOUKES, H., *Teenage Religion*, SCM Press, 1961

    New Ground in Christian Education, SCM Press, 1965

MAY, P. R. and JOHNSTON, D. R., 'Parental Attitudes to RE in State Schools', *Durham Research Review*, 18 (1967)

PRICHARD, E. C., 'The Extent of RI in the Secondary School', *Learning for Living*, 6, 4 (1967)

REES, R. J., *Background and Belief*, SCM Press, 1967

SCHOOLS COUNCIL, *CSE Trial Exams: RK*, HMSO, 1967

SHEFFIELD UNIVERSITY INSTITUTE OF EDUCATION, *Religious Education in Secondary Schools*, Nelson, 1961

UNION COLLEGE CHARACTER RESEARCH PROJECT, *Children's Religious Concepts* (Schenectady, NY), 1959

WRIGHT, D. S., 'A Study of Religious Belief in Sixth Form Boys', *Researches and Studies*, No. 24 (1962)

B *A selection of books and articles touching on the problems of RE*

ACLAND, R., *We Teach them Wrong*, Gollancz, 1963
    Curriculum or Life?, Gollancz, 1966

ALLPORT, G. W., *The Individual and His Religion*, Constable, 1951

ALVES, C., *et al.*, articles on 'Theology in education', *Theology*, LXVII, 532 (1964)

ARGYLE, M., *Religious Behaviour*, Routledge and Kegan Paul, 1958

BALLARD, P. H., *et al.*, *Man in Society*, Congregational Church in England and Wales, 1967

BEREDAY, G. Z. F. and LAUWERYS, J. A., eds., *Church and State in Education*, Evans Bros, 1966

BLISS, K., *et al.*, *Education and the Nature of Man*, WCC/WCCE, 1967

BRISTOL COUNTY BOROUGH, *Agreed Syllabus of Christian Education*, BCBC, 1960

BROPHY, B., *RE in State Schools*, Fabian Tract 374, 1967

BRUCE, V. R. and TOOKE, J., *Lord of the Dance*, Pergamon, 1966

CASTLE, E. B., *Moral Education in Christian Times*, Allen & Unwin, 1958

CENTRAL JOINT EDUCATION POLICY COMMITTEE, *Christian Teaching in Schools*, National Society, 1963

COCKIN, F. A., *et al.*, articles on 'Christian education in state schools', *Theology*, LXVIII, 541 (1965)

COLLEGE OF PRECEPTORS, 'Introduction' in *Teachers' Guide, 1966–67*, 1967

CORNWALL C.C., *Agreed Syllabus of Religious Education*, Darton, Longman & Todd, 1964

COUSINS, P., *et al.*, *The Bible and the Open Approach to Religious Education*, Tyndale Press, 1968

COX, E., *Changing Aims in RE*, Routledge & Kegan Paul, 1966

DAVIES, R. E., ed., *An Approach to Christian Education*, Epworth, 1956

DEPARTMENT OF EDUCATION AND SCIENCE, *Children and their Primary Schools* (Plowden Report), HMSO, 1967

DEWAR, D., *Backward Christian Soldiers*, Hutchinson, 1964

ELVIN, H. L., *Education and Contemporary Society*, Watts, 1965

GLOUCESTER CITY and GLOUCESTERSHIRE C.C., *Agreed Syllabus of Religious Instruction*, GCC, 1962

GOLDMAN, R. J., *What is Religious Knowledge?*, National Froebel Foundation Bulletin 117, 1959
    Readiness for Religion, Routledge & Kegan Paul, 1965

GOLDMAN, R. J., *et al.*, *An Open Letter to LEA Religious Education Advisory Committees*, 1965 (available from Didsbury College of Education, Manchester)

GRECH, P., *Educating Christians*, Herder, 1960

HAMILTON, H. A., *Religious Needs of Children in Care*, National Children's Home, 1963

HILLIARD, F. H., *The Teacher and Religion*, J. Clarke, 1963

HILLIARD, F. H., *et al.*, *Christianity in Education*, Allen & Unwin, 1966

HOWKINS, K. G., *Religious Thinking and RE*, Tyndale, 1966

HUBERY, D. S., *Teaching the Christian Faith Today*, Chester House, 1965
    Christian Education and the Bible, REP, 1967

HUNTER D. R. *Christian Education as Engagement*, Seabury Press (N.Y.), 1963

JAHODA, M. and WARREN, N., ed., *Attitudes*, Penguin, 1966

JEBB, P., ed., *Religious Education* (a symposium from Downside), Darton, Longman & Todd, 1968

JEFFREYS, M. V. C., *Glaucon*, Pitman, 1955
    Personal Values in the Modern World, Penguin, 1962
    Religion and Morality, REP, 1968

JOHNSON, P. E., *Personality and Religion*, Abingdon Press (N.Y.), 1957

JONES, C. M., *Teaching the Bible Today*, SCM Press, 1963

LEESON, S., *Christian Education Reviewed*, Longmans, 1957

MARRATT, H. W., *et al.*, *Religious and Moral Education*, 1965 (available from Borough Road College, Isleworth)

MARTIN, D., *A Sociology of English Religion*, SCM Press, 1967

MATHEWS, H. F., *Revolution in RE*, REP, 1966

MAY, P. R., *et al.*, *Another Open Letter to LEA Religious Education Advisory Committees*, 1965 (available from Department of Education, Durham University)

MINISTRY OF EDUCATION, *15 to 18* (Crowther Report), HMSO, 1959

MINISTRY OF EDUCATION, *Half Our Future* (Newsom Report), HMSO, 1963

NIBLETT, W. R., *Christian Education in a Secular Society*, OUP, 1960

NIBLETT, W. R., ed., *Moral Education in a Changing Society*, Faber, 1963

PATEY, E., *Young People Now*, SCM Press, 1964

SCHOOLS COUNCIL, *Some Suggestions for Teachers and Examiners*, HMSO, 1963
    Raising the School Leaving Age, HMSO, 1965
    Society and the Young School Leaver, HMSO, 1967

SMART, N., *The Teacher and Christian Belief*, J. Clarke, 1966

STANFORD, E. C. D., *Education in Focus*, REP, 1965

TILLICH, P., 'A Theology of Education', *Theology of Culture*, OUP (N.Y.), 1964

WEDDERSPOON, A. G., ed., *R.E. 1944–1984*, Allen & Unwin, 1966

WEST RIDING OF YORKSHIRE, *Suggestions for R.E.*, WRCC, 1966

WILSON, B. R., *Religion in Secular Society*, Watts, 1966

WILSON, J., *Introduction to Moral Education*, Penguin, 1968

WORLD COUNCIL OF CHURCHES, 'Christian education in an ecumenical age', *Risk* II, 1 (1966) (see also *World Christian Education* XXIII, 1 [1968])

See also editorials and articles in *Learning for Living*, SCM Press (first published September 1961; five issues a year).